OAKWOOD REMINISCENCES SERIES

WEST COUNTRY RAILWAY MEMORIES

Rose-tinted reflections of some rural railways past and present

by
Robert Penrose Prance

THE OAKWOOD PRESS

© Oakwood Press & Robert Penrose Prance 2013

British Library Cataloguing in Publication Data
A Record for this book is available from the British Library
ISBN 978 0 85361 731 0

Typeset by Oakwood Graphics.
Repro by PKmediaworks, Cranborne, Dorset.
Printed by Gomer Press, Llandysul, Ceredigion.

This book is dedicated to the memory of:

Eric Gray – one of the last signalmen at Bere Alston and Tavistock North.

Ronald Hooper – last station master of Tavistock North and Tavistock South.

Frank Quant – local JP, goods checker, permanent way inspector, at Tavistock North.

All professional railway gentlemen to the fingertips, and kind friends who encouraged my enthusiasm.

Also with huge gratitude to:

My parents, my wife Susie plus family Katie, Gyles and Cameron together with my special friends who have been kind enough and patient enough to loiter with me on various occasions.

And to the memory of my very dear son Ben, who only occasionally complained that we had stopped at too many stations on our travels together!

Above right: Benjamin Prance, the author's son alongside St Erth's down starting signal in 2009. A postcard was written by Ben to his grandmother, 'Dear Granny, We're having a wonderful time here at St Ives although it took a long time to get here since Dad stopped to photograph a lot of stations on the way!' *Author*

Front Cover: 'Passing St Winnow' GWR 0-4-2 No. 1419 heads an auto-train to Lostwithiel along the bank of the River Fowey opposite St Winnow church where relatives of the author are buried *(see Chapter Nine).* *Reproduced by very kind permission of Mrs Don Breckon*

Rear cover, top: 'N' class 2-6-0 No. 31859 on the 1.00 pm Padstow-Okehampton service at Otterham on 22nd August, 1964. *Peter W. Gray*

Rear cover, bottom: 'N' class 2-6-0 No. 31855 coming off the viaduct at Meldon with the 9.00 am Waterloo-Plymouth service on 4th August, 1964. *Peter W. Gray*

Published by The Oakwood Press (Usk), P.O. Box 13, Usk, Mon., NP15 1YS.
E-mail: sales@oakwoodpress.co.uk
Website: www.oakwoodpress.co.uk

Contents

Preface

This book is not in any way a technical work about railways. Nor really so much about the trains themselves, but rather more about the stations, signal boxes and places by which and through which the lines passed. Nor is it intended to be a comprehensive survey of any kind. The Bibliography at the end lists just a few of the many books which I am proud to have on my bookshelves and which have helped me check some of the details lacking in my memory. I am amazed, and stand in awe of, those brilliant writers who have the ability to put together such minute comprehensive details of the lines about which they have written.

To some extent what I have written is totally subjective, since it is a personal pilgrimage from my early childhood of how my passion for railways has grown and developed, and in no way do I believe I am saying anything particularly new or unique. But it is now 50 years since the Beeching report brought about such huge changes to our once vast railway system of the country and I felt the need to capture on paper my own memories of those changing years before the little grey cells lose their power to recall and the memories are lost forever.

So I offer an apology in advance to those who will find the many gaps in this book an irritation. On the other hand I hope there will be some reminiscences which will strike a chord or two and bring back memories both for rural railway enthusiasts and together with those who simply appreciated those small stations from which they travelled or stood waiting for loved ones to alight, as the station clock ticked the precious waiting minutes away, unless permanently stuck at ten to three, in those familiar musty and often empty waiting rooms, or on a seat alongside a lovingly tended and colourful piece of station garden.

The purpose of this publication therefore is first an attempt to recapture memories of just a few of those West Country railways which played such a large part in my life and which will never be seen again. Secondly, to remind readers that there remain some wonderful places, and not just on preserved lines, where it is still possible to linger and savour the joys of the rural railway. Although I may mention in passing some preserved lines (and have been tempted to say even more) this is another world and therefore possible material for another book. So I have largely stuck with railways on the main network.

So, please linger and enjoy!

Robert Penrose Prance
Farnham
Blandford Forum
Dorset
2013

Introduction

I was born in Plymouth in 1947, and at an early age, despite having screamed my way through Mutley tunnel as a baby, it was clear I was attracted to railways. True to form I was given a trainspotters' book and was duly taken to the bridge near the Laira depot in Plymouth where I remember being told, 'There is always an engine moving here'. It was true, and there was no doubt, I liked looking at trains, but as I trundled home with my 'Manors', 'Halls' and Granges' all duly ticked, and with a soot-covered face from the railings above the railway, I think even then, I was conscious that I was not really a trainspotter, I was a station spotter, and more than that, a small station spotter rather than big station spotter. This will become evident as the book progresses, but I remember, even as a very young child, being extraordinarily aware of, and alive to, places like Gara Bridge on the Kingsbridge branch, Gunnislake on the Callington branch or Dousland on the Princetown branch. There was something about the small country station which absolutely captivated me, and still does. Hundreds, of course, have been closed and now lie forgotten 'as though they had never been'. But to me 'their name liveth for evermore'.

My bookshelves are already overgrown heavy with books and photo albums about rural railways and signalling. And since I am no technical expert as are so many of the fine writers who have put pen to paper about these things, why the need for another book? Why should I be arrogant enough to think I can add anything further? Well, indeed, not for a moment do I suggest or do I think, I can supersede anything written by so many erudite good folk. None the less I do believe I have a story to tell, some of it by its very nature semi-autobiographical, which might just complement what has already been written down elsewhere. And I hope I am not being arrogant when I say I would be sad if my story were lost.

The fact that I was brought up in the west country, and at Tavistock in particular, meant that from an early age I was influenced by both the former Southern (SR) and Great Western (GWR) railways. Of course that intense jealous rivalry between the two companies had long since diminished by my teenage years of the 1960s. But the gentle, and very occasionally not so gentle, banter of divided loyalties still continued, not least in signal boxes, and differences in bell codes, a badge on a hat, or the efficiency of a type of locomotive, might still give rise to a comment from a GWR man, 'Well, what can you expect from the Southern Region?', or vice-versa. But generally by 1960 this all said with good humour.

Quite apart from the actual railways themselves, an over-riding factor which struck me at a young age was the honest decency of so many railwaymen. So often the image of people like Ronald Hooper comes to mind, the last station master of Tavistock South on the GWR route, and upon its closure transferred to Tavistock North on the Southern route. Always immaculate in his uniform, always polite and helpful, always with a smile and a professional to the fingertips, he was one of those good men who was only too happy to encourage my interest in his station and its workings. So too Percy Skinner, one station down the line at Bere Alston. Or signalman Eric Gray who became a good friend, or Frank Quant, chief linesman at Tavistock for many years. Frank was a wonderfully intelligent and widely read man who also served on the town council, indeed had been Chairman of the town council. He had had opportunities to rise through the ranks of railway hierarchy but chose to stay where he was because he loved what he did and where he did it. These were but four of a host of similar railway employees who took such pride in their work to the extent that it was as much a vocation as a job, and as such were people whom one would always treat with the utmost respect.

Railway enthusiasts can be a nuisance to hard-working railwaymen, perhaps to signalmen in particular who are trained to be wary of the stranger who may come knocking on the private door into their little kingdom. But old fashioned good manners can get you a long way and experience taught me that once they were aware you had a real interest in what they did and observed the common courtesies, railway folk were, and indeed are, some the nicest people on God's earth and I shall be for ever grateful to the many who have made me welcome, encouraged my interest and allowed me to linger within their special domain.

For the casual reader who loves railways but who does not consider him or herself an 'enthusiast' I have included a list of certain technical terms used at the end of the book which may be helpful. For those who know about railways some of my observations may strike them as a touch obvious or puerile. To the less enthusiastic some of the detail may become tedious or boring. In both cases you have full permission to just skip over those bits and pick up further on!

Frank Quant, JP, Chairman of the local council, goods checker and permanent way inspector at Tavistock North. A truly great railwayman and Christian gentleman.
By kind permission of his daughter Valerie

In the summer of 1960 the afternoon down train pauses at Meeth Halt before proceeding over the unguarded crossing towards Hatherleigh, the next stop.   *Roger Joanes*

Meeth Halt as it is today.   *Author*

Chapter One

Meeth Halt ... and a lingering seed is sown

In the beginning was the holiday! One week at Easter and two in the summer; as regular as clockwork, as if carved in stone. You could even say it started before the beginning for long before I was born, it was to Croyde Bay in North Devon that the family had made their bi-annual pilgrimage. Croyde was a sort of Prance-type Mecca for nearly 100 years until about 1970, from long before my father's birth in 1895 and for most of his 83 years. Cyril Prance was a much loved, hardworking ear, nose and throat surgeon, well known in the West Country, a fact which, as will be seen later, was to be a helpful asset to entrance into more than one signal box in later years. His whole life was given over to public service as surgeon, city and local councillor and on numerous voluntary public service committees. But like his father before him Croyde was where, for a short time each year, time stood still and he actually relaxed. When he married my mother, Delma, it was inevitable that they would honeymoon at, well, where else, Croyde. I doubt if my mother had any say in the matter!

The build-up to this great event was so special and exciting. It was always early to bed for me, although excitement made it hard to sleep knowing that the familiar holiday objects were being pulled from distant cupboards and seldom used drawers, thence to be meticulously packed by my perfectionist mother into two large suitcases, her's black, Dad's brown. In the morning my father would walk along the landing singing the same little made-up song, which went vaguely to the tune of Mendelssohn's *Spinning Song*: 'Tavistock, Hatherleigh, Torrington, Bideford, Barnstaple, Braunton, Saunton and Croyde', thus geographically indicating in musical vein the route our journey by car would take.

A 90 mile journey is 'as an evening gone' in today's fast moving world, but to a young child in the 1950s, the journey from the bottom of Devon to the top might have been to the other end of the world. And, 'Tavistock, Hatherleigh, Torrington, Bideford, Barnstaple, Braunton, Saunton and Croyde' were magical steps on my own Harry Potter-type journey and nothing could ever be so good. Each turn, each village, each town, each landmark was somehow special; the place where we always bought an ice cream, the house my mother always admired, even the place where I had once been sick, each had a significance, culminating in journey's end when a mile beyond Saunton, with its tiny church dedicated to St Anne on the right, and the sand dunes on the left , finally Baggy Point and Croyde Bay heaved into view amidst speculative competition as to who could spot and shout out 'Baggy' first!

Well, no trains in sight yet. Little did I then know how special the stations at 'Tavistock, Hatherleigh, Torrington, Bideford, Barnstaple, and Braunton for Saunton Sands and Croyde Bay' would become over the following years. But the art of loitering is a slow process and learning how to loiter was going to take time.

My mother was a fantastic picnic maker and although latterly, and in wet weather, we would stop for a pub lunch, in my early years it was always my mother's picnic which was another traditional jewel along this magical journey. And the jewel within the picnic itself were the pasties which had to be seen to be believed. Now having turned 66, I consider myself an authority on pasties; I dread to think how many I have consumed and I certainly would not confirm the amount in writing to Dr Sandi Malpas my charming but cholestrally aware doctor. When in later years I regularly bought pasties at Dartington Post Office while on duty at

Staverton station on the South Devon Railway, I considered these to be the best pasties available anywhere, yet even these were as nothing compared to those produced by my mother.

By the time the Morris Oxford had passed Tavistock, the aroma of newly made pasties was beginning to take hold. Another 20 miles, now passing Hatherleigh and the strain was becoming too much. Thus it was, and at long last there is a railway drawing near, we paused for lunch, and the stopping place was, as often as not, just beyond the gateway of a tiny railway halt just outside the mid-Devon village of Meeth.

Meeth Halt marked the midway point on one of Devon's most extraordinary railways between Torrington and Halwill Junction. Completed as late as 1925, and with its main function being to serve the Peters Marland Clay works, passenger services were always sparse on the upper end of the line beyond the picturesque station of Petrockstow, with just two passenger trains each day. Meeth Halt was in this quiet, upper section.

Meeth was not the smallest station in Devon. First prize for that would probably go to Watergate Halt, four stations down the line towards Torrington with only a station name board on its tiny platform. But it was a little gem. Facing south, Meeth with its platform bending back on itself as the track curved through and with a clump of rhododendron bushes on the other side of the line, had a small waiting room and a seldom used little booking office all under the same roof, built of local stone. It even had a siding shooting off behind the building from the up side, controlled from a small ground frame. Curving away towards Hatherleigh, Hole and Halwill Junction, the line crossed the main A386 Hatherleigh-Torrington road via an unguarded level crossing and into a cutting before being quickly lost to sight beneath an unsubstantial wooden bridge. From the Torrington direction, however, the line made a superb quarter-mile, sort of question mark curve in its approach to the station with an impressive backdrop of rolling Devon countryside, and it was in this direction that one instinctively looked.

For several years, it seemed, we paused here expectantly as our pasty crumbs fell off the edge of the concrete single platform. But never a train. Enquiring fingers would traverse the familiar large white Southern Region poster with its black print of train times. Usually tucked away in the bottom corner, cowering underneath the far superior spacious Waterloo-Plymouth train times, were the seemingly insignificant timings of this little branch line, and nearly always it seemed that there would be no train for at least two hours, too long for us to wait, although I have waited longer since!

It wasn't until about 1957 when for some reason or other we arrived later than usual, possibly we had stopped for lunch at Tavistock, that the impossible happened. Fingering the timetable yet again, it seemed a train was due at 4.44 pm, the 4.00 pm from Torrington, and the second and last down train of the day. It was as if discovering that there really were fairies at the bottom the garden and that Father Christmas was real. There were! He is!

The train appeared out of the sun slightly early, a Southern Region Ivatt 2-6-2 tank engine with one solitary green coach. The track is rising at 1 in 50 at this point but the train appeared effortlessly from around the distant curve. I was in heaven. I don't know how long it took to snake its way into the platform but I can still see it now as time stood still. The train stopped in the halt a few feet short of the crossing. Guard and driver stepped onto the platform surprised to see three potential travellers. Alas we were not travelling that day. Was there time for a photo? 'All the time in the world' came the unhurried reply. I was later to discover that a hugely generous 1 hour and 20 minutes was allowed for the train to travel its 20 miles so this reply was something of an understatement. The photo was duly taken and in due, leisurely time, the train departed with much tooting from driver and much waving from us. Then silence for another hour an a half until the final train of the day back the other way would again disturb, momentarily, the gentle peace of the little station. We were not there to see it!

Meeth Halt closed on 1st March, 1965 although the section below remained for freight until 1982. The two passenger trains continued faithfully to the end as they had for many years at more or less the same times: down to Halwill at 9.38 am and 4.44 pm, and up to Torrington at 11.16 am and 7.08 pm. In addition an up freight would rumble past around 1.30 pm returning back down from Halwill around 4.00 pm. Amazingly, however, the station building still stands today and in remarkably good order, and visiting it last summer it is quite extraordinary how standing on the platform still evokes such strong memories of that bygone age when little trains arrived, paused and chuffed on, even though now it is largely bikers who puff their way up from the Petrockstow direction to the end of the Tarka Trail. The station nameboard has been reinstated and the platform is almost exactly as it was. The rhododendron bushes on the opposite side of the former track are still there, if a touch unkempt. For me, this oasis on a remote piece of railway was a starting point for a lifelong pilgrimage and passion of loitering with intent, a passion for the small rural station which quietly and patiently waited for that two or three minute flurry of excitement which linked it to something infinitely bigger in a faraway world. And waiting for those brief flurries still holds for me, all the excitement of waiting for Christmas morning to dawn, the first mouthful of a delicious meal, or waiting for the familiar figure of a much loved friend to appear in the distance.

It had taken some five years of loitering to see a one-coach train arrive and depart from the tiny world of Meeth Halt, but it had been well worth the wait, for a tiny lingering seed had been sown. And the chapters which follow are to the memory of countless subsequent further loiterings at similar locations, some of which are long gone. But also a reminder that for those who want to search them out, there are still good observing haunts to be discovered.

In 2012 a station sign still remains *in situ* although not the original one.   *G. Guild*

'West Country' class Pacific No. 34025 *Whimple* on an up train bound for Exeter in the summer of 1958 showing the level crossing and signal box at the down end.   *Author*

Braunton station in the summer of 1968. Georgeham Gates can be seen in the far distance. By this time the down line through the platform has been removed and only the up platform is in use with the signal box reduced to the status of a ground frame crossing box.   *Delma Prance*

Chapter Two

Braunton... where seeds for signals and signal boxes are sown

If diminutive Meeth Halt was where I discovered a dawning devotion to remote wayside stations, it was at a station further north in Devon, on towards the tip of the Southern Region's line to Ilfracombe, where I first became conscious of the world of signal boxes and signals, a world which was to play such a huge part of my formative railway life. And by 'signals', I mean of course the real thing; not some passive coloured light affair, so often nowadays just changed to 'off' by the flick of a tiny electronic switch by some far away official from some characterless concrete structure, an official who probably goes happily home at the end of the day to his awaiting spouse, having never in his life set eyes on the signal in his faraway care. I am speaking, of course, of a proper, manually operated semaphore signal, whose 45 degree change from 'on' to 'off' ('stop' to 'go' in layman's terms) has necessitated some real effort as a gleaming silver-topped lever with red or yellow base, joined in turn to a succession of safety devices beneath the box to emerge triumphantly into the world again to be attached to steel wire extending anything from two to 2,000 yards to its signal mate, is firmly pulled by the man in charge. A man who knows each signal, who has nurtured, oiled, and adjusted it, in fair weather and in foul, one of that wonderful body of men and women, the signalman!

It was at Braunton (or as the vast station sign proclaimed 'Braunton, for Saunton Sands and Croyde Bay'), two stations short of the Southern Region's Ilfracombe terminus, that I at the age of about seven, was first invited into the magical world of the signal box. C.S. Lewis may have needed his wardrobe by way of entrance to another world, but for me as a small child, my Narnia was the signal box!

Braunton was in many ways a perfect example of a semi-rural station on a semi-main line. It was set firmly at the heart of the community it was built to serve, not several miles down a country lane to get there, as was the case of Mortehoe one stop down the line, set remotely on the top of a lonely rural landscape. The station was surrounded by a collection of small shops alongside the busy road which beckoned excited holidaymakers towards Saunton with its matchless white beach and luxurious sand dunes, picturesque Croyde Bay and quaint Georgeham. A hundred yards further back, traffic turned north towards Ilfracombe, largely following the course of the railway. Alongside a small stream chattered its watery way towards the Braunton Burrows and the sea. So it was a busy spot; and yet the station retained a delightful feeling of spaciousness without any sense of being encroached upon or hemmed in. The station platforms stood at the end of a straight quarter-mile run from the Ilfracombe end which gave up trains an impressive approach to the station, especially in the days of steam. Moreover no less than three level crossings graced the length of the visible track. The main station crossing (Caen Street) stood at the foot of the down side, beside which stood Braunton's most perfect example of a fine Southern Railway signal box. To the south, in the up direction stood Braunton Gates, just as the line started a gentle curve away to the left. This little ground frame box was not permanently manned and it was a member of the station staff who, by bicycle, made his way to this location to close the gates by means of the wheel and lock them by the levers in the box, in order that the Braunton signalman could then pull off his signals. To the north, towards Ilfracombe, and somewhat further away at the point where the line curved sharply away out of sight to the left, stood

Looking in the up direction after closure. Gates and signals have all been removed although the buildings remain. *Author*

The interior of Georgeham Gates crossing box with its five-lever frame. *Author*

Georgeham Gates with its own crossing keeper and attractive crossing keeper's cottage, still easily spotted today long after closure. Between and beyond these three crossings were an array of wonderful signals, and in my memory all were Southern Region design, upper quadrant with metal posts.

The signal which dominated Braunton station was the 'down starter', impressive but not too tall, unlike the vast up home, to be intimidating. On the same post and just below it was the yellow down distant signal operated from Georgeham gates. This starting signal was the first signal lever I was ever allowed to pull; I say 'pull' for in practice it was far too heavy for a seven-year old to manage on his own. But with the friendly arm of my new-found, god-like, friend the signalman, and the immortal reminder, 'always use the duster', across came lever 22 (there were 24 levers altogether), and with it came this little boy, hooked for life. And for those who are unaware, the signalman's duster is always used in order to keep the shining metal silver spotless since it was considered a blasphemy, as blasphemous as a gloveless surgeon, to ever pull a lever without the holy duster. I have also been told that the use of such a duster for those whose hands are making continual contact with hard steel, is a good preventive against rheumatism. As to whether this is true or not you must ask your doctor!

In Braunton box there were, 'Four signal levers to pull for a down train and four levers to pull for an up' my new friend impressed upon me. 'The three reds first and the yellow one last'. Educational advisers need to take heed here, how strange a thing the memory is. When, just a few years later, I was struggling to recall facts, figures and concepts for English, Maths or Theology, painstakingly thrust upon me by devoted professional teachers, and as often as not failing to do so, why was it that the minutiae of a country signal box, enthusiastically imparted to me by a virtual stranger still remain as clear as a bell within the little grey cells?, Such is the mystery of life!

With less than two months before closure, a dmu awaits departure from Braunton with an Exeter-bound train in August 1970. *Author's Collection*

Of course I did not then fully appreciate what exactly the red or yellow levers, home signals and distant signals, actual meant at that early stage - nor more the black point levers or the blue point lock levers, let alone the white levers indicating they were out of use, although in those days white levers were far less common than they are today, so many sidings and signals having been made redundant. But I did know that this was a good, safe place to be! And it was for so many reasons starting with the steps themselves which led up into this very special world with its matching stair rail alongside. Then there was the smell! Oh the bliss of grease and lamp oil combined with polished linoleum floor, although my mother was not so enthusiastic about this when I once tried to imitate the same effect in my bedroom at home via the use of various spirit-filled containers and tins of brown Kiwi polish! Then the sudden break into silence of a bell with its clear direct message in code that a train was either approaching, or was about to approach, and not just one bell but one from each direction and each in a slightly different key note or timbre, depending what type of bell it was. In response there was the tapping in reply of the signalman to his neighbouring colleague, in the case of Braunton to Mortehoe or Wrafton, acknowledging or sending the clearly understood message. Then there was, what seemed to a child, like the secret book, for which the Braunton signalman had to reach for his horn-rimmed spectacles, writing with neat precision the time trains entered section, arrived, departed, cleared section, a book poised, bible-like, on its well-polished, lecterned stand. Braunton too boasted one of those great wheels, like something from an old fashioned fairground, controlling the crossing gates across the road, white with large circular red discs in the middle and with a great red oil lamp on the top of each gate. On a busy summer's day it was no mean feat to find a slot in the traffic to get the gates across in time and it was a long time before I was ever allowed to get a hand on that wheel! But over and above all this it was of course the quiet, friendly confidence of an avuncular figure who was happy, if off the record unofficially, to allow 'ME' into this wonderful world, which made this place so special. Father Christmas himself could not have done better!

From this wonderful vantage point (signal boxes were naturally always placed at that point which gave best vantage to the area they controlled), all the six red stop signals could be clearly seen. It was a while before I got to know them as 'home', 'starter' and 'advanced starter', but I was quick to learn which lever did what and in which precise order they had to be pulled. The up advanced starting signal, 400 yards from the box, also supported the Vellator Gates crossing up distant signal, and I always looked out of the south window to see this distant signal pulled 'off' beneath the advanced starter, as an up train pulled away from Braunton, Vellator Gates being a mile up the line, a ground frame crossing midway between Braunton and Wrafton, the next station towards Barnstaple, whose main purpose was to serve the adjacent Chivenor RAF base.

I was also gradually to learn the mystery of those most reclusive of signals, the yellow distant, whose yellow levers complemented one another at each end of the row of levers.

Distant signals are warning signals, positioned a little less or rather more than a mile outside the station or signal box they protect. They act as a warning to drivers if the way ahead is clear or not, and if not, the driver is given ample warning to slow, and if need be stop, before the next signal. Because these signals were the furthest away, they were also the toughest to pull. And because they were nearly always out of sight of the box they served, there was a little repeater needle fixed in a circular glass casing, which indicated by a 90 degree swing, if the signal was pulled properly 'off'. The two Braunton distants were 789 yards from the station in the Ilfracombe direction, and a little more in the Barnstaple direction.

It was quite a long time before I mastered these since they required considerable force and I dare not say how many times, despite my best efforts, that the little repeater needle drooped pathetically down to indicate the signal had not been pulled properly 'off'. However, I do take heart from the fact that I have seen many a stronger man than I take several pulls before getting it right, especially in the hot weather when the wiring to these far-out signal expands.

At busy moments at Braunton with an engine in the up siding and trains coming from both directions (and when usually the signalman would politely but firmly ask me to sit in the chair quietly), the whole place would erupt into non-stop activity. Georgeham gates and Braunton gates were probably already closed to cars before the busier main road crossing by the station box; the great wheel would be turning, gates would be locked from the lever in the box, signal levers would crash across, and within minutes two magnificent locomotives would curve into view. If one was really lucky to be there at the right time, it could even be the 'Atlantic Coast Express', the most important train of the day, the down one now with far fewer coaches than when at Waterloo, portions having already been detached towards Plymouth, Bude, Padstow and Torrington.

In the days of steam there was an added bonus for heavy trains bound for Ilfracombe who would need banking assistance up the hugely demanding gradients of Mortehoe bank. The engine in the up siding would move forwards and attach itself to rear of the down train in order to ensure safe passage up to Mortehoe. Bells were sent and exchanged and eventually peace would once again descend upon the signal box until the next little flurry. Less than 30 minutes later, the banking engine would quietly reappear from Mortehoe, and return to rest and wait again until required in the up siding. Or if time permitted, the engine would pause for a few minutes in the platform while a soot-encrusted and oil-speckled driver and his fireman, would exchange railway gossip in the box over the inevitable recharge of the readily available caffeine. After all, 'the good signalman always has the kettle boiling' as Eric Gray of Bere Alston would later often remind me.

Here then at Braunton I was initiated into the joys and excitements of the signal box world. And I suppose the one special thing about Braunton's box in addition to its mysterious workings and atmosphere was the fact it was such a friendly box; it *had* to be, situated as it was by the level crossing and at the entrance to the station amidst this busy little town. The signalman knew everyone and everyone knew him. Hoots from cars, waves from passing pedestrians were responded to by a courteous salute from the box, often duster in hand. Sounds, smells, mysterious books and polished surfaces, tradition, professional efficiency coupled with old fashioned courtesies, all this was thrillingly infused into the mind of an impressionable growing boy, and 50 years on that thrill is still as captivating as ever.

When in the 1960s, Devon's railway system was cut down by the Beeching report, in such a way as to make the last few minutes of Butch Cassidy and Sundance Kid look like tea at the vicarage, it was inevitable that certain stations, and Meeth Halt might be such an example, would be axed. The idea of stations such as these was delightful and possibly at one time desirable; but in all common sense it could no longer be justified. Yet while one accepted this, there was, surely, no way in which it might even be contemplated, that North Devon's main artery from Waterloo to Ilfracombe, via Exeter, Crediton and Barnstaple, could ever be severed. Of course there had to be, and there were, cut backs. Several stations between Crediton and Barnstaple lost their crossing loops, signal boxes, and with it any human presence. This was sad but sadly realistic and I shall return to this section in a later chapter.

Vellator crossing after closure with the down signals optimistically 'off. The lower signal is the down distant for Braunton, a few hundred yards around the corner.   *Author*

The interior of Vellator Crossing signal box after closure showing the gate wheel and levers. Brambles have found their way through the broken windows.   *Author*

But the problem was between Barnstaple and Ifracombe: how could cutbacks be made here? There were still two signal boxes at Barnstaple which could have been overcome, but there was no mentionable cutbacks with the expensive-to-maintain Barnstaple bridge across the river, 10 level crossings, eight of which had resident keepers, five stations all of which, with the possible exception of Wrafton, produced reasonable custom, a tunnel towards Ilfracombe and a swing bridge at Pottington. What was there to cut back?

Well of course the line could be singled. And so it was, but with little real thought. A once busy semi-main line was now reduced, in practice, to a 16 mile siding with the result that once a train had left Barnstaple for Ilfracombe, no other train could enter the line until that train had returned, at very best 90 minutes later. This might have worked for a winter season but in the still busy summer it was pretty hopeless. Further cuts were, however, made. Mortehoe and Ilfracombe, where there were no level crossings, lost their signal boxes, but everything else remained much as it was. With long term vision and financial input at least eight level crossings could have been automated and a crossing loop installed at Braunton to ensure a better train service. But it gradually became clear that the far off powers-that-be had put the writing on the wall, and that finance from an already stretched and creaking budget was not going to be forthcoming.

Thus it was that Braunton station limped without much dignity into old age. The track through the down platform was now scarred into disuse with all trains using the up platform. Gone were any through trains from Waterloo and diesel-hauled trains were replaced largely by diesel railcars.

A small mercy was that the signal box at Braunton remained intact until the very end although reduced to ground frame status, purely to control the level crossings whilst at Ilfracombe and Mortehoe, signals and signalling equipment lay rusting, redundant, along the track and on the platform.

This once great section of the Southern Railway was being starved to death, and it was finally put out of its misery on 5th October, 1970.

Visiting Braunton today and standing where trains once passed over the busy holiday road is like coming to pay respects at a churchyard and being unable to find the grave on which to lay flowers. There is little to tell the unknowing passer-by that, 'Just here, not so long ago, you could have turned the brass handle of green Southern Region railway carriage, and been carried away in comfort to Exeter, Basingstoke, Waterloo, and all stations betwixt'. There is still a station house and goods shed with those with eyes to see. But these now blend into a very different vista of parks, gardens and walkways, and it has been very tastefully done, I would not deny that for a moment. The stream is still there, unchanged, and seemingly unaware of the changes and ravages of time. And Braunton remains an attractive small town with bustling shops and friendly faces.

But .... oh the buts of this world ... on a hot summer's day as cars wait patiently, and not so patiently at those busy Braunton traffic lights, moving slowly yard by yard towards Ilfracombe or Saunton as engines boil and tempers rise, one cannot help but ask if it was really worth it? And if not now then what in another 10 years? How indeed might one then again long for that duster, waving from a signalman's hand in response to a friendly toot rather than the frustrated blast on the horn from a exasperated driver who is starting to wish he had never set out on this infernal journey.

And who will ever know, here, where you dear weary motorist sit angrily at your wheel, that once upon a time there was another way to travel and that it was at this very spot a small boy's strange passion for that other way was kindled.

Chapter Three

Plymouth to Launceston
... the 'pretty' way to Tavistock

Plymouth Millbay (0m. 0ch.) - Plymouth North Road (0m. 68ch.) - Laira Junction (2m. 62 ch.) - Tavistock Junction (3m. 54 ch.) - Marsh Mills (3m. 72ch.) - Lee Moor Tramway Crossing (4m. 65 ch.) - Plym Bridge Platform (5m. 13ch.) - Bickleigh (7m. 63 ch.) - Shaugh Bridge Platform (8m. 53 ch.) - Clearbrook Halt (9m. 79 ch.) - Yelverton (11m. 11ch.) - Horrabridge (12m. 51ch.) - Whitchurch Down Platform (15m. 39 ch.) - Tavistock South (16m. 45 ch.) - Pitts Cleave Quarry Sidings (18m. 07 ch.) - Mary Tavy and Blackdown Halt (19m. 77 ch.) - Lydford (23m. 17 ch.) - Liddaton Halt (26m. 9 ch.) - Coryton (27m. 50ch.) - Lifton (30m. 68ch.) - Launceston (35m. 41 ch.)

If Braunton was where I discovered the delights of the signal box, and if Meeth Halt was where I first discovered the delights of 'loitering', then it was along the tracks of the former Great Western Railway's Plymouth to Launceston branch, that I began to discover that every station, like every human being, has its own personality.

There are some stations that overwhelm you immediately as being warm, characterful and lovable. Some are quaint. Some have a chocolate box appeal and are readily accessible while others, even some of the smallest, are tough and rugged. Others take more time to grow on you, while a few feel cold, frigid and unyielding. The Central Wales line remains a haven for the station enthusiast with the purest of gems such as Dolau. And yet try as I might I find Knighton dark and soulless. Tenby on the attractive Pembroke branch is another, or Torquay on the way to Kingswear, stations which, despite their fine architecture and often attractive situation, remain to me somewhat austere. If I offend anyone here I apologise for being rude about their favourite station.

From an early age I realised there were two ways to get to Tavistock from Plymouth. But it was confusing because each left Plymouth in different directions. The one which seemed to be going to Cornwall was the 'big' line and the one we initially at least, never travelled by.

As a later chapter will show, in time I came to know well and love this ex-Southern Railway route, travelling on to Okehampton, Yeoford and Exeter. But to a young child this was the line which seemed rather superior, with longer trains and bigger tender engines. The 'other way' to Tavistock was a gentler affair, with tank engines puffing their way slowly from station to station at a much more leisurely pace. This line veered its way off the main Plymouth-Paddington line four miles east from Plymouth, before setting off via Bickleigh and Yelverton, reaching Tavistock 16 miles away, then continuing a further 19 miles to Launceston, just over the Cornish border.

This was then the 'pretty' way to Tavistock, which may seem a bit unfair on the Southern Railway route which was far from unattractive. But the branch line pace was slower and there was time to become more familiar with every station. Not only was it pretty it was also a truly substantial branch line, 35 miles long supporting 14 very different, intermediate stations, each with its own personality.

It was also a well-serviced line with some 12 trains each day to Tavistock of which only three went on to Launceston, with an extra two or three on Saturdays. Trains to Tavistock were often drawn by small pannier tanks with a single auto-coach, pulled to Tavistock and reversed back to Plymouth. Launceston-bound trains were drawn by bigger tank engines, looking a touch grander with two coaches.

As many will be aware, intermediate branch line stations can be generally divided into two types: a) single-platformed stations or halts, and b) signalled crossing stations with, usually, two platforms. There are exceptions since single-platformed stations can also be signalled, especially if they boast a level crossing. Today, however, the number of this very special breed of station surviving is tiny. Between Plymouth and Launceston Marsh Mills, Bickleigh, Yelverton, Horrabridge, Tavistock, Tavistock, Lydford and Lifton were crossing stations, while Plym Bridge Platform, Shaugh Bridge Platform, Clearbrook Halt, Liddaton Halt and Coryton were single platforms. Coryton also boasted a small goods siding. Mary Tavy & Blackdown had once had a crossing loop but was reduced to a single platform in 1890.

My first experience of lingering on this line was at **Plym Bridge Platform**, seven miles from Plymouth and the second intermediate station on the line. In the winter few passengers alighted here, but in the summer this was an idyllic and popular area for enjoying picnics and walking through the verdant pine woods along the river. It was here my mother would take both me and the tea basket catching the 3.10 pm Plymouth to Launceston. Majestically positioned, the single platform, by this date built of concrete with a small waiting shelter, stood proudly on the up side of the line, facing southwards into the sunshine, perched on a high embankment, overlooking a lush green Devonian field with the river and bridge from which the station derived its name. A small path led down from the station at the down Tavistock end, leading to the road which, having passed under the railway, crossed over the river. In those days cars could cross this bridge and make a short-cut across from Plympton to Roborough. Today bollards across the road prohibit this. It was from this bridge I believe I took my first railway photo with my newly acquired Box Brownie camera which I had been given as a tenth birthday present in 1957. Climbing up from the previous station, Marsh Mills, the line snaked its way for a few hundred yards up through the station before gently curving away to the left and into the woods above the river.

On arriving at Plym Bridge at around 3.20, my mother and I performed a regular ritual of watching the little train set off on its way, curving off into the trees and up towards Bickleigh four miles away. But there was time to linger, for at Bickleigh our train crossed with the afternoon train from Launceston. This train passed our little station, non-stop at about 3.35 pm and part of our ritual was to sit on the platform to watch it rattle past. Plym Bridge was the only station at which this train did not stop and I remember my child-like mind wondering if it felt upset by the fact! The anticipation of this moment was always exciting. Coming down the gradient, we did not always hear the train until it was almost out of the trees. With a whistle and usually often a wave the train rushed past away to Marsh Mills leaving us to wander for an hour among the trees and for tea on the riverbank. However, on one occasion a kindly-minded driver brought the train to a sudden halt just off the up side of the platform, thinking that we were hoping to catch his train.

Five pm would see us back at the station for the return home on the 4.30 pm from Tavistock. The journey would rattle us back over **Lee Moor Crossing**, still with its disused ground frame box *in situ* plus an armless signal post, before slowing to cautiously approach the tall **Marsh Mills** wooden up home signal with the fixed distant for Tavistock Junction beneath. Often this signal would be at 'stop' and although on slow approach the signal might be dropped to 'off' the train would arrive in the platform to discover the starting signal was also at danger, with another fixed distant for the junction beneath.

With the main line only a quarter of a mile away, at busy periods the Marsh Mills signalman was sometimes hard pushed to obtain 'line clear' towards Plymouth.

The afternoon Plymouth to Launceston train pauses at Plym Bridge Platform in March 1957, the first railway photograph ever taken by the author.   *Author*

Plym Bridge Platform looking in the down direction towards Bickleigh.   *Author*

In 2010 progress is being made relaying the track from March Mills to Plym Bridge, seen here at Lee Moor Crossing. *Author*

Thus there could be five minutes or so to linger while we waited for things to happen. One particular signalman who knew us, would allow me to wait in the box and, once the line to the junction was freed, let me pull the up starting signal off, before I shot down the steps and back into the waiting train. Marsh Mills was essentially a branch line station although it struggled a little to keep this identity. The huge restless sidings of Tavistock Junction, just screened by the road bridge on the up side, and the lengthy sidings leading off to China Clay areas, covering at times I recall the station with a white dusty coating, served as reminders that we had not quite got to the countryside as yet.

To stand at the end of the curving down platform waiting for a Tavistock-bound train, was always an excitement as one watched for three well-spaced starting signals to drop to off, in nodding agreement that the road to Bickleigh was clear. The last of these, over a quarter of a mile away, stood at the point where the now single line curved away towards the woods, enticing the would-be traveller onwards into the delights of this enchanting rural railway.

How exciting it is that that same stretch of line is once more seeing a new era of life, with track now reaching its way from Marsh Mills towards Plym Bridge, thanks to the Plym Bridge Preservation Society, a magnificent achievement. Bickleigh the next stop one day?

Two of the first letters of the alphabet which I was conscious of writing were 'a' and 't'. I will explain. As already mentioned, my father was an ENT surgeon. Saturday was his regular day for operating at Tavistock and on Friday evenings, as regular as clockwork, the Tavistock hospital matron, Diana Davey, an old family friend, would ring our Plymouth number telling my father how many operations he would be performing next day. In time I was allowed to take this 'phone message and would carefully write down the number against 't' for tonsils' and 'a' for adenoids! At about the same time my mother would once again be preparing the picnic for the next day. At 8.00 am on Saturday the familiar wicker basket, carefully covered by a cloth, was loaded into the car and my father set off to Tavistock while my mother and I followed later and, of course, by train. On Saturdays there was a choice of either the 12.12 pm which went on to Launceston or the 12.42 pm to Tavistock only. I preferred the former because the two-coached train had easier windows from which to look out!

The charming crossing station of Bickleigh looking towards Plymouth from the bridge on the down side.   *Author*

Thus it was I began my relationship with the stations further up the line towards Tavistock. Curving sharply again off the busy main line at Tavistock Junction and past the short Marsh Mills down home signal, on again through Plym Bridge, over viaducts and through cuttings with magnificent views of wooded hills and valleys from the north side of the train, all now a cycle path, finally into the station of **Bickleigh.** This was the most perfect example of a station with warm and friendly personality, the epitome of a GWR rural crossing station, with two straight platforms, rambling roses over the railings, a station house, a perfect signal box on the up platform, a compact station building on the down side, complete with awning, all set against the most spectacular views across to Shaugh Prior, the Dewerstone Rock, and Dartmoor beyond. Waiting for trains here to cross was always a pleasure. Trains from Tavistock rounded a curve half a mile away and over Bickleigh viaduct before straightening up past a long siding, a tall home signal, under a rather severe black metal road bridge and into the platform. Down trains squeezed their way out of a tight little rock cutting on an uphill 1 in 60 climb, past a cheeky little home signal, high up on the bank on the up side, before curving sharply into the platform, where the little engine would blow off a steamy sigh of relief. Seldom could there ever have been a more perfect spot where to pause and linger.

The next station, **Shaugh Bridge Platform** was literally just around the corner, a mile and a quarter from Bickleigh, with the latter's tall up fixed distant signal clearly visible from the end of the up platform. Here was another of those stations which could be busy with walkers, picnickers, and river lovers in the summer months. As with Bickleigh, so too here there was a quite stunning view. The long platform was built on a gentle reverse curve bending back on itself flanked by rhododendrons and GWR railings. The pagoda-type waiting room even boasted a tiny booking office included within, possibly a reminder of the days when excursion trains brought large numbers of passengers to this most beautiful setting. Fields climbed sharply up in front of the station while on the up side a substantial road bridge dominated the platform, rising up at a slight angle as the road climbed up the hill beyond; the platform itself extended under and beyond the bridge. From the bridge itself and in the down direction, the line curved away to disappear eventually into the mouth of Shaugh tunnel, 308 yards long.

The difference between the perfectly constructed halt at Shaugh Bridge and that at **Clearbrook**, a twisting, hill-hugging, mile and half away, was in marked contrast. Clearbrook, like Shaugh, was in a charming setting well-positioned for the little village it served. But the station itself was more basic, darkly north-facing on the down side, with a short wood-edged platform topped by earth and cinder. Trains from Plymouth entered the station on a blind left-hand curve and more than once I recall a driver overshooting and having to reverse back. Although not that attractive, this was a station that had a tough little personality which might have appeared more at home up on the Princetown branch, on the upper reaches of Dartmoor rather than in this cosy village.

Two miles on and **Yelverton** was reached, until 1956 the starting point of the magical Princetown branch. Like Bickleigh, Yelverton was a perfect example of a GWR branch crossing station but with the added bonus of also being a rural junction. We shall return here in Chapter Four, except to say that in 1958, after the Princetown branch ended, Yelverton's lovely signal box was closed, the up loop spiked and padlocked and only the down platform was used. The poor old up platform was left to rust and rot. I remember being so upset by this that at the age of 11 I wrote to the *Western Morning News* as 'Yours Disgusted' about the issue. Despite this being one of the greatest of regional newspapers, my letter was never published! In retrospect,

Yelverton station looking towards Plymouth in 1958 before the up track was abandoned. The former bay platform for Princetown is on the left.   *Roger Joanes*

however, with the crossing loop at Horrabridge less than two miles away, it was inevitable that one or other box would have to go. And with more freight being handled at Horrabridge than at Yelverton, it was the latter that lost out, sadly.

The gentle straight approach to Yelverton, rising at 1 in 60, combined with its picturesque view of the rolling countryside, was in sharp contrast to the down side as the line started to drop down into the austere mouth of Yelverton tunnel, 641 yards long. When trains crossed here and travelling from Plymouth, I always hoped our down train would be there first to allow me to get out and see the up train appear from that tiny circle of light at the far end of this straight-bore tunnel, before blacking out the light and reappearing a minute later on the station side amidst a deluge of smoke.

Horrabridge, 12 miles from Plymouth, was set up high above the village it served, necessitating a short but very steep climb for aspiring passengers. Trains from Plymouth curved sharply into the station over a black bowstring bridge which became a familiar landmark for those who knew the A386 well, and as a child when travelling by car, I would always try to catch a glimpse of the wooden down home signal as we passed under the bridge, and observe if it were 'on' or 'off'. The curving down platform was set firmly into the Dartmoor hillside and I can just remember the heavy level crossing gates on the up side which were taken out of use in the 1950s, shutting off access to the station from the road above. Horrabridge could be a cold place in winter, highly exposed as it was, and, unlike Yelverton or Bickleigh, the tired and weathered GWR paintwork reflected this. But the staff here were always incredibly friendly, especially to the young enthusiast, and the station building set close to the signal box on the up platform was not without appeal. The fairly blind approach to the station by trains from Plymouth was more than compensated for by the view of an up train puffing its way past the distant signal, across Magpie Bridge viaduct, past the goods shed and into the platform.

Two magnificent viaducts, one stone and one metal with stone piers, the latter replacing the wooden Brunel gem in 1910, followed by Grenofen tunnel, carried the line across the stunningly beautiful Walkham valley, also so popular for picnickers in the summer months. Once through the 374 yard tunnel, the line curved to the left affording a first glimpse of the outskirts of Tavistock and its attractive suburb of Whitchurch.

The 351 ft-long **Whitchurch Down Platform** into which trains from Plymouth curved before straightening up for a long straight run through a cutting and past the clearly visible down distant for Tavistock, was set on a slight embankment facing south. As a child I often used my pennies from pocket money to travel the mile from Tavistock to Whitchurch by the mid-morning train, the 10.15 am from Launceston, and sit and wait by the metal pagoda waiting room for the up train it crossed with at Horrabridge at about 11.15 am, arriving at Whitchurch Down just after 11.20 am. On a summer's day this was a glorious setting looking over the fields of western Tavistock with sometimes a glimpse of trains on the main line making their way between Tavistock and Bere Alston. Behind the station was a succession of the back of small houses with gardens lovingly tended, crammed with vegetables and flowers. But this was not a station on which to loiter in winter when the south-westerlies whipped around every nook and cranny of this exposed halt.

Three minutes further on and the train rattled its way into Tavistock, **Tavistock South** (GWR) of course not to be confused with Tavistock North (SR) on the other side of the town. The fact that Tavistock South was not on the Southern Region route understandably proved more than confusing to some unsure passengers! The approach to Tavistock South was past extensive sidings and a disused former signal box with no less than three starting signals from the station in the up direction. Tavistock South, the most important station between Plymouth and Launceston, could not really be described as attractive. But it was impressive and it demanded your respect. The two platforms, with a third running line in the middle, were wide and solidly built exuding a sense of importance and reliability. The covered footbridge was a fine example of GWR architecture, and all was dominated by a vast, all-embracing roof, which eclipsed everything into deep shadow, even on a sunny day. The spacious offices and facilities were all on the up platform with a large signal box off the up end. The often one-coached auto trains which largely terminated at Tavistock looked dwarfed under this great canopy as they hissed patiently at the end of the down platform while they took water. Once refreshed, and possibly having waited for an up train to pass from Launceston, they would move forward onto the single line in the down direction, wait for the arm of the tall up home signal to drop, thence back into the up platform and there to simmer, sometimes for an hour, before returning to Plymouth. At a busy time of day the train might even be shunted onto the middle running line until the lines were clear again.

Meanwhile on those Saturdays when my mother and I would have arrived off the 12.12 or 12.42 pm* from Plymouth, as the train took water we would be on our way down the short hill into the town to find my father, the picnic basket and the pasties!

For some years, the second distinctive half of the Plymouth to Launceston line was something of foreign territory, and in my very young mind there was a perceived bravery for those slightly bigger trains which journeyed away from Tavistock towards the further six stations to Lydford and Launceston. There was some truth in this since there was soon to be a definite change in the landscape. The path to Tavistock had been generally warm and friendly. The next few miles would become, for a while, much bleaker. From Tavistock the line followed the river Tavy below the playing fields of Kelly College before slowly curving to the left to draw closer to the

* Times of trains varied slightly from year to year but these and other times quoted are as they were around 1960.

Tavistock South looking towards Launceston in 1960. *Author*

Southern Region line with which it would run parallel for several miles from near the unstationed village of Peter Tavy, past Mary Tavy and Brentor, and as far as Lydford, hugging the edge of Dartmoor.

In 1956 I won the first prize for being the best junior treble in the Cornwall Singing Festival held at Launceston. As a reward (and we had come here by a school car), my mother told me we would travel home by train. I had not really realized how well I had done at this festival, and was quite overwhelmed next day when, in assembly, my headmaster Major Bartlett, asked the whole school in Plymouth to stand and applaud me as he placed an awarded medal around my neck. It all rather went totally over my head. Far more important was the treat to travel home by train from Launceston to Plymouth with my mother; no medal and no applause could have made up for this, my first real introduction to the second part of the line.

Having mentioned my mother, I might at this point tell how, as an assistant matron at a school in Launceston during the war she often travelled from Plymouth to Launceston on the line. Since she was getting out at the terminus it wasn't a problem for her, but in those darkened black-out days when the many remote stations were shrouded in darkness, she recalled how many a passenger was known to leave the train only to discover they had got out at the wrong station!

Later, between 1960 and 1961 I was housed at Hazeldon House, near **Pitt's Cleave Quarry Siding**, a couple of miles outside Tavistock. And twice a day I would cycle from here along the A386 to school at Kelly College, turning up the college drive opposite Tavistock's fixed up distant signal.

With road, rail and river all squeezed tight together, there were great stopping places to see if the salmon were jumping up the weir opposite Newton House, or to watch a train negotiate the tight curve past what was then the Cottage Inn, more recently known as the Trout and Tipple.

I recently discovered, scribbled in an old railway note book from school days, the times trains passed this point although at that time I knew the weekday times off by heart. Since these times do not quite tie up with the timetable, I believe I must have estimated them as two minutes for a down train departing from Tavistock and three minutes for an up train departing from Mary Tavy. The times ran:

Mondays-Fridays

7.53	*am*	Up	Passenger
8.02		Down	Passenger
8.18		Down	Freight to Launceston
8.47		Down	Freight to Quarry Sidings
9.40		Up	Freight from Quarry Sidings
10.55		Up	Passenger
4.02	*pm*	Down	Passenger
4.35		Up	Freight from Launceston
6.28		Up	Passenger
7.15		Down	Passenger

Saturdays

7.53	*am*	Up	Passenger
8.02		Down	Passenger
8.18		Down	Freight to Launceston
8.47		Down	Freight to Quarry Sidings
9.40		Up	Freight from Quarry Sidings
10.55		Up	Passenger
11.32		Down	Passenger
1.07	*pm*	Down	Passenger
1.30		Up	Passenger
2.50		Up	Passenger
3.43		Up	Freight from Launceston
4.02		Down	Passenger
6.28		Up	Passenger
7.15		Down	Passenger
9.14		Up	Passenger
9.32		Down	Passenger

As can be seen, the line was twice as busy on a Saturday. I vividly recall the time of the last weekday down train since it was just after the bell rang for prep to start. As often or not my head was turned in the direction of the south-facing window, which in those strict school days might well have been a punishable offence during prep time! I was also always somewhat nonplussed that there was something of a five hour gap on weekdays in the middle of the day on this part of the line, making it difficult during 'free time' to nip out and watch a train go by.

'**Mary Tavy for Blackdown**', as the overlarge station nameboard proudly proclaimed, was the station whose character gave the impression of an elderly widow, once beautiful and long-bereaved but which was determined to hold onto her dignity despite lack of make-up. Seemingly remote and yet in fact not so far downhill from the village it served, the station faced south, some seven minutes and five miles from Tavistock. Although the down loop had been taken out of use as far back as 1890, amazingly the platform and ivy-clad waiting room still remained intact, as did the leverless signal box on the up platform. The compact station building also remained to the end although the windows had been boarded up since the station became an unstaffed halt in 1941. Mary Tavy was unique in having been the only station on the line which had suffered such rigorous cut backs in its facilities; none the less there was a wonderfully sleepy, peaceful quality about this remote little halt which it never lost. Close alongside, the former station house was still occupied with a well tended garden, giving credence to the sense that there was still life here. I well remember the up freight one glorious summer's afternoon, a little after four o'clock, rumbling slowly through,

The morning train from Launceston to Plymouth leaves Mary Tavy and Blackdown in September 1961 with 0-6-0PT No. 4658. The original down platform was still standing decades after the loop had been removed. The former Southern Railway line is in the cutting running behind the station. *Peter W. Gray*

the driver giving a few friendly toots on his whistle as a former employee responded with a wave of an earthy shovel from his vegetable garden. It was one of those tiny railway moments where one felt God was in his heaven and all was well with the world... and why not? After all the GWR was God's Wonderful Railway!

Today this remains a tranquil spot, and although no trains rumble through, the old platform is still discernible alongside a smartly modernized station house.

Only a few yards to the north, in a deep cutting behind, Southern Railway trains roared past, and would do so for a few more years after Mary Tavy closed, oblivious it seemed to the little GWR halt nearby. From here up to Lydford three miles on, the two railways snaked up the valley together, and two miles on it was the turn of the Southern line to halt at the station at Brentor while the GWR sailed on past.

At this point I must digress for a moment, about a crow-flown mile to the south-west, and give a moment to this small but utterly distinctive tor, above the village of Brentor itself, with its tiny church crowning the top, dedicated to St Michael de Rupe, and where the faithful still climb every Sunday evening between spring and autumn for gloriously rural Anglican Evensong. This unique spot on the very western tip of Dartmoor, with views on a clear day which embrace both Bodmin Moor in Cornwall and Exmoor in Somerset, is one of the most magical places in the world and to be there at sunset is beyond description.

From this point until closure, the two lines could be traced all the way from just beyond Mary Tavy right up to Lydford with Brentor's pretty station visible a mile below. In fact the beautifully restored station house can still be clearly seen from here. Although the trains have gone, for those of us who can still remember, this remains a wonderful place to dream dreams of the past and still peacefully to linger.

Having passed by, but not through, the Southern Railway station at Brentor, the GWR line now climbed northwards across bleak moorland countryside, towards the lonely station of Lydford, passing first its own wooden fixed distant signal for **Lydford,** with the squat Southern Railway upper quadrant distant not far to the right, before passing an array of long sidings also on the right coming away from the Southern Railway. These sidings had been extended during the war and gave the station and the area around it, a sense of quite massive proportions. Passing an array of signals for both lines, respectively upper and lower quadrant, the GWR arrived at the windswept platform at Lydford, a lonely two miles from the little village it served. This wonderful outpost, where the two railway systems had learnt to work together, has been brilliantly chronicled by far greater pens than mine as acknowledged in the Bibliography and possibly my memories of the 1960s, when things were coming to an end may not seem so important. And yet how I cherish those hours spent, technically illegally, in that signal box where Great Western levers faced west and Southern Railway faced east in ecumenical harmony. Both sets of platforms had been battered by the Dartmoor winter weather; both the Southern green and the Great Western chocolate and cream had seen better days, and in those last years when staff, apart from the signalman on duty, were sparse, the station buildings and waiting rooms were often eerily silent and might have been the setting for a thriller novel.

Yet there were still flurries of excitement. Because far fewer trains ran beyond Tavistock, the GWR line was always less busy than the Southern. I seldom recall seeing passenger trains cross here, although the afternoon down passenger did so with the waiting up freight, suddenly causing a much active changing of points and pulling of signals. On summer Saturdays the 12.12 pm from Plymouth crossed the 12.40 pm from Launceston here. We shall return to this station in a later chapter.

It was at this point the two routes bade farewell, the Exeter line continuing northwards along the bleaker Dartmoor route towards Okehampton, while the GWR

At 1,110 ft above sea level and the fourth smallest complete parish church in England, Brentor church also marks the western extremity of Dartmoor with views on a fine day to Bodmin Moor in Cornwall and Exmoor in Somerset. Like other churches on high places (for example the mount at Glastonbury or St Michael's Mount in Cornwall) the church is dedicated to St Michael de Rupe, meaning 'of the rock'. Many legends have been ascribed to the church, the most well-known being that of a merchant, possibly one Robert Giffard, returning from a sea voyage and on being caught in a fearful storm while entering Plymouth Sound vowed that if his life were spared he would build a church on the highest visible point from the Sound. Brentor may have been that, being some 18 miles away. For many years the Great Western and Southern railways ran side by side for a few miles from Mary Tavy up past Brentor to Lydford in ecumenical harmony below the eastern side of the tor. *(Both) Author*

curved sharply away to the west in the direction of Cornwall via the verdant pastureland of the Lyd valley. At 1 in 55 this was the steepest section of the branch as well as longest distance between two block posts (Lydford-Lifton) of some seven miles. The two little non-block post stations which followed, displayed as with Shaugh and Clearbrook, how varied single-platformed stations could be in design. **Liddaton Halt** was a simple single platform built entirely of wood as was the tiny waiting room, and with three much needed oil lamps for pitch black winter nights. This was the last station on the line to be built in April 1938, 73 years after the line opened! This remote halt backed out onto a minor road east of a metal overbridge. The countryside behind with its scattered farmsteads presented a stunning view especially in the spring, and the prospect of a down train in the summer evening light, descending down the gradient on the straight approach to this tiny stopping place was a fine sight.

Just over a mile further, the line still descending, was the charming **Coryton** station, latterly Coryton Halt. This was the sort of station at which, from another generation, characters from a Jane Austin novel might have alighted, with its spacious meadows and woodlands, going on perhaps to attend Sunday Morning Mattins and to sing *Onward Christian Soldiers* at nearby Lewtrenchard church where its author Baring Gould had been vicar and where the delightful Father Tom Curry has continued the tradition of fine priestly care in this parish. This gem of a station was, amazingly, manned by a porter right up until 1959 and was the only single-platformed station on the line where the goods trains were booked to stop. There was a small loop controlled from a tiny ground frame on the down side where trains would shunt wagons. The up goods would arrive here at about 3.40 pm and had been allowed some 15 minutes to shunt if required. I recall riding here on my bike via Brentor on a day when there was no shunting and while the train simmered in the platform with half a dozen wagons, fireman and driver sat on the platform enjoying the sun and the inevitable cup of tea! The guard was kind enough to allow me and my bike to travel back in the guard's van with him to Tavistock, crossing the down passenger at Lydford on the way and rattling non-stop through both Liddaton and Mary Tavy. On another occasion I rode again to Coryton but this time waited for the down train at 4.30 pm and going on to Launceston, there to wait for an hour before returning to Tavistock on the same train, the last of the three up trains of the day, leaving Launceston at 5.40 pm and arriving at Tavistock at 6.30 pm.

A majority of the stations on the line have now totally vanished. Coryton, however, has not. As at Mary Tavy a private house now stands on the old station but the layout is still clearly visible and the old weighbridge shed still stands patiently waiting for the freight trains which no longer come. In his detailed book *The Branch*, Bernard Mills concludes his section on Coryton, delightfully, as follows: 'Time has taken Coryton from a peaceful crossroads to a private place in the country. It still has the look of a railway station but it has slipped peacefully into history'.

The penultimate station was **Lifton** which Anthony Kingdom neatly describes as a 'modeller's delight' and with its relatively small proportions, such it was: a small signal box, small platforms, small waiting room, small level crossing, and a small arched bridge on the down side, over which a long gone quarry line once ran and through which trains would, so it seemed, squeeze their way on towards Launceston. The signal box was smaller than the others on the line because the single-line token instruments, as with some of the stations on the North Cornwall Railway, were housed in the booking office. It might have been a quiet spot had it not been for the often noisy Ambrosia factory alongside for which three sidings were provided off the up side of the station. I always felt this was possibly the poor relation amongst the crossing stations of the line. Yet like many a poor relation, it outlived the others by four years after the line closed to passengers, thanks to

'4575' class 2-6-2T No. 5531 stands at the Launceston terminus waiting to return to Plymouth in the spring of 1960. For Southern Region trains Launceston was a through station for the line to Padstow from Okehampton. By this date both routes used the Southern Region platforms. The signal box is just visible to the right of the train with levers at both ends of the box for the SR and GWR routes. *Roger Joanes*

the milk factory, running in the Lydford direction until 1964 when the signal box was reduced to ground frame status, and in the Launceston direction until February 1966, eight months before Launceston itself and the North Cornwall line tragically closed.

Between Lifton and Launcestion the line reached its lowest point since around Plym Bridge, and it had been downhill all the way since leaving Lydford, although there was a slight climb up to Launceston from about mile post 29 for the final three miles. Compared with the high ground around Brentor, the countryside could now, certainly in the summer, be described as positively 'lush'. Watching from a slight distance a Launceston-bound train curving past Lifton's up distant signal, through verdant fields and around the little hamlet of Leat, was like viewing a model train moving across a green tablecloth. And as if for a reward for having had to stop at 13 stations under a speed restriction of 40 mph, the little train was now given the treat of an extra five miles per hour before reaching the terminus!

Crossing now from Devon into Cornwall, there was always the anticipation of watching for the North Cornwall line to come curving into view, running down the gradient to our train's right, from Tower Hill. The up main outer advanced starting signal was 982 yards from the signal box and coming from the Lifton direction, the train curved past the back of this signal before the two-armed down outer home signal at 730 yards, just before the North Cornwall Railway crossed over it. Until the war all GWR would have simply gone straight on to its own station at **Launceston** (North). As at Lydford the two stations would have stood side by side independent of each other. But in 1943 a connection was made to the Southern Railway and for the last 10 years of its life all passenger trains veered left over the point beyond this bridge and up to the (now) Southern Region station, passing the first of the only two upper quadrant signals on its journey, the other being Launceston's up starter. Goods trains continued to use the often very busy original station, a stone's throw to the north.

More about this station will be written in the chapter on the North Cornwall line, but for the GWR line, this was the terminus, although without buffer stops since for Southern trains it was a passing loop on the long line to Padstow. If Southern trains were crossing here, manoevering the Plymouth train into position for its return journey could prove complicated although, as at Lydford, everything was controlled from the one signal box on the up platform. Here, literally side by side GWR tank engines and larger SR engines would simmer together and happily let off steam. The Southern Region up starting gantry signal, one for Plymouth on the left and for Okehampton on the right were both at equal height suggesting both lines were of the same importance, which of course they were. But I always felt this was a friendly and ecumenical gesture on the part of the Southern Region! Latterly Western Region trains arriving and departing from Launceston were as follows:

Weekdays
Arrive: 8.43, 10.05 am (freight), 4.39, 7.55 pm
Depart: 7.05, 10.15 am, 2.50 (freight), 5.40 pm

Saturdays
Arrive: 8.43, 10.05 am (freight), 12.15, 1.47, 4.39, 7.55, 10.10 pm
Depart: 7.05, 10.15 am, 12.40, 2.05, 2.20 (freight), 5.40 pm, 8.35 pm

Although GWR freight still used the old station to the north, one can appreciate that on summer Saturdays, with North Cornwall trains also using the cramped Launceston station with only two platforms, the signalman would have deserved his supper by the time he got home.

Thus the conclusion of this wonderful 35 mile journey achieved in, on average, about a leisurely hour and a half; and it was on this line that I started to nurture a sense of what I can only describe as 'station personalities' or 'auras': the austere importance of Tavistock South, the elderly widow of Mary Tavy, the rural graciousness of Bickleigh or Yelverton, the rugged blasted courage of Lydford,the rural aristocratic charm of Coryton, the romantic beauty of Shaugh Bridge, the simplicity of Clearbrook or Liddaton, and so on. They became friends and acquaintances with whom I was content to loiter and take time, and when they closed, there was a real bereavement.

The former GWR terminus at Launceston looking in the up direction from the buffer stops.

Chapter Four

Yelverton to Princetown
... the bravest little branch line of all

*Yelverton (0m. 0ch.) - Dousland (1m. 47ch.) - Prowse's Crossing (2m. 1ch.) - Burrator &
Sheepstor Halt (2m. 72ch.) - Lowery Road Crossing (3m. 58ch.) - Ingra Tor Halt (6m. 20ch.) -
Swell Tor Sidings (7m. 63ch.) - King Tor Halt (8m. 74ch.) - Princetown (10m. 43ch.)*

It would be impossible to leave the Plymouth to Launceston railway without another
chapter devoted to the other branch line which ran from the already mentioned
Yelverton, 11 miles from Plymouth and seven miles from Tavistock Junction.

The 10 mile-long branch to Princetown closed just one week short of my ninth
birthday on 3rd March, 1956, and by the time I was 10 most of the track had been
removed. That was some 57 years ago. Yet of all the GWR branch lines I have known,
and so many now closed, this one lives on in my mind in a most extraordinary way, and
even after such a passage of time particular memories remain with child-like clarity.

There are several reasons why this is so. The first is simply that it was the first
railway I remember being closed, and it seemed so very sad. Secondly, and the
casual reader may have just to accept this, it was a branch line off another branch
line, a sort of 'twig' line! Although this was not exceptional, it put it in a very special
category for the branch line enthusiast. Thirdly, there was the sheer romance that
this was the only railway brave enough to negotiate the rugged tors of Dartmoor.
Some will be quick to remind me that there had been the terrifyingly remote
Rattlebrook Peatworks Railway, which ran seven miles out into the heart of bleakest
Dartmoor from Bridestowe, closed in 1931, and described in T.W.E. Roche's
unsurpassable book *The Withered Arm* in the chapter 'Rabbits and Peat'. The
Princetown line, however, was the only passenger line to do so, venturing even
further and higher than the Rattlebrook Railway, to very heart of this wild terrain
which, although utterly glorious in the summer, was a fearsome landscape in the
depth of winter. Fourthly, not only was Princetown the highest railway station in
England, 1,373 ft above sea level, its very name, 'Princetown', was synonymous with
the history and mystery of the infamous prison. Built by, and for, prisoners from the
Napoleonic wars this formidable building is still in use today with the Latin
inscription 'Spare the Vanquished' carved in stone over the thick-walled entrance.
My father had been surgeon to the prison in the 1930s and had been present in the
prison on the night of the riots in 1933 when he thought he was going to be killed by
the prisoners who had broken out and had captured the inner wall of the prison.
Fortunately the warders had managed to hold on to the outer wall until the police
arrived who, with truncheons drawn and led by Plymouth's Chief Constable, were
able to restore order. So Dad survived but he was up most of the night and next day
tending to the numerous fractured bones of prisoners as a result of the skirmish, a
night he would never, understandably forget. He himself used the railway from time
to time and often saw prisoners being escorted to or from the prison, travelling in a
reserved compartment kept specially for this purpose.

The final reason why this line still captures the memory is that while over the
passing of time many closed lines have become unwalkable, in this case it is still
possible to wander over some eight of the 10 miles of the line, from Yennadon Down,
2¼ miles from Yelverton, right up to Princetown itself, allowing only for a very
occasional obstacle or removed bridge. Because of the natural geographical setting

of the route, the views remain exactly the same as they were when the line closed, come summer or winter. Thus nothing has changed.

Before the war, my father had bought his sister, my aunt Hilda, and her husband Clem, a small cottage in the hamlet of Welltown, near Walkhampton, and since this was not far from Dousland station, this little railway found its way into my rather hazy memory from my earliest years. The railway passed two fields above this cottage, and I vividly recall regularly going out across a tiny bridge over the stream which ran through the garden, and into the field to watch the afternoon train to Princetown travel by above us, after my post lunch rest. We certainly travelled on the line from Dousland on a number of occasions. I was too young to remember too much detail but I do recall the engine at Princetown running forward from the train, parallel to Station Road in order to run around its single coach and a cheerful toot and wave from the driver.

But to start a description of the journey from the other end at **Yelverton**, almost the whole journey was uphill, nonetheless it was always 'down' to Princetown and 'up' to Yelverton in railway jargon, 'up' on most railways always being towards London. The first train of the day always came 'up' from Princetown arriving bunker first at Yelverton a little after 8.00 am. The two termini were 10 miles apart, six as the crow flies. In character however the stations were worlds apart. Yelverton nestled comfortably amongst luxurious trees and well nurtured fields while Princetown was terrifyingly exposed and unprotected from the worst of Dartmoor weather with winds and rain from every direction, not to mention snow!

The actual village of Yelverton, mid-way between Plymouth and Tavistock by road as well as by train, today still retains an atmosphere of amiable gentility, with a spacious village green where Dartmoor ponies roam freely, and gracious houses opposite a neat line of shops. The approach to the station was down a spacious, luxuriously leafy drive, with the station clearly visible at the bottom. The station also reflected the genteel atmosphere of the village with crossing loop, traditional architecture and signals, but above all, with its own branch line. All sang the praises to the glories of Great Western perfection.

One exciting memory I have, although in essence it is really a sad one, comes from the autumn of 1956, after the Princetown line had closed. My parents and I walked the delightful footpath from Clearbrook to Yelverton, to discover to our surprise a short freight train in the branch platform. I was offered a ride in the cab to Dousland and back and allowed to pull the whistle! Alas, it was of course part of the whole horrible business of demolition and when we drove home later, I realised that I would never travel that line again.

Yelverton's bay platform for Princetown hugged, rather shyly, the curving outer face of the up platform to Plymouth. On arrival from Princetown the engine would back the coach out of the platform, and, having ensured that the guard or fireman had put the brakes on the coach, would uncouple and run forward into the siding. The coach would then be gravity shunted back into the platform, after which the locomotive would move out of the siding and reverse onto the coach, (two coaches on special days and Saturdays) ready for the journey up, sorry 'down', to Princetown!

If one were in the right place, the pull out of Yelverton was an impressive sight. The first half-mile made a complete semi-circle over a steep embankment past the seldom-photographed down advanced starting signal. Despite the challenges of the open moorland still to come, at a climb of 1 in 40, this was as steep as anywhere else on the line. After this embankment the line plunged through some deep cuttings which included both the distant signals for **Dousland** and Yelverton before levelling out to run parallel to the Yelverton-Princetown road on the approach to Dousland station.

It was unusual, although understandable, that while the line was 10, often very lonely, miles long, the only intermediate block post on the journey, and this is the unusual bit, was just two miles away. However, bearing in mind that the terrain beyond Dousland was so wild and remote, and this is the understandable bit, it did indeed make sense. I went to Dousland a couple of times before closure and by this time I do have some clearer memories than from my very early years. The toy-like signal box was on the platform with a loop beyond on the Princetown side, in which it was only permissible to pass a freight train. In practice there was seldom more than one train on the line at a time apart from wintry weather when a light engine was sometimes in use with a snow plough. A second rather unattractive signal box stood a little further on although for many years this was only a ground frame box protecting the level crossing.

Dousland was an absolute gem and a fine example of the now almost extinct, and already mentioned, breed of single-platformed stations, fully signalled with the bonus of a level crossing. The small goods yard on the down side added to the sense of quiet well-being this station enjoyed, a veritable oasis before the rigours of the moor. There were three 'stop' signals in each direction although the furthest two on the down side were controlled by the level crossing box. I recall clearly on this occasion we could hear the train whistle as it left Yelverton two miles away but there was no two rings on the bell from the Yelverton box to inform us that the train was entering the section. The signalman told me that a long serving and much respected signalman was on duty at Yelverton who often forgot to notice that the branch train had departed and that the driver would always give an extra loud blast to let Dousland know he was on the way to avoid being halted at the down home signal! The train curved into the platform and after a moment the signalman joined the driver on the engine, and travelled the 200 yards to the crossing box in order to open the gates while I, a small boy, remained alone and trusted in the geranium-fronted signal box with its 14 levers and with its familiar sign on the front bearing the station's original name of 'Dousland Barn'.

A sharp right-hand curve beyond the level crossing and the train was quickly out of sight from the station, passing behind the comfortable houses along the Meavy Road and lining itself up for the straight section over **Prowse's Crossing** where another level crossing ensured safe passage across the seldom used little lane off the Meavy Road which led up to Yennadon Down. A tiny ground frame here provided a gate lock and two other levers which worked the distant signals in each direction. The down distant for Prowse's Crossing was back at Dousland beneath the home signal which protected the crossing there, and there are a number of photos of this signal not least during periods of snowdrifts. But I have never seen any photo of the up distant 530 yards from Prowse's crossing, although I can still remember it well. Situated on the very edge of Yennadon Down this signal was, to a small boy at least, a tall impressive structure. As the train came back off the moors it would have been the first operational signal the driver would have seen since leaving Princetown eight miles behind him, and what a welcoming friend its flickering light must have been on a cold winter's night reassuring that all was clear through to Dousland, even though there would still have been the final down train to negotiate a little later back to Princetown.

Walking with my parents from Yennadon to Burrator in what I guess must have been late 1956 I vividly recall this signal lying demolished alongside the track, like a soldier slain in battle, with fragments of coloured glass from the lamp optics confettied around it. It seemed such a sad, ignominious end to this faithful warrior who had stood guard against the elements of the cold east winds throughout the years, safeguarding the well-being of the trains, welcoming each one back to the warmer lower climes.

Although one thinks of the Princetown branch in terms of the wild open spaces of Dartmoor, one should not forget that at the lower end of the branch there was a rich variety of changing landscape. After scurrying amongst the scattered houses of Dousland, the train, passing this up distant signal, burst onto the moor for the first time but this was a much gentler terrain than what lay beyond the fourth milepost. At two and a quarter miles out, curving gently from the east and around to the north, passengers were treated to the spectacular view over the beautiful Meavy valley and just a little further on around to Burrator reservoir, cradled by a series of majestic tors.

Perched on wooden stilts above this magnificent reservoir for Plymouth, with its dam holding back the waters unless full when there is a cascade of waterfalls crashing over the sharply sloping dark granite stone edifice, **Burrator & Sheepstor Halt** was placed in an idyllic and alpine-like setting. The wooden platform with its two tall electric lamps, station name board, seat and waiting hut just off the platform (it could hardly be called a waiting room), all added to the charm of this spot. Access to the station was via a rough road leading up from the reservoir below and onto the platform via steps and a kissing gate. Opposite the platform, the line could be crossed to steps up the steep bank to another kissing gate at the top and onto Yennadon Down again. Both kissing gate and steps remain clearly visible and are still in use to this day.

A quarter of a mile on and the train plunged into a gloriously mysterious wood of towering mature conifers. This was a uniquely magical mile of the journey where imagination could run wild as shadows danced against the carriage windows amidst an ever-changing pattern of mossy greens with the towering trunks of trees and little glimpses of dancing light in-between. A little further on in the woods stood a tired fixed distant signal giving warning to the approach to **Lowery Road Crossing.** For many years, a crossing keeper lived here in the house provided alongside, opening and shutting the gates for passing trains, surely the remotest railway employment in the West Country. Life at this extraordinary outpost has been wonderfully preserved and chronicled in a chapter of Grace Horseman's lovely book *Growing Up on the Railway in the South West.* Chapter Nine is given over to an

A train bound for Princetown rounds the curve into Burrator and Sheepstor Halt on a somewhat damp day. The steps leading up to a kissing gate at the top are still in evidence today. The view from here overlooking the reservoir was, and is, quite stunning.

Author's Collection

interview with Mrs Phyllis Tarr who lived in the crossing house from about 1929 to 1939. It is a superb record of life at this lonely outpost. Eric Shepherd, in his first volume of *Branch Line Memories*, graces the front cover with a painting by Arthur Read of a train passing Lowery Road.

Having long had a fascination for out of the way spots on the railway like this, I again discovered in an old notebook from schooldays, the times that trains passed this spot, taken, I think, from the final years. It reads:

Lowery Road Crossing (approximate train times)

Weekdays

7.57	am	Up
9.18		Down
10.53		Up
11.32		Down
12.30	pm	Up (Tuesdays & Thursdays)
1.18		Up freight (Mondays, Wednesdays, Fridays)
2.43		Down
4.23		Up
5.05		Down
6.32		Up
7.15		Down

Saturdays

7.57	am	Up
9.21		Down
10.53		Up
11.36		Down
12.30	pm	Up
1.39		Down
2.35		Up
3.07		Down
4.23		Up
5.05		Down
6.32		Up
7.15		Down

Once the crossing became unmanned the two, once operated, distant signals were fixed at caution, the down signal 460 yards back in the woods and the up signal 630 yards out on the edge of the fields which led to the moor. From then on it became the job of the occasional motorist to open and close the gates.

For the unaware walker lingering near this lonely spot, it could have been unnerving when the silence was suddenly broken by a the ringing of a lonely bell. This bell, close to the gates, was set off by treadles near the distant signals when an approaching train passed. Down trains to Princetown experienced a 1 in 40 climb at this point and to view a train climbing up the straight section through the trees towards Lowery Road was a fine sight.

If this was a slightly eerie spot in the days of the train, then certainly it was even more so afterwards when the house became empty and was eventually pulled down. On the Princetown side, the deep cutting, heralding the entrance to the open countryside which was to dominate the rest of the journey, has been filled in and for a few hundred yards the old track here vanishes, although there is a footpath over the top of the infill. But the approach up from the Yelverton direction is still clearly visible, the old track bed looking like a neatly laid green tablecloth lying amidst the now somewhat thinned-out conifer woodlands.

Curving away through the cutting from Lowery crossing, the train now burst out into a totally different setting with views stretching way away into Cornwall, Walkhampton, Horrabridge clearly visible, and Brentor on the horizon with the Walkham valley stretching out far below. It was around this point that I would have been standing two fields below at Welltown Cottage with my mother or aunt, watching the afternoon train climb its way towards the next stop at Ingra Tor. I say 'climb' but in fact it was around this point that the train briefly had the one and only piece of respite with a short downhill run before resuming the climb which then continued all the way to Princetown.

I have two copies of Anthony Kingdom's definitive book about the railway; one which sits in pristine condition on the bookshelf and the other which is rather more battered. This latter copy travels around with me whenever I revisit the line, and with this in hand one can fully appreciate every twist and turn of the track from the outskirts of Dousland right up to Princetown. Thus one can quickly rediscover remains of platelayers' huts and battered farm crossings such as the one down to remote Rountrundle Farm at 5½ miles, and not least the sights of the three little halts en route. No walker should travel without it!

Some halfway along the line and the train would be heading for the friendly if somewhat remote face of Ingra Tor. There were many wonderful vantage points along the line but Ingra Tor for me was probably the best. To find it for the first time by car, or as close as one could by car, required careful map reading and the confidence not to say too often, 'Am I *sure* this is the way?!' Passing the tiny hamlet of Samford Spinney on the hill to the west of Ingra Tor, a narrow lane drops down to picturesque Ward Bridge before climbing up steeply to a parking spot within 10 minutes walk to the tor, the bumpy road continuing down again to a lonely farm below Swell Tor. From the top, easily climbed, one could watch the train for about five miles over a period of some 20 minutes, from the moment it shot out of the trees beyond Lowery Road to the moment it curved out of sight beyond the penultimate stop at King Tor Halt. Only for a few minutes would the train be lost from sight beyond Swell Tor Siding across to the north of the vantage point.

The half-mile approach to **Ingra Tor Halt** required a huge semi-circle sweep around the west face of the tor to pause at the tiny halt on the north side, four miles since our last stop at Burrator and six miles from Yelverton. Like Burrator the platform was completely wooden, standing on stilts, but unlike Burrator access was only by foot and the two lamps fired by oil and not electricity, these lit by the guard of the 4.00 pm from Princetown at about 4.15 pm and extinguished by the guard of the final train of the day at about 7.25 pm.

Every commentary on the line quotes the famous sign which stood at the station entrance: 'In the interest of game preservation and for their protection against snakes etc, dogs should be kept on a lead'. I always wondered what the 'etc' might have stood for?!

The superb horseshoe curve which led the down train away from this little halt was a highlight of the line and many fine photographs have been taken from this spot. The next station was 2½ miles by train, but as the crow flies it was just one. I was told that, at a fast pace, one could alight at Ingra Tor and catch the train again at King Tor. One mile directly across the valley from Ingra Tor, known as Yes Tor Bottom, stood an isolated yellow ground frame controlling the points to the quarry sidings of **Swell Tor.** This little outpost, the base of which can still be discovered today, must surely have been the most

Ingra Tor Halt then and now. Many hundreds more people pass this point today by bike or on foot than ever did when the trains were running.   *Author's Collection/Author*

'45XX' class 2-6-2T No. 4568 with the 2.51 pm from Yelverton is seen departing Ingra Tor from just below Swell Tor Siding. In another five minutes the train will be passing this spot.
Peter W. Gray

In this wintery scene '45XX' class 2-6-2T No. 4524 heads the 11.20 am from Yelverton between Ingra Tor and King Tor halts on 2nd March, 1954.   *Peter W. Gray*

Swell Tor Siding ground frame on 31st December, 1955. *Peter W. Gray*

All that remains of the base of Swell Tor Sidings today. In the middle distance are the rocks of Vixen Tor. *Author*

weathered of signalling equipment anywhere in England, open to the elements in every direction, not least the prevailing south-westerlies blowing straight up from distant Cornwall. It was so prominent that it was clearly visible from many miles away, not least from Pew Tor, standing way across the valley and a popular climb for walkers. The thrice-weekly freight from Princetown was booked to call here 'if required' until the line closed from 12.45 until 1.00 pm on Mondays, Wednesdays and Fridays, a passenger train running half an hour earlier on the other three days. However, since the quarries had ceased to be active, so far as I am aware this never happened latterly, and the extensive sidings lay gently rusting until they were lifted in November 1956.

Because of the severe gradients on the line which were as much as 1 in 41 between Ingra Tor and Swell Tor, down trains to Princetown never stopped here. Freight wagons went forward to Princetown and were later brought back down the gradient to Swell Tor, to be backed in off the main running line towards buffer stops at the end of a long siding. Once shut in off the main line, the train then moved forward towards the extensive quarry sidings where a run-round loop was provided. The track bed of these sidings as well as that running back off the main line can still be clearly seen today, although the quarry area into which the tracks ran are silently austere for any passing traveller.

Continuing from Swell Tor Siding, the line crossed a still standing small granite bridge before making another complete semi-circle through a sharply curving cutting, bringing the line up the north side of King Tor. The curves here were the sharpest of the whole line, and as the train squealed its way around this remote and rocky section, seldom reached by the sun in winter, the route changed its course to an easterly direction with Great Mis Tor off to the left, and across the valley the quarry community of Merrrivale. The road from Tavistock to Princetown climbed, and still does, steeply up a long winding hill to the south of which, near the top, there still runs a roughly made up cul-de-sac road which, unknown by many, bumped its way across the inhospitable countryside to meet the railway at **King Tor Halt**.

Standing on this lonely station, the penultimate before Princetown, the would-be passenger would have been able to watch his train for some ¾ mile, pulling up the steep climb from the tor after which the station took its name, although sitting on the tiny platform he would have also seen it a few minutes earlier, setting off from Ingra Tor Halt, a mile below. In passing, I wonder how many people had spotted the railway track bed at this point making a brief appearance in the film of *Sense and Sensibility*, partly filmed in this area, in which a Jane Austen-type carriage trundled across a rough track above Merrivale hill. King Tor Halt was topped with a dark cinder and gravel covering, the platform edged with sleepers, and once again it was the job of the guard to light and extinguish the two oil lamps.

On a clear day the quite magnificent view to the south stretched way away to Plymouth, Staddon Heights and the sea; but with a backdrop of rough, muddy track beds running back into the former workings of Foggitor Quarry, and the countryside to the north littered with pile after pile of discarded granite stone, on a wet winter's day, this was probably the most desolate place on the whole line, with Dartmoor rain showing little respect even for the tiny waiting shelter just off the down side of the platform. This was probably the least photographed station on the line; however, there is a magnificent picture which forms the rear endpapers of Paul Karau's book on GWR termini, as a Princetown-bound single-coach train pulls away from the halt, around the 'S' bend towards the terminus, passing a wooden platelayers' hut on the left and with mile post nine to the right. It is one of those photos of which it is impossible to tire and captures to perfection the genre of the line.

The single-coach branch train hauled by a '45XX' class 2-6-2T approaches its destination at Princetown. The photograph has been ironically captioned 'The Princetown Express'.
John Marshall Collection/Kidderminster Railway Museum

A view from the station throat at Princetown. The signal box, station building and platform, goods shed and engine shed are all visible.   *R.J. Leonard/Kidderminster Railway Museum*

Still climbing at an average of 1 in 50, the train was now less than two miles from the buffer stops, and as it climbed, so now the road from Yelverton, which the had been crossed a little after Lowery Road crossing, reappeared to the right of the train, gradually moving closer towards the line. The curves now became gentler and on the horizon appeared a welcome sight for the engine in the form of a cluster of conifers which marked the outskirts of **Princetown**. The station was approached on a graceful quarter mile curve at the start of which stood the lonely wooden distant signal. Again I recall this signal clearly but have never seen a photo of it, or can I just detect it, part-obscured, in the photograph on the back cover of Anthony Kingdom's book?

One solitary home signal on the wrong side of the track, guarded the entrance to the station with a ground signal for the crossover to the sidings at its foot, levers 14 and 12 respectively from the 14-lever signal box, past which the train now moved before coming to a halt in the station. Originally lever 14 had controlled the distant signal in those long gone days when a distant signal, even for a terminus, was workable. The signal box itself stood a little off the platform austerely constructed of rendered stone.

The single platform, devoid of much of the architectural niceties of Yelverton, consisted of one long building, squarely and sturdily built, but with some protection for waiting passengers in the form of a wooden canopy with timber screens at the side giving some protection against the winter weather. There were no entrances into the building from the back of the station but on the platform side there were doors to a waiting room which led to the ladies toilet. Another door, also under the canopy, led into the booking hall which also served as a waiting room, complete with familiar ticket window, no station complete without one. Beyond the canopy was the door to the main office and another to the parcels office, originally the lamp room. Despite the bleak setting of the station, facing across a spacious goods yard with a run-round loop and three sidings, on all accounts passengers always received the warmest of welcomes from staff who were utterly dedicated to their job. Various livestock sometimes also wandered the platform, not least a free range goat whom I remember well and which, I read, belonged to the well-known guard Frank Price, and which appears in a number of photographs. As departing passengers made their way from the station towards the village, so the engine, now uncoupled from its coach, would move forward with them towards the buffers, as if bidding its own polite farewell to the traveller.

Apart from Saturdays, there was usually plenty of time between arrival and departure, during which the engine would not only run around its train, but would as often as not fill up with water from the tower by the engine shed on the far side of the goods yard, and busy itself with wagons which might have accompanied the train from Yelverton, or which had to be positioned for the return trip.

In latter days trains departure and arrival times were as follows:

Weekdays
Arrive: 9.45 am, 12 noon, 3.10, 5.32, 7.41 pm
Depart: 7.35, 10.30 am, 12.08, (Tues, Thurs), 12.35 (freight Mon, Wed, Fri), 4.00, 6.10 pm

Saturdays
Arrive: 9.45, 12 noon, 2.03, 3.33, 5.32, 7.41 pm
Depart: 7.35, 10.30 am, 12.08, 2.12, 4.00, 6.10 pm

Since the first train of the day started here, it was here also that the engine was housed for the night, and a magnificent desciption of the early morning activity, and train workings from Princetown can be found in Paul Karau's superb book entitled *Great Western Branch Line Termini* with a wealth of information about the station, its architecture and method of working; a book, so rich in detail that I would have to take it with me, were I ever cast away on the proverbial desert island!

Thirty-five minutes was the usual time allowed for the journey to Yelverton with just over 40 for the return working, the block section to Dousland being generally 30 minutes from Princetown and about 35 minutes for the return working. An extra three minutes was given to the 4.00 pm from Princetown, presumably to allow time for the guard to light the lamps at King Tor and Ingra Tor.

On a normal evening, after the last train had arrived at Princetown somewhere around 7.40 pm, the signalman had a busy few minutes pulling points to allow the engine to shunt its coach before retiring to the engine shed for the night. But on 3rd March, 1956 there was an unadvertised return working back to Yelverton. The Princetown signalman would have asked Dousland for 'line clear' and pulled lever number one, the solitary starting signal, before going down the steps of the box to hand the driver the staff for the journey to Dousland. As the train moved out of the station, passing the signal just beyond the box and under the metal bridge, he would have sent the usual two beats to the Dousland signalman for 'train entering section'. Throwing back lever number one, he would have watched the red tail lamp disappear from sight into the night across the moor. Half an hour later he would have received the 'two pause one' on his own bell from Dousland to announce the train was safely out of section, signifying also that he could lock up and go home. Within some 15 minutes of the train's departure, the oil lamps at King Tor and Ingra Tor would have been extinguished by the guard for the last time, and as he did, so the lights went out forever on the Princetown railway.

Re-walking the route again recently from Burrator, I made a photographic record of all that remains down to Princetown. From a photographic point of view this is probably the best way to walk, with the light behind one most of the way. But it is the uphill way, and ending at Princetown station is hugely depressing where no glimmer of the tracks remain, only a muddy void of grass, nothing that is except one old railway building originally used as a stable and nearby an overgrown hillock where once there were buffer stops.

Yelverton station was, as noted in the previous chapter, to live on for another seven years. However, after the signalling went and the loop was taken out of use, this station was reduced to the likeness of some sad elder who had suffered a stroke after seeing better days. After final closure, the ravages of nature have swallowed up the skeletonic remains, and today, as a private nature reserve, the station is lost amidst unchecked undergrowth.

Dousland station remains domestically intact, now as a bungalow, with a welcoming owner who is obviously used to railway eccentrics like me appearing from nowhere, as also was his friendly dog. The platform is still easily discernible from the down side; there are a few pieces of memorabilia, including an old home signal, and the station name remains in white letters below the old platform. But around the old station, all has been swallowed up by new houses, and not until Yennadon Down is the track truly recognisable. And from here on there is still much to enjoy and with Anthony Kingdom's book in hand, the three halts at Burrator, Ingra Tor and King Tor, are easily recaptured in the mind's eye.

As for me... well, I can still dream my dreams on a hot summer afternoon, at around three o'clock, with possibly a glass of white wine and a sandwich in hand, leaning against the rocks of Ingra Tor amidst the granite, the heather and the bracken, and with the sound of skylarks high above, can I still hear the whistle of a little 2-6-2 tank engine making its way out of the woods near Lowery Road, again curving and climbing its way up across the moor towards Ingra Tor Halt?

Dear reader, please don't disturb my dreams and wake me up!

Chapter Five

The North Cornwall Railway
... the Southern's longest tentacle

Okehampton to Halwill Junction
Okehampton (0m. 0ch.) - Meldon Quarry (2m. 4ch.) - Meldon Junction (2m. 52ch.) - Maddaford Moor Halt (4m. 70ch.) - Venn Gates Crossing - Ashbury (8m. 51ch.) - Halwill Junction (12m. 36ch.)

Halwill Junction to Torrington
Hole (15m. 43ch.) - Hatherleigh (20m. 7ch.) - Meeth Halt (22m. 37ch.) - Meeth Clay Co. Siding (23m. 7ch.) - Petrockstow (24m. 95ch.) - Marland Clay Siding (26m. 91ch.) - Dunsbear Halt (27m. 14ch.) - Yarde Halt (28m. 41c.) - Watergate Halt (31m. 5 ch.) - Torrington (31m. 83ch.)

Halwill Junction to Padstow
Ashwater (17m. 44ch.) - Tower Hill (21m. 13ch.) - Launceston (26m. 13ch.) - Egloskerry (30m. 36ch.) - Tresmeer (34m. 8ch.) - Otterham (38m. 78ch.) - Camelford (43m. 34ch.) - Delabole (45m. 63ch.) - Port Isaac Road (49m. 71ch.) - St Kew Highway (52m. 42ch.) - Wadebridge (56m. 51ch.) - Padstow (62m. 23ch. - 259m. 54ch. from London Waterloo)

Halwill Junction to Bude
Dunsland Cross (15m. 65ch.) - Holsworthy (20m. 30ch.) - Whitstone & Bridgerule (25m. 27ch.) - Bude (30m. 73ch.)

If the Princetown branch was the first line to have been firmly instilled into my childhood memories, another which made a similar never-to-be forgotten impression from teenage years was that of the dramatic line which began its course high up over Okehampton in Devon to wend its way over 62 miles towards the north Cornish coast to far off Padstow, the furthest point of the former Southern Railway. The North Cornwall Railway was a line which I came to know well over the last eight years of its life.

I have to start by saying that nothing I could ever write could possibly compare with the matchless work produced by the late David Wroe in 1995 and so magnificently updated by George Reeve in 2008 in which no stone of detail is left unturned. Not only the detail but the descriptive narrative too is quite superb, and this would have to be another book for me if stranded on a desert island!

But my own memories of this line remain so vibrant that I feel a need to commit them to paper and hopefully there may be something amidst my rose-tinted reflections which may strike a chord or two with others. Because it is such a long line, the process of my getting to know it was somewhat fragmented, a bit here and a bit there, as may become confusingly evident. However, I hope by the end there will be some continuity.

It was a late distinguished parishioner of mine, Lord David Cecil, formerly Professor of English Literature at Oxford and close friend of the Cornish devotee John Betjeman, himself a great admirer of the North Cornwall Railway, who suggested that he always thought South Cornwall reflected the music of Mozart while North Cornwall was more Wagnerian. Certainly if you travel today to Penzance through genteel Liskeard, Bodmin, Lostwithiel, Par, and so on, passing those little fingers which stretch down to Looe, Fowey and Falmouth, there is certainly the serenity of a Mozart symphony and sense of comfort. And although Cornwall is a smaller county than its much larger next door neighbour, like Devonshire the dramatic north coast contrasts hugely with the southern side. With legendary historical and literary landmarks such as Tintagel, Boscastle, and

Bodmin Moor with its Jamaica Inn, here is a world of mists, mystery, driving Atlantic gales and wild open spaces. And it was into this world that the North Cornwall Railway slowly made its way.

The Southern Railway's most westerly station at Padstow, 260 miles from Waterloo was not finally reached until March 1899, even though its starting point at Meldon Junction had begun 20 years earlier. Sixty-two miles embraced 15 stations as it wound its way through the largely rural landscape, stations which, for the most part, merely served a wide, scattered countryside of small villages and hamlets or in the case of Port Isaac, adding 'Road', which was always a giveaway that the station was far away from the community after which it was named, as for example Bodmin Road or Grampound Road. Launceston and Wadebridge were the two major places on the journey, Wadebridge being well-positioned for the town, Launceston slightly less so at the bottom of a very steep hill. Delabole and Egloskerry were the two villages best served by their station's location. Tower Hill was merely named after an adjacent farm, Tresmeer, Otterham, Port Isaac Road and St Kew Highway were all some distances from their nomenclature. Yet each provided a vital lifeline in this remote south-western outpost where the winters were fierce and towns of any size were few and far between.

Although I began to be aware of this line in the 1950s, it was from 1960 until closure in 1966 that I started to become really familiar with almost every station. In 1960 the line was still steam worked and busy, boasting the daily 'Atlantic Coast Express', with much freight, and with staff and signalling at every station except the single-platformed Maddaford Moor Halt which, strangely, lost its crossing loop in 1921 before it even had a station! By the last year of its life, Ashwater, Tresmeer, Otterham and St Kew had all lost their crossing loops together with their last member of staff, as also had Dunsland Cross on the Bude branch.

Freight had gone as had the 'Atlantic Coast Express', and of course by now, all steam. The final year of service had dwindled to a thrice-daily, often single, diesel railcar, with one extra train as far as Launceston at the start and end of the day. The line had just escaped closure in 1964 but it was living very much on borrowed time.

Otterham

However, going back in time, my first real encounter with this line was one summer in the late 1950s. Every six weeks my Father had an ENT surgery at Stratton hospital near Bude, and in the holidays my Mother and I would spend the day with friends on the beach at Widemouth Bay until Dad rejoined us in the afternoon. The way home varied. The usual way was along the B3254 via Whitstone and on to Launceston. However, if the weather was fine we went home via the slightly longer route taking, initially, the A39 Bude-Wadebridge road , but turning off towards Hallworthy and over Wilsey Down where we sometimes stopped to see if the lapwings were nesting. It was at this turn off that the road crossed the exposed station of **Otterham**, 850 feet above sea level. Here, for miles around there was nothing but wide open spaces of fields, hamlets and farmsteads. But on a clear day, as it often was when we drove this way, visible from miles away, stood this extraordinary oasis of a lifeline to a bigger world, fringed on the south side by a distinctive row of conifers above the down platform, planted to give some slight protection from the ruthless south-westerly gales.

Although the highest station on the line, the actual summit was a mile to the west near the up distant signal, and on a clear day, this tall, brave beacon of safety could be seen from the bridge silhouetted far away against an evening sun, and to see a

Beautiful remote Otterham in 1962 looking up the line towards Launceston. The author's father is waving his handkerchief on the platform, as was his wont! *Author*

Waterloo-bound train come over the crest of the hill and down into the long slow curve towards the station was a sight to behold.

At that first visit, I clearly recall our turning left off the main road and along the short cul-de-sac towards the station. Typical of its breed, the station was two storey, built of Delabole stone. Immediately ahead and to the left two sidings stretched back from the running line off the up loop, a couple of elderly looking wagons sitting in the siding waiting for further instructions, bearing witness to the old phrase that, 'They also serve who only stand and wait'. The signal box, visible from the road, was set just off the up platform and the down home signal beyond the points at the top of the climb up from Tresmeer, the next station, was 'off' announcing the fact that a train was expected.

The platform had an air of spaciousness, made even more so by the fact that there was not a solitary passenger in sight. There was a magnificent down starting signal with a co-acting arm, which towered over the bridge to give the driver better sighting as down trains came up the gradient. This signal was 'on'.

Two friendly employees of the railway company were standing chatting outside the entrance to the main waiting room and they greeted us warmly while already in the distance the sound of a train could be heard pulling up the 1 in 73 gradient. It turned out to be a small goods train pulled I think by an 'N' class locomotive. It curved over the points and into the station, stopping slightly short of the road bridge. Various greetings were made from cab to platform as the signalman caught, with accustomed ease it seemed, the pouch with the key token from Tresmeer, lobbed across from the locomotive. 'Come on', said the signalman to myself, 'You can come and help'. We walked the length of the up platform, off the end and then up inside the sacred box and the tablet instruments, and after returning the tablet to Tresmeer, another was procured for Camelford, to the accompaniment of bells, lever turning, and the clanking of metal discs being returned and withdrawn. Then with a heave lever number three was pulled over and the two-armed signal raised to 'off'. 'Now go and give this to the driver', said the signalman, thrusting the pouch with the encased tablet into my hand. 'Cross the line down there', indicating a sleepered crossing on the upside of the platform. I recall a sense of huge responsibility as I half ran the length of the down platform. 'Are you sure it's the right one?', asked the driver, not unkindly. I was not sure what to say. 'Always check', he continued, as he pointed out the clearly embossed words on the token – 'OTTERHAM-CAMELFORD'. A throaty whistle, a shower of smoke as the steam hit the bridge, and the train was off, over the down points, through the cutting and away out of sight, although not for a while out of hearing, as it made its way towards the summit.

'Better put the signals back', called the signalman. No need to ask twice. Back down the platform, up the steps and into the box to be handed the familiar duster. Signals two and three were not many yards from the box but both were heavy and I remember the force with which they flew back, somewhat to the signalman's amusement. 'All quiet for a while now', he added taking back the duster and changing the points, before we descended the steps to rejoin loitering parents.

Memory is an odd thing and I surprise myself that I can still recall this visit with such clarity. And although some of the detail is retrospective, the gradient or the signal numbers, none the less the substance is certain. Again, in retrospect, I am not quite sure why the starting signal was 'on' or why the tablet to Camelford had not been obtained before the train's arrival. Presumably no driver wants to see the down home for Otterham against him on that gradient. Possibly the last train from Camelford had not cleared the section. Possibly too the signalman had pulled the down home off earlier to save an extra walk back to the box. I remember this practice happening at the remote station of Hole on the Torrington branch, where points and signals were sometimes set long before the train had entered the section, and left long after, to save walking down the platform again.

All this is really of no matter. What was important was that Otterham was firmly embedded in my mind and was the starting point for my life-long interest in this fascinating railway. And although my less railway-minded friends might have thought I ought to have 'got out more', for a while I could think of nothing more exciting in the whole wide world than that of becoming the signalman at Otterham station!

Key places on the North Cornwall line

The North Cornwall line was twice as long as the former GWR Launceston branch. Being Southern Region the stations were of a different style, but here again each had different characteristics and different 'feels' to them. Some were cosier, some were more austere. Some were busy, others more tranquil. From the point of view of being busy, one has to start with famous **Halwill Junction**, 210 miles from Waterloo; famous because in one sense it was a tiny outpost, and yet in railway terms it was revered as one of the most significant junctions anywhere in the rural railway world.

Because I had heard of it for a long time before actually being there, rather like my first visit to hear the choir at King's College, Cambridge, when I finally arrived for the first time I had to pinch myself to ensure I was not dreaming! In fact, unlike the architecture at King's College, the buildings at Halwill were a touch disappointing. I suppose I had expected something a bit grander. The main station buildings were modest compared even with some of the quieter stations.

But this was essentially a junction for three railways set in a very small village through which people passed, like Adlestrop, or where people changed trains, unlike Adlestrop! So passenger numbers waiting to board here were not huge and thus there was no great need for large buildings. None the less the all dominating, wooden, 40-levered signal box, taller than the station buildings, left one in no doubt that this was somewhere special!

Not that it was always hustle and bustle. Like all the stations on the line there were periods of tranquillity and silence. But unlike most of the others, with the possible

Halwill Junction looking towards the triple junction in the down direction. Trains to Padstow went away to the left and straight ahead to Bude. The Torrington branch with its diminutive platform (far right) curved away to the right.   *Author's Collection*

exception of Wadebridge, there were a few half-hours in the day when there were tornadoes of activity with as many as four trains arriving and departing, especially around 10.00 am and 5.00 pm when the one-coach train from Torrington twice daily meandered into its own tiny unsheltered platform off the down side of Halwill's up platform. The guard of a train from Hole was, unusually, allowed to deliver and collect the token to the signalman; Maiden Newton on the Bridport branch was the other station where this was permissible. In practice, the signalman would recover the token by hanging a rope out of the west-facing window of the signal box and haul it up.

From within the box with its steep, straight flight of steps on the east side, there was a spectacular view of everything that was happening. To the south there was a magnificent sweep over the level crossing and away down the long straight, past the distant signal and curving away in the distance to the left towards Ashbury. Ahead of the box was a bay platform and a set of compact and often crowded sidings, while to the north, the Padstow line curved sharply away past the distinctive down advanced starter, back to back with the up home at the top of the steep climb up from Ashwater. Also to the west, the Bude branch strode away in a straight line, parallel to the Torrington branch for a few hundred yards before the latter curved gently away to the right towards Hole and all stations to Torrington.

Some mention has already been made of **Launceston** in a previous chapter where since 1952 WR and SR shared the same two, sharply curving and slightly cramped platforms. The former GWR station to the north was far more spacious, and there was even more space after its only use was for freight. With buffer stops at the west end, the sidings on the east side had plenty of room to embrace the busy coming and goings of the daily freights without being in the way of passenger trains. The Southern Region line, with the main buildings on the up platform and shared signal box on the down, squeezed its way out of the platform and out of sight in the down direction, under a succession of bridges, now the home of the Launceston Steam Railway. The sidings were out of view from the station which to the casual viewer gave a slightly misleading picture of the shunting facilities which were greater than one imagined. Despite the business of the station the Southern route signalling was, surprisingly, of the basic minimum with just the usual home, starter and distant in each direction. As with Halwill there were lulls in the day, but even in 1961 as things were just starting to slow down, summer Saturdays could be very busy:

Launceston signal box with its levers for SR and GWR lines and at either end.

Author's Collection

Launceston, Summer Saturdays 1961

SR	Down	6.12-6.16 am	Waterloo-Padstow (overnight)
WR	Up	7.05 am	Depart to Plymouth
SR	Down	7.48-8.05 am	Waterloo-Padstow (overnight)
SR	Down	8.15 am	Freight depart to Wadebridge
SR	Up	8.20 am	Depart to Okehampton
WR	Down.	8.43 am	Ex-Plymouth terminates
SR	Up	9.18-9.22 am	Wadebridge-Waterloo
SR	Up	9.50-9.58 am	Padstow-Waterloo
WR	Down	10.05 am	Freight ex-Plymouth terminates
WR	Up	10.15 am	Depart to Plymouth
SR	Down	11.09-11.13 am	Okehampton-Padstow
WR	Down	12.15 pm	Ex-Plymouth terminates
SR	Up	12.18-12.22 pm	Padstow-Waterloo
WR	Up	12.40 pm	Depart to Plymouth
SR	Down	12.49-12.53 pm	Waterloo-Padstow
WR	Down	1.47 pm	Ex-Plymouth terminates
WR	Up	2.05 pm	Depart to Plymouth
SR	Down	2.15 pm	Ex-Halwill terminates
WR	Up	2.20 pm	Freight depart to Plymouth
SR	Up	2.19-2.23 pm	Padstow-Waterloo
SR	Up	2.48 pm	Depart, light engine to Halwill
SR	Down	3.29-3.36 pm	Waterloo-Padstow
SR	Up	3.52-3.55 pm	Light engine Wadebridge-Exmouth Junction
WR	Down	4.39 pm	Ex-Plymouth terminates
SR	Up	4.49-4.54 pm	Padstow-Okehampton
SR	Down	4.51-4.56 pm	Waterloo-Padstow
WR	Up	5.40 pm	Depart to Plymouth
SR	Up	6.45 pm	Freight ex-Wadebridge arrives
SR	Down	6.46-6.51 pm	Okehampton-Padstow
SR	Up	7.23-7.29 pm	Padstow-Okehampton
SR	Up	7.40 pm	Freight depart to Exmouth Junction
WR	Down	7.55 pm	Ex-Plymouth terminates
WR	Up	8.35 pm	Depart to Plymouth
SR	Down	8.42 pm	Ex-Okehampton terminates
WR	Down	10.10 pm	Ex-Plymouth terminates

As can be seen a little later at Padstow, the contrast of this with the final year in 1966, just five years later, is tragically extraordinary:

Launceston, Summer 1966

7.22 am	Down to Wadebridge from Okehampton
7.48 am	Up to Halwill from Launceston
9.56 am	Up to Okehampton from Wadebridge
12.31 pm	Down to Wadebridge from Halwill
3.27 pm	Up to Okehampton from Wadebridge
5.37 pm	Down to Wadebridge from Okehampton
7.21 pm	Down from Halwill terminates
7.45 pm	Up from Wadebridge to Okehampton

At the far end of the line **Wadebridge** too could be a busy place as trains from Bodmin North and Bodmin Road, together with trains from the North Cornwall line steamed in side by side from the south-east, having converged a mile up the line where for a few short years Wadebridge Junction signal box had stood until 1907, to be replaced by two parallel lines and two gantried outer and inner home signals, controlled from the handsome brick-built Wadebridge East signal box.

Graced with an island platform as well as a down main platform, the view eastwards displayed spacious water meadows surrounding the still, at this point, relatively narrow River Camel, extensive sidings and an impressive four-armed gantry signal for up trains. All this contrasted with the narrow opening through which down trains departed on their way to Padstow. Passing another wonderful tall double-armed, lower quadrant, co-acting signal, standing a few yards short of the platform edge and back onto single line, trains squeezed their way towards cramped Wadebridge West box, with its shortened gates, protected by the advanced starting signal in the down direction and a tall gantried up home, on the wrong side of the line, giving drivers a better view as they approached from Padstow.

From here it was away for the final magnificent six miles towards the terminus, as the River Camel now opened up its vistas for spectacular views across the estuary, preparing the river for its final journey out to the Atlantic Ocean via Padstow on one side and Daymer Bay and Trebetherick on the other. These final six miles were totally different to anything else on the line. There were no gradients to negotiate and the views were warm and lushly scenic as opposed to the windswept barrenness of the Otterham-Delabole area. One writer compares this section as being like the Teignmouth-Dawlish route on the GWR main line.

Although the Dawlish sea wall is impressive, for me this was rather more beautiful. The pace was less rushed, the countryside unspoilt, there were fewer houses and the colours more varied. To be fair one was largely sea and the other estuary. But whatever the preference this was a quite unique piece of line.

I say 'was' but it is still possible to re-live the views passengers enjoyed right up to 1967 (the Wadebridge -Padstow section having lived on for a further three months after the rest of the line) by cycling here along the Camel Trail. Many tell-tale signs of the railway can still be spotted along the route and none more so than the fine Petherick viaduct ¾ mile from the terminus. No longer does a battered and slightly leaning fixed distant signal stand at the upside approach to the bridge, but the view has not changed and riders can still relive the pleasure that thousands before them would have felt, knowing that journey's end is near, as they pedal the final curving yards around the coastline, before a sharp left curve into what was once Padstow station.

With only two months before the closure of the North Cornwall Railway, the afternoon return trip to Halwill Junction sits in the platform at Wadebridge facing the gantry signal which directs trains either towards Halwill (left) or to Bodmin (right). *Author*

Padstow looking along its single platform towards the buffer stops. *Author's Collection*

Although **Padstow** was well provided for with a run-round loop, long sidings and considerable facilities for manoeuvring freight over its 60-plus years of life, not least fish, there was only one long straight platform at journey's end, which at times necessitated considerable shunting movements as trains came and went, bearing in mind that trains from the Bodmin lines also terminated here.

Trains approached Padstow via a sharp curve past the signal box into the platform with the result that both the home signal and the advanced starter were out of view around the initial curve which hugged the cliff face. None the less the signalman could look directly out of his box and see an approaching train for some miles the other side of the estuary. Although the signal box, situated where it was, was rather in the shadows, the view northwards over the waters towards Wadebridge was stunning.

The station had all the dignity of a Southern Railway structure and as at Launceston and Camelford, boasted a typical protective awning over its single platform. Although the station could be filled to full-length capacity by long trains from Waterloo, on my final steam visit in 1964 I recall being taken by a local train back to Wadebridge with a 'West Country' class and just one single coach! How were the mighty fallen!

In the last year of its life, the North Cornwall line had to bear the sad insult of its miniscule train workings even being left out of the public timetable. But already by 1964, with freight totally withdrawn from Padstow, the writing was on the wall.

One can see how quickly things changed between 1962 and 1965 by comparing the following three sets of normal weekday timetabling. The demise from summer Saturday workings was of course even greater. The North Cornwall line trains have been indicated by *italics*.

Padstow (SX) trains - September 1962

Arrive	Depart
7.34 am freight from Wadebridge	
(Ex-Yeoford previous day)	
8.00 am from Bodmin General	8.12 am to Bodmin General
	8.30 am to Waterloo
8.50 am from Bodmin Road	9.03 am to Bodmin Road
9.22 am from Waterloo	
	10.10 am freight to Yeoford
10.49 am from Bodmin Road	10.57 am to Bodmin Road
11.50 am from Bodmin North	
12.09 pm from Okehampton	*12.58 pm to Waterloo*
1.29 pm from Wadebridge	
2.34 pm from Bodmin North	2.52 pm to Bodmin North
	3.13 pm to Exeter
4.29 pm school train from	
Wadebridge (Unadvertised)*	
4.55 pm from Bodmin North	5.02 pm to Bodmin North
5.21 pm from Waterloo	
	5.35 pm light engine to Wadebridge
6.22 pm from Wadebridge	*6.00 pm to Okehampton*
	6.35 pm light engine to Wadebridge
7.09 pm from Bodmin Road	7.35 pm to Bodmin General
7.58 pm from Okehampton	8.30 pm to Wadebridge
10.26 pm from Bodmin Road	10.22 pm to Wadebridge

* On non-school days this ran as a light engine or empty stock. SX- Saturdays-excepted.

Padstow weekday trains - September 1964

Arrive	Depart
7.54 am light engine	
8.09 am empty coaching stock from Wadebridge*	8.10 am to Bodmin Road
8.29 am from Bodmin North	8.35 am to Wadebridge
	8.48 am to Exeter
9.14 am from Okehampton	
10.48 am from Bodmin Road	*11.05 am to Okehampton*
	11.20 am to Bodmin Road
12.17 pm from Okehampton	
12.42 pm from Bodmin Road	12.45 pm to Bodmin Road
	3.45 pm to Okehampton
4.09 pm from Exeter	
4.37 pm from Bodmin Road	4.50 pm empty coaching stock
5.10 pm from Bodmin Road	5.15 pm to Bodmin Road
5.49 pm from Wadebridge	
	6.20 pm to Okehampton
7.02 pm from Bodmin Road	7.05 pm to Bodmin Road

* This coaching stock worked the 8.48 am to Exeter. It had arrived at Wadebridge the night before as the 6.55 pm from Okehampton which terminated at Wadebridge at 9.00 pm. Thus only three trains *from* Okehampton and four *to* Okehampton.

Padstow weekday trains - September 1965

Arrive	Depart
	8.16 am to Bodmin General*
8.40 am from Wadebridge	8.45 am to Bodmin Road
10.30 am from Bodmin Road	10.45 am to Bodmin Road
12.20 pm from Bodmin Road	12.45 pm to Bodmin Road
2.32 pm from Bodmin Road	2.37 pm to Bodmin Road
4.18 pm from Halwill	
4.45 pm from Bodmin General*	5.00 pm to Wadebridge
5.21 pm from Wadebridge	*5.30 pm to Halwill*
6.43 pm from Bodmin Road	6.55 pm to Bodmin Road

* Unadvertised school train.

For those who loved this railway, it was heart-breaking how the North Cornwall line was strangled out of its furthest outpost in those last years: no freight, barely any service to Exeter and only one train a day beyond Wadebridge. Latterly even this was cut back to Wadebridge with only one connection a day from Padstow from 8.45 am, and two in the down direction arriving at Padstow at 8.41 am and 6.54 pm.

Padstow signal box was closed on 9th January, 1966 and the line thereafter was run under 'One Engine in Steam' regulations until total closure just over a year later.

Travelling down the line

Years ago I attended a series of lectures at Durham University by an obscure but delightful academic, on the subject of Milton's *Paradise Lost*. The first lecture turned out to be simply about the very first word 'Of'', as in 'Of man's first disobedience....'

It was heavy stuff but because of his natural enthusiasm, he had the gift to hold us for an hour, relating to later passages as to the importance of this initial word. I remember enjoying the whole experience hugely although often losing the thread of a brain much more capable than mine. But what made the lecture was at the end, when this delightful elderly scholar removed his glasses from his nose and himself from his notes, looked at us with a wonderfully humble smile and said, 'Well, I don't imagine that anything I've said tonight is going to change the world. But I find it quite fascinating and thank you for bearing with me!' We stood and cheered.

Now, I always had a fascination about the way in which branch lines depart from their main line. Well yes, perhaps I should get out more. But for some odd reason this really does stir the old grey cells, although I doubt if any university will ever invite me to lecture on the topic! The, still alive and still with semaphore signals at St Erth, St Ives branch curves away from the main line, out of its bay platform, in a dignified traditional way, as Thomas the Tank Engine might have puffed out of his platform and away from Gordon on the main line! The former branch line from Gwinear Road to Helston, arrogantly strode out of its platform on a dead straight departure forcing the main line to take a steep curve. The radical little Looe branch rudely turns its back on the main line at Liskeard as it stands in its own platform. The Bodmin branch curves away from the former Bodmin Road, now Bodmin Parkway, into a mysteriously romantic woodland setting. While the Plymouth-Launceston branch, as we have already seen, chunters happily along the big main line for a while before curving away at Tavistock Junction. I could go on much longer!

Like the Launceston branch, the North Cornwall Railway used the main line for a mile or so, before setting off on its own independent way, and **Meldon Junction** where this happened, was one of the most wonderful junction points of any railway I have known. If I were a better musician, I would love to have been able to capture in music the scene of, perhaps, a 'T9' class 4-4-0 making its long, visible sweep towards this junction from the Padstow direction. From the delightful, if totally exposed, west-facing Meldon Junction signal box, the train could be seen for over half a mile away, as it plunged out of a cutting with the fixed distant signal high up on the top of the bank. From this point the line curved sharply over an impressively high embankment to cross the A30 Launceston-Okehampton road, (today almost unrecognisable through road changes) , then to slow as it swept round to meet the Plymouth line, passing the branch up home signal with Meldon Quarry's fixed distant beneath. Clattering over the main line points and still slowing, by this time the signalman would have crossed the line and have been waiting to catch the token from Ashbury, standing on a raised platform on the up side of the line. For the final months of the railway's life, North Cornwall drivers would have had to not only give up the token but also exchange it for the short journey to the next signal box at Meldon Quarry, the double track over the magnificent Meldon viaduct having been singled.

The line east of Halwill was always slightly busier than the stations beyond Halwill with a mixture of Bude and Padstow trains. Diminutive **Maddaford Moor Halt for Thornton Cross**, some two miles from Meldon, was the only 'halt' on the line and the last station to be built in 1927. This was an idyllic spot on a summer afternoon but lonely in the extreme in the depths of winter with only a solitary couple of lamps and a small unsubstantial waiting hut on the down side.

The little platform stood at the mouth of the upper end of a former crossing loop which had been taken out of use after just 20 years of service in 1919, seven years before the station was built. Today the line to the west of the station makes a pleasant walk and the track is easily discernible. It takes a moment or two to realize that one

Meldon Junction signal box in 1964 from the top of the down inner home signal. The North Cornwall Railway sweeps off to the right while the line to Plymouth vanishes away to the left.
Author

Maddaford Moor Halt looking in the down direction. This is the only photograph I have ever seen looking this way. Long before there was a station here there had been a crossing loop. The station arrived after this had closed and was the only single-platformed station on the line. Despite its size it was well patronized until the end. *Roger Joanes*

has eventually stumbled upon the old station itself, but the familiar road bridge just beyond, under which the train curved, suddenly makes the walker aware that those strange grassy mounds and projecting edges all point to the mortal remains of this little station. The view is as it ever was!

Almost as remote, and possibly the least known location on the whole journey, was **Venn Gates Crossing**, the only crossing box on the line, situated near the 204 mile post, two miles before Ashbury and four miles from Meldon. With no passengers to deal with and with only the bells from neighbouring boxes for company, the crossing keeper's job here would have been one of the easiest and loneliest over the whole length of the line. The small signal box had five levers with home signals and working distants in each direction, lever three locking the gates. The down distant to the east was clearly visible from the box around a fine 60 chain curve, while the tall up distant stood out clearly at the top of a long straight section near the 875 ft summit. This was not a block post so the signalman did not have to respond to the bells between Meldon and Ashbury, merely note that a train was on its way, close the gates and pull off the two signals. In practice, however, and certainly latterly, since the crossing was little used, the signals were often left 'off' in both directions with the gates closed to road traffic unless a car needed to cross over.

One of my huge regrets is not having taken more photographs at this time but as a pocket-moneyed teenager, well before the days of carefree digital photography, economy was an important factor! However, I can boast that the only two photos I have ever seen at this location are my own, taking in the early 1960s. But pride may come before a fall and I am more than happy to be proved wrong!

Since this was, rather like Lowery Road on the GWR to Princetown, the least noticed spot of the line, I had again made note of the times trains passed here in 1964 during the final summer of both freight and the 'Atlantic Coast Express'. Although somewhat out of the way, there was still a good deal of traffic going by. However, after September of the same year, things would start to become somewhat quieter.

Approximate times at Venn Gates Crossing. Weekdays (SX), Summer 1964
4.59 am down mail and freight, Okehampton-Bude
6.02 am down mail and freight, Exeter-Launceston
6.42 am down passenger and newspapers to Padstow
7.37 am down freight Exmouth Junction-Bude
8.37 am up passenger Bude-Okehampton
10.16 am down passenger to Padstow.
10.52 am up passenger Padstow-Exeter
11.18 am up Padstow-Waterloo 'Atlantic Coast Express'
12.02 pm down freight to Launceston
1.45 pm down passenger to Bude.
2.59 pm up passenger Padstow-Okehampton.
3.24 pm down passenger to Padstow 'Atlantic Coast Express'
3.48 pm down passenger to Padstow
4.34 pm up passenger Bude-Okehampton
5.25 pm down passenger to Bude
5.38 pm up passenger Padstow-Exeter
6.11 pm down passenger to Wadebridge
6.20 pm up freight Bude-Exmouth Junction
7.21 pm up freight Wadebridge-Okehampton
7.56 pm down passenger to Bude
8.30 pm up passenger Padstow-Okehampton
8.58 pm up freight Launceston-Exmouth Junction
9.11 pm up light engine Halwill-Okehampton

Venn Gates Crossing in September 1962. An evening train for Bude approaches this lonely outpost on the line, the only level crossing box of its type on the whole route. It was not a block post and the gates and signals were left in favour of the trains most of the time unless cars needed to cross.   *Author*

Tower Hill looking down towards Launceston in 1965. Only the up line on the right was in use by this time. The author's parents stand by the station nameboard with his mother trying to encourage a rambling rose … as was her wont!   *Author*

At a little over eight miles from Okehampton, **Ashbury for North Lew** was a cottage-like gem of a station which remained as such until the final closure in 1966. With its single-storey, cream-painted long main building on the down side and its wide drive approach, together with neatly kept flower beds, this was a wonderful project for an aspiring modeller looking for something simple but attractive, including as it did a couple of sidings, and a small goods shed alongside an agricultural store.

The station was on a straight run through the up platform rising on a 1 in 73 from the down direction and disappearing to the right beyond the up distant signal, giving the road bridge on the up side a wonderful vantage point to watch an evening train climb up out of the sun, on under the bridge, passing the squat little up home signal, over the points and away to the right towards a backdrop of Dartmoor beyond. On the up platform was a waiting room and towards the down end a delightful, small platform-level box which latterly also housed the ticket office. Passengers catching a down train therefore usually used the barrow crossing on the down side to obtain their tickets before crossing back to await their train. Manned and well-kept to the end by courteous staff, this little station served a wide area of villages, and not just tiny little Ashbury some distance away.

On through Halwill which has already been described, the line took a sharp curve to the south-west; it was downhill, almost, the whole way to Launceston some 15 miles away via two delightful stations, Ashwater and Tower Hill; the former station I shall return to in the next section.

David Wroe's detailed description of **Tower Hill** shows how this unlikely station, typically serving such a wide area of tiny habitations, had a series of changes throughout its life, mainly due to the changing necessities of freight during its history. In the early 1960s the long siding off the up platform towards Launceston was still in evidence. The loop here was the longest on the whole line capable of holding up to 40 wagons as did also the long up refuge siding. Although the view under the bridge in the up direction did not give much warning of a train's approach, the view in the down direction was the longest straight stretch on the whole line of some two miles.

My memory of trains crossing here was most poignant on a gloriously sunny day in the summer of 1963. Viewing from the road bridge with the small up starter just beneath, I recall the clatter of a freight train coming down the Carey valley from Ashwater several minutes before it came into view. Since it was due to cross with an non-stop up train, the home signal was 'on' and therefore having passed the down distant, at caution, the approaching train gave a long throaty whistle which echoed down the valley. A minute later it rounded the curve as the home signal was pulled 'off', thence into the platform where the signalman waiting on the up side was all set to catch the token, deftly thrown across as if a cricketer aiming for the stumps. Way away in the long distance the smoke of the approaching up train could just be seen.

In 1920 the original box at Tower Hill had been closed and soon after the sidings were worked from a ground frame. The loop and signals were re-instated in 1943 but incorporated into the booking office with a rather attractive bow window, a merciful bonus for the signalman in wet and wild wintry weather, saving him a run to the signal box as was the case at many other stations.

Back to that summer day in 1963, the signalman returned to the booking office and signal frame where he worked hard to replace and extract the tokens, making it in time to pull off the two stop signals, followed by the distant just before the train

Charming Egloskerry only a few months before closure in 1966. The diminutive railcar had to wait for some 45 minutes for a pilotman to arrive after the failure of the tablet instrument to Camelford, even though there was no other train on the line. *Author*

The following year the signal box at Egloskerry is in decay. A view looking from the signal box towards Launceston. *Author*

reached it. The driver dutifully responded with a long, mile away 'toot', undoubtedly gratified that he now had a clear run through the station. Back on the platform the signalman poised himself for the familiar give and take of the tokens.

On a rising gradient and with a heavy load, the drivers of non-stop trains were reluctant to slow down too much for the exchange which, at speed, demanded both focused eye and steady hand. With the one hand held high to give the token for Ashwater, and lower arm outstretched to receive the token from Launceston, the train stormed through the platform and the exchange was done. Blink and you would have missed it. With renewed energy the engine regained full momentum and was away around the curve and up towards Ashwater while the down freight hissed patiently on the other side, waiting for the line to be cleared down to Launceston. But there was, it seemed no rush. After a series of bells and tokens in and out again, the signalman, having pulled off the down starter, crossed to the down platform. No throwing across this time. Signalman, driver and fireman exchanged news while the guard sat on the station seat. A few minutes passed at which point there seemed to be a common understanding that it was time to move on. A flagless guard gave a wave to the driver and with the barest suggestion of a whistle the train moved off effortlessly, down the long straight to Launceston, disappearing out of vision after several minutes. And once again peace descended upon this tranquil backwater. There was a quiet efficiency about this little station, modest though it was, also a certain warmth despite its remoteness, possibly because of the combined working area of booking office and signals all as one. As with Ashwater, the station once again lost its box in the final year of its life in November 1965 and the station became unstaffed.

In 2009 I happened to cross the old bridge on my way from Launceston to Okehampton, taking a somewhat circuitous route. But it wasn't until I had crossed the bridge that I realised where I was. Even then it was hard to get any sense of bearings so much had changed. Indeed of all the stations between Halwill and Padstow, more, if not everything, at Tower Hill has probably vanished than at any other location. So, cherished are the memories.

Launceston was the lowest point on the journey until the line was getting towards the coast, lying between the two summits, the one above Venn Gates and the other above Otterham. The two stations which followed were Egloskerry and Tresmeer. Just as Ashwater and Tower Hill were slightly similar, so too these two stations had similarities, both being of red brick. Of all the stations on the line, **Egloskerry** was probably one of the most idyllic, situated in verdant pastureland and perfectly situated to serve the village after which it was named.

This was the only station between Halwill and Wadebridge to boast a level crossing which was just off the down end. The main station buildings were on the up side with the signal box just off the up end of the up platform. This signal box was typical of many on the line, being a Southern Region type 3. Many similar boxes were built in the 1880s when the railways were fast expanding although as the line progressed towards Padstow there were some slight variations in style. Generally roomier than previous styles of box, type '3' boxes were brick based with the windowed top half in wood; they were square-shaped with a multitude of latticed window panes which gave good light to the interior but could be fearfully cold in winter without some form of heating. The station nameboard, as at Egloskerry, was normally fixed to the wooden boarding immediately below the windows and above the brickwork. However because of the battering these little structures received from the winter's winds and rains, this boarding often became weathered and was replaced by brickwork as could be seen at Tresmeer, Otterham or Camelford, for example. In latter days at these smaller stations when there was only one member of staff on duty, it seemed that the heart of the station was, often as not, in the signal box, rather than in the booking office. But at both Egloskerry and Tresmeer the token instruments were in the booking office and it was here that the porter/signalman spent most of his time.

South facing with well kept flower beds there was a real rural warmth about this station, close to its nearby village community, pub and church, and a stark contrast with those stations on the higher reaches which lay ahead in the down direction. Were Egloskerry up and running today, it would be the perfect setting for the producers of those films and TV programmes in which actors ascended or descended in their period costumes to awaiting horse-drawn carriages or a long outdated grand vintage car. Up trains entered the station from around a sharp curve as they approached the level crossing, with the up home signal almost out of sight. Trains from Launceston could be viewed from the platform over a gentle curve from beneath a bridge a quarter of a mile away, and rising on a 1 in 120 gradient, this soon to quickly increase a mile after the station to as much as 1 in 70, from there until the summit beyond Otterham.

In the summer of 1966 there were only three trains each way arriving at Egloskerry at approximately: 7.30 am down, 9.45 am up, 12.40 pm down, 3.20 pm up, 5.45 pm down and 7.35 pm up. I simply note these to show what huge gaps there were between trains in that final year and the one remaining booking clerk/signalman needed to be happy with his own company. On one beautiful summer's day, three of us travelled from Launceston to Wadebridge on the 11.25 am from Okehampton. Sitting in the front of the single diesel rail car we had a superb view of the journey. As we approached Egloskerry we saw the down home was 'off'. But the down starter was 'on' despite the level crossing gates being open. Could it be that even at this late date there was another train with which we were going to cross, even though no other train was booked for another, almost, three hours? Alas no! The token system had failed between here and Camelford and we had to wait for a pilotman who had to drive from, yes indeed, Camelford! The delightful and apologetic signalman who, in a few months time would be redundant, was quick to point out that the realignment of the block section after Tresmeer signal box had closed back in November had been badly done and 'it never should have happened', adding again for emphasis and with heartfelt Cornish wisdom 'it never should have happened'.

It seemed extraordinary that the despite the fact that this single coach diesel railcar was the only train on the whole 40 mile section between Halwill and Wadebridge, none the less we had to wait 40 minutes in order to secure pilot working to see us safely to Camelford! But then 'rules is rules' I suppose. In fact nobody seemed to mind, not least the guard and driver who knew they had over an hour to spare once they arrived at Wadebridge before the return journey. And it was 40 minutes well spent loitering around the station, over the level crossing, looking in the signal box ('make yourself at home' we were told, and we did), and looking in the booking office where the malfunctioning tablet instrument sat innocently looking back at us. It was hard to believe on that idyllic summer's afternoon, as we savoured the beauty of that one-coach train, patiently waiting in the down platform amidst a perfect rural setting of flowers and grassy woodland, that within three months that heavenly scene would never be recaptured again, except in the pages of the photograph album. So it does, and it remains a favourite image.

I could stay much longer here but it's time to move on up the 3½ miles towards **Tresmeer,** in which the train climbed 155 ft. Although similar architecturally, Tresmeer was yet another station some distance from the village after which it took its name, the wonderfully sounding nearby hamlets of Splatt and Three Hammers being in fact slightly closer, but I suppose 'Tresmeer' sounded rather more Cornish. 'By Tre, Pol and Pen, ye shall know all Cornishmen' as my mother used to remind me.

The signal box was on the up platform, and the main buildings here were on the down side, but since these faced north-west, the red brick only warmed to the sunlight towards the end of the day. While the approach from the down side was around a long curve for almost a mile as the line fell down from the Otterham direction, the view from the up side was almost blind because of a sharp left-hand curve and through a steep cutting which necessitated the down home signal being positioned on the wrong side to allow better vision for the driver. The up starter was the shortest signal on the line, crouched between the road bridge. I always wished I had bought it for the garden! The up platform with its typical waiting shelter was flanked by a row of rhododendrons and some trees, beyond which was a fabulous view of rolling North Cornwall hills.

My first visit to Tresmeer was in the late 1950s returning home with my parents from Bude via a roundabout way. We stumbled upon the station by chance, not an easy thing to do since it was fairly secluded, and I recall the excitement of seeing trains being signalled in both directions. The excitement was short-lived when I realised they were the two starting signals and the trains had departed some minutes before. Since the token instruments were again here in the booking office, the signalman had yet to return to the box to set the signals back. In fact he was waiting for the trains to clear Otterham and Egloskerry so that he could go home! Thus it was I learnt that the last two trains of the day for many years crossed at Tresmeer a little after seven, and that the signalman here was the first on the line to set off homewards!

It was almost six miles from here to the summit and in bad weather with a heavy load this was a demanding climb for the driver and his fireman, even more so with the normally required stop at Otterham some five miles up the gradient. But these were engines and drivers who knew what was expected and how to get to that 237 milepost from which began the long descent to Camelford and finally the sea.

In the late summer of 1962, I travelled down on the 'Atlantic Coast Express' to visit a friend at Port Isaac. Despite being the summer, it was the foulest of days, blowing a gale, and with driving rain and mist. Of course this did not prevent me sticking my head out of the window as we travelled down the gradient at a spanking pace! As we approached Camelford's down distant, enveloped in mist, there below it was a gallant fog-signalman, buttoned up to the neck, with his flag in hand. I imagined this was one of the most miserable jobs possible. A day or two later, however, and on an equally dismal foggy day, I visited **Camelford,** arriving at a relatively quiet moment. As always the staff were friendly and welcoming. There in the signal box was the same fog-signalman with the inevitable cup of tea. I expressed empathy with the job he had to do. This was dismissed by a loud Cornish laugh. He made it clear that the worse the weather the more he liked the job. He explained that he could time his arrival at the signal to within minutes of the train's arrival, setting off at about the time the train left Tresmeer. However, in extremely bad weather, he told me, a sympathetic driver of an up train would sometimes take him on the footplate and drop him off on the way if trains were crossing at Otterham, or in the case of an unhurried down train, pick him up and return him to the station for another 'cuppa'

Tresmeer station in 1964 showing the main station buildings on the down side. In its final year the up loop was taken out of use and the station became unstaffed.   *Author's Collection*

With the author's father again waving, this is Camelford in 1962 looking up towards Launceston. Although similar in style, Camelford had slightly superior facilities to those at Otterham.   *Author*

before his next trek up the line. Like so many of his ilk, here was a genuinely happy man and a true railwayman who would never win riches or fame, but who loved what he did and was proud of his railway. Would that the world was filled with more like him.

Camelford was an important railhead. The village after which it was named was some distance the south, the station standing in the hamlet of Melorne. To the north however lay the popular coastal resorts of Tintagel, Boscastle and Trebarwith. Crackington, a little further up the coast was closer to Otterham. Camelford was at times therefore, and especially in the summer, an extremely busy place.

The typical and delightful signal box at the end of the up platform, had 17 levers, and the well provisioned, often busy, goods yard off the up end of the down platform contained a loop, which meant the signalling was slightly more complicated than at other smaller stations. Although this required the usual three signals in each direction, the down ground signal, lever four, for the loop was also pulled off for down trains as well as levers one, two and three. The main buildings were also on the up platform with easy access from the wide car park outside. A fine awning stood on four columns over the up platform, providing what must have been welcome shelter for passengers on a rainy and crowded day, an addition afforded to very few stations on the line and underlining its importance, an importance, however, which also reflected what a blow the railway's closure was to those for whom this was a vital lifeline in a somewhat inaccessible area. As at Otterham, the up starter was a distinctive lower quadrant signal which, at Camelford, survived to the very end.

The impressive approach to the station of a train from the up direction was of it curving around and under a private road bridge, with the unusual name of Horragutter, some ¼ mile away, on a 40 chain curve before straightening up for the run into the station. The view of a departing down train was similar to that at Otterham, under a road bridge and through a cutting past a tall up home signal, then curving away and down to Delabole. Although the journey from Otterham was largely downhill for the remainder of the journey, there was a gentle 1 in 330 up though the station before the line again descended the short 2½ miles down to Delabole, the shortest distance between any two stations on the whole journey although both were fully signalled until the end, as indeed was the next station at Port Isaac Road. Bearing in the mind the signal boxes that were closed in 1965, it was strange that the boxes at these very close distances were kept working.

Of all the stations on the line **Delabole** was in some ways historically the most interesting. Although perfectly positioned for the village it served it was perhaps the least attractive station. The vast slate quarries off the up side of the down loop were, of course, the reason for Delabole's existence and the reason the line followed this particular route. The main buildings on the down side were facing north, adding to the somewhat sombre, grey feelings about the whole station campus, reflecting the greyness of its main resource. The vast gaping upturned mouth of the quarry, above which sidings precariously ran, could have been the backdrop for some dastardly plot of a James Bond movie. Up trains made an impressive half-mile curve in the quarry direction and the station just beyond, passing heaps of discarded slate together with the only advanced starting signal on the line between Halwill and Wadebridge. This signal was for up trains and allowed for the shunting and departure of freight trains from the quarry.

In the down direction, as at the two previous stations, the line passed under a road bridge and a tall up home signal before swiftly curving away out of sight. The line

Delabole looking in the up direction. *Author's Collection*

'N' Class 2-6-0 No. 31832 enters Port Isaac with an up freight in September 1961. *Roger Joanes*

descended 300 ft in the four miles down to **Port Isaac Road,** approaching this delightful rural outpost via a magnificent one mile curve which continued through the station before straightening up and dropping down steeply away at 1 in 73, through a deep cutting, passing yet another very tall up home signal, while a siding stretched away in the down direction on the up side, shelved above the falling main line.

Situated at the top of a lonely twisty lane the station was some four miles from Port Isaac itself. But despite the distance, even in its final year it remained well served by holiday makers. Today, although inhabited and still in good repair, it has been largely forgotten. Even the wonderfully ebullient recent rector's wife, Liz Bartlett, well-educated on local matters, had no idea where the station had been situated; she now knows! The down platform, curving back on itself with its typical 20 ft-wide stone waiting shelter, and a slightly off-centre station sign nearby, was set against an attractive backdrop of rolling green fields, while the stations buildings and signal box, set close together and just separated by the entrance from the car park, graced the curving up platform.

Continuing to drop down sharply from Port Isaac Road, passing through Trelill tunnel, the only tunnel on the line and with Port Isaac's diminutive up distant signal close against the up-side entrance, by the time **St Kew Highway** was reached, crossing the A39 road, a window gazing passenger would have been aware that slightly larger pockets of population were starting to appear on the scene. While being less remote, St Kew was almost identical to Port Isaac with again the main buildings on the up side, the only main difference being that here the signal box was off the end of the up platform on the down side and not on it, another type '3' signal box with a tall brick base and with fully glazed wooden encased windows; as at Port Isaac, it contained 17 levers. This was another signal box casualty, less than a year before closure, in November 1965 after which only the down platform was left in use, the only one of the stations to lose their crossing loop where the platform with the main buildings was not used.

'N' class 2-6-0 No. 31840 stands at St Kew Highway with a train for Wadebridge on 22nd April, 1960. 'Battle of Britain' class Pacific No. 34085 *501 Squadron* approaches with the up 'Atlantic Coast Express'. *Roger Joanes*

Ashwater station in 1964 looking up towards Halwill Junction.   *Author*

Ashwater station looking down towards Launceston in 1964.   *Author*

Although only four miles from Wadebridge and its estuary, there was no respite for up trains with continuing steep gradients and a succession of sharp curves. Down trains which had earlier worked hard up to Otterham now had the easy run and at around milepost 253 the line from Bodmin could be seen coming in from the left while Wadebridge's down fixed distant flashed past the windows as brakes began to be applied. The two lines approached Wadebridge for about a mile side by side, giving an impression of a double track line, each passing its respective two-armed gantry outer home signal. The larger four-armed inner home controlled signals for both lines guarding a plethora of point work towards the sidings and the three platforms. The East signal box was on the right-hand side of down trains, as was the West box beyond, but with the luxury of two boxes, the token had only to be surrendered and not retrieved. Thence into the platform either to terminate or, with usually a few minutes grace, to continue to Padstow, as already described.

Ashwater

I have left this penultimate section to what latterly became my favourite station on the line, although I have to admit that Otterham was always a close first equal. Ashwater was an absolute rural gem although strangely enough I did not visit it until 1963, and then totally by chance.

The cunning plan was, having been dropped off at Launceston by a kind dad who had driven me from Tavistock, to catch the mid-morning train up to Halwill and then explore the Bude branch which I did not know very well. As chance would have it, everything was running late and by the time the up train arrived at Launceston it was clear I would not make the connection and would have to wait some while for the next train. However, Halwill was always an exciting place at which to pause so that was not a worry. Thus I set off, over once again the now-starting-to-rust rails of the GWR line, up the long straight to Tower Hill, on up that beautifully wooded valley towards Ashwater. What it was I shall never really know, but for some reason, possibly the guilty fact which suddenly struck me, that this was the only station on the whole line I had never visited, I opened the door and alighted. It was confusing that the station below Halwill was *Ashwater* and the station above *Ashbury*, with the result that in more than one book these locations have been confused.

Although Ashwater was not in fact far from the tiny village it served, it actually stood in an area called Ash Mill with a superb village shop just opposite by the name of Moon's which seemed to sell everything and where I regularly went to spend my pocket money. I know memory plays tricks but this shop had a wonderful atmosphere with little nooks and crannies which Charles Dickens would, I am sure, have been able to describe in narrative equal to that of *The Old Curiosity Shop*.

On this particular day at Ashwater, a pleasant-faced porter-signalman called Walter Slade was on duty, and once my up train had departed, he crossed back over the line to the little signal box on the down platform, an oasis of joy which I came to know so well over two or three years. Close alongside was another typical stone waiting shed complete with oil lamp over the entrance. A steep bank backed up behind this platform which in the summer was a mass of wild flowers and grasses.

Since I was obviously loitering, the friendly and outgoing Mr Slade soon returned across to ask if I needed anything, and having ascertained that I was just there to admire the station, was only too happy to show me the booking office, the lamp room and of course the signal box. My delayed up train was crossing with another down train, also running late, at Halwill, the next station up the line so it wasn't long before there was more activity with points being set and the three signals set to 'off'. Just as at Tower Hill next down the line, the narrow wooded valley running down from Halwill meant that on a still day, down trains could be heard rattling down the hill long before they appeared at the station. If the wind was in the other direction, however, the train could appear around the sharp curve on the upside without warning so that signalmen had to be ready and waiting with the token to Tower Hill, even more so if a train was non-stop. As at Tresmeer the down home was on the 'wrong' side of the line in order to give the driver of an approaching train better visibility. However, here at Ashwater the signal was perched high up on top of the bank making it possibly the highest signal on the line. In the down direction the line dropped away for a quarter of a mile at 1 in 73 after the relatively gentle gradient through the platform before curving away to the right and though a series of sharp curves down the Carey valley.

With over an hour before the next train I was offered my first cup of tea in Ashwater signal box. By choice I am not a tea drinker but I never refused a cup when offered one in a signal box having always felt this to be something of an honour and to refuse would have displayed the manners of a cad! Over the tea Walter Slade, on discovering that I was called 'Prance' enquired if I was related to the ENT surgeon of the same name who had treated him some years previously, and when it turned out I was his son, I was very definitely 'in'. As becomes evident in the next chapter, the same thing happened when I first encountered Eric Gray at Bere Alston signal box at around the same time! This Walter was due to finish his early turn after the 'up fast' had gone by just after 12.30 pm at which point the box would be locked and the station unmanned for an hour. However, he informed me that his colleague Walter Harris would be on duty to take up the late turn and that he would ring him to say I was 'OK'! The signal box was duly locked once the up train had cleared Halwill and the key hidden under a plant pot. However, on later occasions as the two Walters got to know me, I was, amazingly, allowed to stay in the box between these two shifts. Eat your heart out health and safety!

During that first lone hour I visited the wonderful Moon's Stores for the first time and walked all over the simple goods yard comprising of one siding running down off the up loop, with another siding running back towards the goods shed and loading bay. Coal and fertiliser products were both in evident supply in the yard and although there were no wagons in the siding on that first visit, it was clear the tracks were still in use. As fate would have it, this would only be for another year.

In another old note book I resurrected some scribbled notes about train times on the summer Saturdays of that time. As they appeared in my book these were:

Ashwater summer Saturday trains, 1963

6.00 am	Down	Non-stop passenger
6.40 am	Down	Non-stop freight
7.27 am	Down	Passenger
8.35 am	Up	Passenger from Launceston
9.21 am	Up	Light engine
9.38 am	Up	Passenger
10.13 am	Up	Passenger
10.55 am	Down	Passenger
12.35 pm	Up	Non-stop passenger

2.20 pm	Down	Passenger to Launceston
2.38 pm	Up	Passenger
3.00 pm	Up	Light engine from Launceston
3.18 pm	Down	Non-stop passenger
4.09 pm	Up	Light engine
4.25 pm	Down	Passenger
5.07 pm	Up	Passenger
6.34 pm	Down	Passenger
7.48 pm	Up	Freight non-stop
8.03 pm	Up	Passenger
8.28 pm	Down	Passenger to Launceston

On those days when my father drove me to Launceston I would usually arrive at Ashwater on the 10.13 am train and returned on the 4.25 pm down. On other occasions I would travel up to Okehampton from Tavistock North early in the morning and arrive at Ashwater at 10.55 am returning on the 5.07 pm up passenger, although on a couple of occasions I stayed until the final up train at 8.03 pm.

Returning however to this first visit, Walter Harris arrived in the due passing of time, walking with a slower, less hurried pace than his early turn colleague. He was also a man of fewer words than Mr Slade and quietly spoken, but one of those good folk who immediately won one's respect. The other Walter had, true to his word, obviously spoken to him since he knew who I was and was happy to accept my company even though I sensed he was a man who was equally happy with his own. The signal box key was duly recovered from the flower pot and the first act of re-entry was, of course, the put the kettle on. The second was to ring Tower Hill to say he was *in situ*.

There was little or no freight in those days on Saturdays but there was always a light engine passing back up from Launceston around 3.00 pm. The time varied slightly, depending on how other trains were running time-wise. Occasionally it paused at Ashwater for a few minutes but usually it went through non-stop, as happened on my first visit. This was my first experience of something called 'Regulation 5' which was a safety measure, usually at smaller stations before a larger, busier station, as was the case at Ashwater with Halwill Junction next stop up the line. In practice what happened was this. When an up train left Tower Hill, the Ashwater signalman would receive two rings on the bell from his colleague at Tower Hill. In order to pull off his signals, the Ashwater signalman then had to ring one beat on the bell to Halwill Junction which the Halwill signalman would acknowledge. In the case of a normal passenger train the Ashwater signalman would beat 3-pause-1 to Halwill. 'Permission for a train to enter section'. The Halwill signalman would respond the same, holding in on the final beat so that the Ashwater signalman could withdraw a token from his token instrument. This enabled him to pull off the up starting signal to show the driver all was clear to the next station, Halwill Junction. If however things were busy at Halwill, the signalman there could only guarantee a clear run as far as the home signal, that is to say as far as the signal protecting the entrance to the station, in which case the driver needed to be warned that he could travel up to Halwill but that he might well be halted outside the station. Thus, instead of replying 3-pause-1 on his bell the Halwill signalman would respond with 3-pause-5-pause-5 which still allowed the token to be withdrawn but indicated 'Regulation 5' was in operation. Normally when a train was accepted under Regulation 5, the train would be checked at the home signal and the driver warned with a green handsignal before the starting signal was

Ashwater station looking down towards Launceston from the top of the down home signal.
Author

BR Standard 2-6-4T No. 80041 arrives at Ashwater with a train from Padstow on 5th December, 1964.   *Roger Joanes*

lowered. Ashwater was one of eight locations listed in the Sectional Appendix where, because of a steep rising gradient, the signalman was authorized to lower all his stop signals.

On this first occasion, Mr Harris allowed me to cross from the signal box to the up platform where he thrust a green flag into my hand, instructing me to stand on the platform and to display it to the driver as the engine came up the gradient. As the coach-less 2-4-2 climbed up into view, passing the up home, the driver gave a hearty blast on his whistle, indicating he had noted the flag and knew that Regulation 5 was in operation up to Halwill.

Oh what power I wielded! Tokens were exchanged in motion and off went the tank engine on its climb up through the woods to Halwill. An hour and a half and three trains later, I said farewell to Mr Harris and was on my way back to Launceston after what would prove to be the first of many visits.

Although I continued to visit other stations over the following few years, it was to Ashwater that I went more often than not and the two Walters became good friends. There were few passengers at Ashwater and such as there were usually locals rather than holiday makers who were more likely to be heading for such as Camelford, Port Isaac or Padstow. Most of these were known to whichever signalman was on duty and while they were issuing tickets I was trusted enough to receive the trains entering our section from Halwill or from Tower Hill, acquiring the token, and pulling off the signals, before placing the token in the pouch and taking it across to whoever was on duty. Occasionally I was allowed to do the token exchange of a stopping train. Initially the signalman would retrieve the old token while I held aloft the new one for the fireman to catch, before I was finally allowed to do both. Once I got it totally wrong and failed to hold the token up correctly with the result it flew across the platform much to my embarrassment. Fortunately driver and fireman both thought this hugely amusing so the only thing damaged was my young pride! I was grateful, however, never to have been entrusted with this task for non-stop trains!

On only one other occasion do I recall overstepping the mark of my capabilities. An upper quadrant signal moves up 45 degrees to the 'off' position and a lower quadrant signal drops 'down'. Although there was still an occasional lower quadrant signal remaining on the North Cornwall Railway, as at Venn Gates, Halwill, Otterham, Camelford and Wadebridge, by this time all signals at Ashwater were upper quadrant. In the hot weather when the wire running from signal box to signal expanded in the heat, some signals did not always rise the full 45 degrees and on this occasion it was obvious to me that the down starter was barely reaching 20 degrees. A signal can be adjusted quite simply by using a tool to tighten the wire. However as this was a section signal, in order to test it, a temporary token needed to be withdrawn from Tower Hill.

The bell code for this was an obscure one which was hardly ever used. Keen to put the signal right, I called one beat to Tower Hill, in order to call attention followed by this bell code. There was a very long pause. Finally the internal phone from Tower Hill rang which I answered. 'What the ************** was that?', came an angry voice down the phone. I grovelled realising that possibly I had been over-eager. Fortunately the Tower Hill man knew who I was and Walter Harris later rang to offer an apology on my behalf. Offering me, bless him, the mildest of rebukes for being a touch over zealous, he told me he wouldn't have had a clue what that particular bell code would have been either. The down starting signal remained at the barely 20 degrees until the cool of the day!

Occasionally I would walk the track with the signalman to change the lamp in the distant signals a mile or so each side of the station. On a fine summer's day this was a pleasant task as we wandered through the wooded countryside, taking about half an hour there and back during a quiet spell in the day between trains.

Sometimes Walter Harris allowed me to change the lamps on the four stop signals which were all within sight of the station. This was not a demanding task unless the weather was foul, apart from the tall down home on top of the bank which required some nerve since as one got higher so the signal started to wobble. Today that kind of signal would have had some protective support on the ladder leading up to the top. Such things were unheard of in those days and poor old health and safety would today have a fit if a totally unqualified 17-year-old did such a thing! However, it was an exciting experience as well as an opportunity to take a fine panoramic photograph from the top, a photograph which I have always treasured.

If I had first learnt the joys of lingering at Meeth Halt as a very young child, it was here at Ashwater that the art was nurtured and developed in the long gaps between the trains. In those periods of inactivity, whichever Walter was on duty would either be dealing with paperwork in the booking office, chatting to a colleague on the internal phone system or reading the newspaper in the comfortable and well worn signal box chair. The box faced comfortably into the sun. A few elderly geraniums adorned the window and around the entrance, and although the two block instruments, tablet to Tower Hill and token to Halwill Junction at each end did not leave a great deal of space in this relatively small box, there was a wonderful peaceful atmosphere of time almost standing still. Already, however, by 1963, with only one member of staff on duty, there was a sense in the booking office and waiting room that the station was in the autumn of its days with the paintwork starting to look just a touch tatty and objects sitting in drawers and cupboards which had long outlived their usefulness or sell-by dates.

In the lamp room there was a strangely shaped, battered old box which had once been affixed to the outside of the signal box and which now lay in long retirement on the floor. This had contained, I was told, the token for the first down train of the day before the box opened. Sure enough, I later discovered the following instructions in the Southern Railway Appendix dated '1934 until further notice'. One needs to bear in mind there was no signal box at Tower Hill at this time.

ASHWATER. Early morning goods and mail train. — The signal box at Ashwater will not be opened for the passing of the early morning goods and mail train, Okehampton to Launceston, and the following arrangements will operate in connection with the passage of that train between Halwill and Launceston:-

After the last train at night has cleared the Halwill-Ashwater section, the Signalman at Halwill must send the appropriate Is line clear signal to Ashwater, and the Signalman there must release a tablet at Halwill for the Halwill-Ashwater section. This tablet must be kept in safe custody at Halwill, and handed by the early turn Signalman there to the Driver of the goods and mail train from Okehampton the following morning.

In like manner, after the last down train at night has cleared the Ashwater-Launceston section, the Signalman at Ashwater must send the appropriate Is line clear signal to Launceston and the Signalman there must release a tablet for that section, which the Ashwater Signalman must withdraw from the instrument and deposit in the slot on top of a special tablet exchange box, which is fixed in front of the signal box in readiness for the Trainmen of the early morning goods and mail train from Okehampton the following day.

The Signalman at Ashwater must, before leaving duty at night, see that the points are correctly set and the outdoor signals lowered for the safe passage of the first down train the following day.

On arrival of the early morning goods and mail train from Okehampton at Ashwater, the Driver must hand the tablet for the Halwill-Ashwater section to the Guard, who must place it in the slot at the side of the special exchange box. This will enable to Guard to withdraw the tablet for the Ashwater-Launceston section from the slot on top of the box by lifting a plunger provided underneath the box, and this tablet he must hand to the Driver, after which the train may proceed to Launceston.

When the Signalman at Ashwater commences duty in the morning he must replace to Danger the outdoor signals, applicable to the down line, ascertain by telephone from Launceston that the goods and mail train has arrived at that station, and accept the Train out of Section signal from the Signalman there. He must then, by means of a special key provided for the purpose, open the door of the special tablet exchange box and obtain the tablet for the Halwill-Ashwater section, re-lock the door and replace the tablet in the instrument and give the Train out of Section signal to Halwill.

With the exception mentioned above, the goods and mail train from Okehampton will not be block signalled between Halwill and Launceston, but the Signalman at Halwill must comminicate by telephone with the Signalman at Launceston, and advise him the time of departure of the train and the Signalman at Launceston must telephone the arrival of the train, with tail lamp attached, to the Signalman at Halwill. In the event of failure of the telephonic communication, the Trainmen must be advised of the circumstances and warned to proceed with caution through the section to Launceston.

I recall Walter Harris remarking, somewhat sadly, that there was a good deal of disused material around the place that needed clearing away. Perhaps even then he was canny enough to realise that it would not be too long before a good deal more would be being discarded. Two years later the little box would be closed, the down loop taken out of use and the station unstaffed.

Meanwhile Ashwater continued to be of loyal service to its small scattered community. The roomy, though sparsely furnished waiting room continued to give shelter from wind and rain, with a couple of posters on the wall, one advertising the delights of the Cornish coast, the other giving warning that trains might be delayed because of FOG, the key word in bright yellow lettering. Over the doorway which led out onto the platform hung the essential round-faced Southern Railway clock which gently ticked away the long minutes from one train until the next, the perpetual and gently therapeutic 'tick-tock' not too fast and not too slow, this being sometimes the sole companion for a lingering traveller, a reminder that time was passing, howbeit slowly. After the box closed in November 1965 it soon stopped since there was nobody to wind it any more. Within a year there would be no trains either and nothing to loiter for.

Finally

In September 1966 I moved to my first job in Dorset as a student teacher, in a delightful Prep School, high up in the Purbeck hills, the start of a long association with the Swanage Railway. Thus I was not around in October when the line came to an end, and in a way I was glad not to have been. I had already said my farewells.

However, I did pay a couple of visits over the summer, the penultimate one being when the already mentioned token failure took place at Egloskerry on a fine summer's day. The final visit was less sunny and the weather reflected the gloom which by now the pervaded the whole line. All freight had long ceased and there were only three trains each way a day with two extra as far as Launceston.

Travelling all six of the remaining trains to and from Wadebridge, my last journey included St Kew Highway which was the station I had least visited. The station house appeared occupied; the up platform on which it stood was now out of use although the track was still *in situ*. The signal box had gone although some vestige of the steps leading up to the box rather oddly remained.

Camelford still had signs of activity with, on this rather dull day weather-wise, lights on in the empty but obviously active booking office and three members of staff enjoying each other's company in the signal box. Only one, I recall was actually on duty, but there was a warm camaraderie of banter. One was retiring, one was to have another job on the railway at Exeter and the third was leaving the railway altogether. There seemed no particular bitterness about the closure, rather a deeply sad resignation. I had travelled up to this point from St Kew, and since there was no down train for over two hours, asked the signalman if I might walk the line to Otterham. He didn't mind in the slightest and so I set off on that last memorable walk , passing the still intact sidings, points and signals before curving away and up towards the down distant and eventually the summit. The damp stillness of the afternoon, was a reminder of how beautiful, remote and isolated this part of the line was, and what a blow its demise would be to those scattered communities who had relied upon it. Walking down the up side from the summit where once Otterham's up distant had stood braving the elements, the familiar row of conifers above the down side of the station came gradually into view as I approached the cutting over which once had towered the tall up home signal. Remembering what a welcome oasis this station had once been, this now had become possibly the saddest station I ever recall in its death throws. It was difficult to tell if anyone was living in the station house but it appeared as silent as the grave. Not a soul was in sight. On the down side, things were still as ever with the waiting shelter longing to welcome a passenger, but now trackless and with weeds adorning its platform. The old waiting room door on the up platform was open but leading to a soulless and empty waiting room area. A battered handwritten notice displaying the six remaining trains each day was fixed to the door. If ever there was a ghost station, this was it.

At some point around 6.00 pm the fifth train of the day, a single coach unit again, pulled slowly into view up the hill bringing the empty station to life for just a brief minute as I climbed aboard, and off we went in the direction from which I had walked an hour before. My intention had been to go to Wadebridge, but realising that this station would remain open for a bit longer after the North Cornwall closure, I changed my mind and alighted for the last time at Port Isaac Road where one other passenger also got off. The train trundled off down through the cutting and I walked the length of both platforms to then be invited into the warmth of the signal box, there to await the return of the last train of the day some 45 minutes later. In due course the familiar 3-pause-1 broke the silence around us, asking for permission to withdraw the Wadebridge-Port Isaac Road token; soon after the 2 beats indicating the train was entering the section. Like a relay race passing the baton from one to another, the Port Isaac signalman now repeated the process up to Delabole for 'permission to enter section', as had happened a thousand times before, and with a new token withdrawn, the three signals were pulled off. The signalman here, also due for retirement, reminisced about earlier days when the platform had been filled with holiday makers and was obviously sad to see the final days of station only a few weeks away. Once again the minimalist train climbed up past the tall up home to stop in the platform. One regular passenger, and obviously well-known to the signalman alighted and exchanged greetings. With no great hurry to rush onwards, guard and signalman chatted for a few minutes before we set off again. The signalman gave us a wave and returned to the box to let Delabole know we were on the way before locking up for the night. On up through Delabole, and Camelford, up to the summit and down through dark deserted Otterham. The train tore down the hill to Tresmeer where no longer did the last trains of the day cross as they had in past, now for the obvious reason, there was no longer a crossing loop here and no more down trains until the next day.

At Egloskerry the distant, home and starter were all set for our passing as were the level crossing gates. The briefest of pauses and on to Launceston where still the one and only 'extra' of the day awaited our arrival in the form of the last down train which terminated at Launceston. At last some action for the signalman as the down train ran over the points in the down direction, and then back onto the rear of our train. The up starter came off, now bereft of the left hand arm which not long ago had beckoned trains forward onto the GWR rails, and we were off again. This was the same train T.W.E. Roche describes in his classic book *The Withered Arm*, on his last visit to the line having travelled down to Launceston from Tower Hill, returning there via this final up train of the day.

Up through deserted Tower Hill and Ashwater and into Halwill Junction where the final up train from Bude was waiting to make us an even bigger train. One of the railcar engines was playing up so there was a few minutes delay before we set off again, but enough time to glance up for a final time at the largest signal box on the line and the tiny Torrington platform beyond, now bereft of any rails.

No comings or goings at Ashbury where the lamps welcomed the final train of the day and as we dropped down through Venn Gates, the signalman stood, leaning over the gates to give the driver a friendly wave. At Maddaford Moor Halt, the smallest stop on the line, several people got off and made their way up the footpath from the station and then we were on the last lap. The orange lamp for Meldon's up distant shone brightly on the top of the bank and the driver seemed to relish a slow approach over that magnificent curve towards the junction where the home signal was 'off'. Although there was a 'catcher' for the tokens of up trains off the branch, with the demise of steam, I believe this was never used again. A few words, tokens were exchanged, and I left the North Cornwall Railway for the last time.

Unlike T.W.E. Roche's final journey to Tower Hill, mine ended at Okehampton which still had six years to run. But his final words in his book *The Withered Arm* sum up what so many who loved this line must have felt in October 1966 as the last train went by:

… and so we came to Tower Hill … where the guard ran up to take my ticket and waved to me as the train ran by; I stood for a while on the platform listening to its sounds growing fainter, then echoing louder again, then dying up the valley of the hanging woods, while the wet Western evening wept for the North Cornwall line.

Chapter Six

The Southern Way to Tavistock
... Beeching's biggest folly

Plymouth North Road - Devonport Junction (where the line to Penzance diverged) (45ch.) - Devonport Kings Road (1m. 16ch.) - Ford (2m. 18ch.) - St Budeaux Victoria Road (3m. 56ch.) - Tamerton Foliot Halt - Bere Ferrers (7m. 70ch.) - Bere Alston (junction for Gunnislake and Callington) (10m. 55ch.) - Tavistock North (17m. 11ch.) - Brentor (22m. 18ch.) - Lydford (23m. 44ch.) - Bridestowe (26m. 61ch.) - Meldon Junction (junction for North Cornwall) (30m. 65ch.) - Meldon Quarry (31m. 33ch.) - Okehampton (33m. 37ch.) - Sampford Courtenay (37m. 12ch.) - North Tawton (39m. 78ch.) - Bow (43m. 9ch.) - Coleford (junction for the North Devon line) (46m. 74ch.) - Yeoford (47m. 71ch.) - Crediton (51m. 42ch.) - Newton St Cyres (54m. 12ch.) - Cowley Bridge Junction (57m. 13ch.) - Exeter St David's (58m. 36ch.).

Before some reflections on specific parts of this route, and hopefully to avoid confusion, it may be helpful to note some particular dates. The 1960s was the decade above all others which was to reduce the size of the railway network forever as a result of the Beeching report. The list of stations above shows the line as it was in the early 1960s. Three small closures of tiny halts near Plymouth had taken place some years before. Between St Budeaux and Ford, Weston Mill Halt closed in 1921 and Camels Head Halt in 1942. Between Ford and Devonport Albert Road Halt closed in 1947. Other cutbacks, closures and changes between Devonport and Yeoford were as follows:

10th June, 1961	Brentor signal box was closed.
10th September, 1962	Tamerton Foliot Halt was closed.
26th January, 1964	Bow signal box was closed.
2nd February, 1964	Sampford Courtenay signal box was closed.
15th June, 1964	Bridestowe signal box was closed.
7th September, 1964	Devonport Kings Road and Ford stations closed after which, trains to Okehampton and beyond were routed onto the ex-GWR line at Devonport Junction via Devonport Albert Road, Dockyard Halt and Keyham, branching off just before St Budeaux Ferry Road to rejoin the old Southern route at St Budeaux Victoria Road.
3rd October, 1966	The North Cornwall line was closed.
7th November, 1966	The branch line to Callington was closed beyond Gunnislake reducing the branch to Bere Alston-Calstock-Gunnislake.
24th September, 1967	North Tawton signal box was closed.
5th May, 1968	Calstock and Gunnislake signal boxes were closed reducing the branch to one long 'siding', once known as 'One Engine in Steam'.
6th May, 1968	The line between Bere Alston and Meldon Quarry was severed and closed resulting in the demise of Tavistock North, Brentor, Lydford, Bridestowe and Meldon Junction. New signalling was installed at the former up end of Bere Alston station to enable branch trains to reverse to Gunnislake.
18th August, 1968	Yeoford signal box was closed.
27th October, 1968	Bere Ferrers signal box was closed.

The goods yard at Bere Alston remained open until February 1968 although at most other stations they had closed earlier including Tavistock in 1966 and Bere Ferrers in 1962.

22nd March, 1970	Meldon Quarry signal box was closed.
7th September, 1970	Bere Alston signal box was closed and a new connection was made at the Plymouth end of the station with a two-lever ground frame installed to be controlled by the train crew.
October 1971	Coleford Junction signal box was closed and the line to Okehampton was henceforth run as a single line from Crediton.
5th June, 1972	All passenger services to Okehampton were stopped resulting in the closure of Bow, North Tawton, Sampford Courtenay and Okehampton.
10th July, 1972	Okehampton signal box was closed and ballast trains ran from Crediton to Meldon Quarry as one single line.

Tamerton Foliot Halt and Bere Ferrers

Although I had been nurtured on the Great Western route to Tavistock, once we had moved there from Plymouth in the 1950s, my interest began to grow towards the 'other way to Tavistock', which departed westwards out of Plymouth as if going to Cornwall before changing direction after St Budeaux and curving under Brunel's great bridge at Saltash then heading northwards via the western outskirts of Dartmoor to Tavistock, Okehampton and beyond.

Although many accepted that cuts had to made on the railways, few imagined that main lines would be affected and certainly not one such as this with the legendary 'Atlantic Coast Express' forging its vital lifeline from London Waterloo to a score of West Country destinations. But not only the 'Atlantic Coast Express', for until the early 1960s there had been a superb service of trains for towns and villages both large and small, and for a rural county like Devon, where roads were often poor and winters bitter, the railway was the heart of community. The mutilation of this line between Bere Alston and Okehampton, and dreadful cutbacks of useful services and connections was probably one of the worse offences perpetrated by the Beeching era. A once great and proud oak of a main line, by the end of the decade had been pruned back to what had become little more than a couple of sad autumnal twigs.

It is not my intention to give a fully detailed description of the line. For that I turn the reader to George Reeve and John Nicholas' magnificent book published by the Irwell Press (see Bibliography). I simply set down my particular memories of the line and hope they may inspire a memory or two in others as well as provide some little information as these memories are retold.

My first early experience of any significance which I can recall of this line was in the 1950s on one of the most diminutive stations on the line, and the least patronized, **Tamerton Foliot Halt.** The village of Tamerton has today been largely engulfed by the vast tentacles of Plymouth, but in the 1950s it was still a community of its own. The station stood on the furthest reaches of the parish almost two miles down a beautifully wooded road alongside an estuary off the Tamar, and it was along this rural retreat that I sometimes went for a walk with my parents. The station was at the end of this road, standing at the edge of a dark cutting with a solid brick bridge on the up side, and with a wonderful riverside location a stone's throw away. There had been a signal box once upon a time but this was closed as far back as 1911, and although the station

Tamerton Foliot Halt shortly before closure in September 1962.   *Author's Collection*

A non-stop Plymouth-bound train enters Bere Ferrers passing a stopping train for Exeter in the up platform in the summer of 1963. With the station on a curve, the tall up starting signal enabled drivers to see it over the top of the embankment on the up side.   *Author*

was staffed for many years by a lady porter called Mrs Angrove, in the late 1950s I never recall ever seeing anyone here; thus there was a distinctly lonely feel to the place through which many trains rushed without stopping, passing the main building on the down side, which was of no particular normal Southern Railway design, resembling a rather dull looking house more than anything else. I remember standing on the down platform one damp afternoon hoping to see a train when there was a strange rumbling sound from beyond the dark sinister curvaceous cutting on the up side. A few minutes later a 'scarily' fast train rushed through the deserted platform. The strange rumbling sound was in fact the train crossing the impressive Tavy Bridge just half a mile around the corner, 1,449 ft-long and one of the most important structures on the line. Near this point the Tamar and Tavy rivers converged, the Tavy flowing under this bridge and then up towards Bere Ferrers and Lopwell.

Tamerton closed in 1962, the only station on the line to do so before final closure apart from the three tiny halts closer to Plymouth previously mentioned. It is still possible to locate the station today although the site remains as lonely as ever. One cannot help but wonder if now, with Tamerton's hugely increased population and with the problems of traffic in and out of Plymouth, possibly many would benefit from its re-opening.

Bere Ferrers, three miles up the line from Tamerton was a wonderful example of a quiet rural station on a main line, with welcoming station approach, and a neat station house and garden serving the delightful village half a mile down the road on the banks of the Tavy estuary, complete with its tiny shop, church and pub. Until 1968 when the station was reduced to an unmanned halt, there were always very friendly staff on duty, Tom Hammett I remember in particular as being only too happy to encourage my interest. The station was on a tight uphill curve in the up direction with a tall up starting signal dominating the station. The height was necessary for up train drivers to be able to see over the top of the embankment, which backed up against the platform, as they pulled up from the Plymouth direction. The attractive signal box with its 17 levers was on the down platform, a few yards down from the main buildings with a couple of small compact sidings leading off from the down end. In this direction the line curved away to the right passing the usual trio of signals with the distant just visible in the distance if you stood on the footbridge. In the up direction there was a good view through the road bridge as the lines snaked away on an 'S' bend' past the advanced starting signal in the distance before disappearing through the trees and up towards Bere Alston, three miles away. This was a very happy and attractive place to be. There were periods of quiet when the kettle in the signal box hissed quietly away to itself followed by periods a great activity with a fast train closely followed by a stopping train in both directions. But there was never any great rush here. God was in his heaven and all was very well with the world. And it remains a good place to be, described in a later chapter, although what was once a busy main line is now a quiet branch line. I have some of my happiest memories at this warm and welcoming place.

Bere Alston

Although I had paused at Bere Alston previously when changing trains to Callington, I hadn't really lingered here until 1961. I caught a morning train down from Tavistock and had been wandering around this sometimes busy station for about an hour and discovering that by far the best vantage point for both up and down trains as well as trains on the Callington branch, was on top of the footbridge. Like Bere Ferrers, the station was on a curve, but here an even steeper one with the down platform, on

A train from Gunnislake climbs up the gradient from Calstock at Bere Alston in 1965 while the main line to Plymouth curves away sharply to the left.   *Author*

Bere Alston station in 1965 with its sharply curving platform looking in the up direction towards Tavistock. The branch platform to Callington is on the left.   *Author*

which the main buildings stood, arching back on itself so that passengers waiting for a down train to Plymouth had no sighting of the train at all until it entered the platform and a fast train could be a surprise for the unsuspecting. The curve away in the down direction was also almost blind. But from the footbridge the view was superb. In the up direction one could watch trains make the almost 90 degree turn away past the distant signal towards Tavistock, and in the down direction there was another sharp curve to the left past the advanced starter high up on a distant bridge which swallowed the train up and out of sight. Branch trains climbed the steep gradient from Calstock before curving sharply up into the branch platform.

Bere Alston station was a mile down the road from the village it served with a stunning view over the Tamar Valley and across to the Cornish hills beyond, so the station had a good rural feel to it. Although there were not the huge gaps in the service as on the North Cornwall line, there were spaces in the day to savour the atmosphere of this country junction. But with some 20 passenger trains in each direction as well the connecting eight branch line trains, it could also be extremely busy and the station was well patronized.

Standing on the bridge in 1961 during a quiet moment of the day, a slightly serious, bespectacled gentleman in railway uniform, with neatly cropped grey hair came past me. 'Interested in railways young man?' 'Yes', I replied, clutching rather obviously my camera. 'Well you'd better come and look at the box then'. I followed him down the steps of the bridge and along the up platform. This was an island platform, from the outer face of which ran the branch line to Gunnislake and Callington.

This was my first encounter with Percy Skinner, the station master at Bere Alston, quietly spoken, modest and held, as I was to discover, in greatest respect. Although I never got to know him well, he it was who gave me my first adult introduction to this part of the railway world and in particular to Eric Gray who was to teach me so much.

On this particular day, a delightful character called Gerry Masters was on the early turn duty in the box; a no nonsense, blunt, but ever jovial man who, in his spare time, swept chimneys, our own included, at Tavistock. Gerry Masters was a relief signalman, that is to say a signalman of no fixed abode but who took over from other signalmen on their day off or on holidays. Thus he might appear at any box along the local network and our paths crossed on a number of subsequent occasions. Indeed he was kind enough at a later date to get me into remote Meldon Junction box. Mr Skinner (and station masters in those days I seem to recall were always referred to as 'Mr' and not by their Christian name, such was their prestige) was a kind man who was happy to take over in the box to give the signalman an extra hour off, especially if they had some distance to travel home. On this day Gerry was off to sweep chimneys in Tavistock, so Mr Skinner took over and I was in the box for the first of many occasions.

Bere Alston was a spacious box with 30 levers, lever No. 30 being the branch up home at the far right hand end of the row. It stood at the up end of the up platform allowing a clear view of the sidings which ran off the up side and back behind the box parallel to the branch platform. There were the usual three stop signals in each direction as well as the two working distants further out. Although the station was on the already mentioned sharp curve, the signal box was well positioned so that all stop signals could be seen from the box apart from the down advanced starter which was well out of sight. However, this was track circuited so the signalman could tell when the train had gone past it.

The branch line had two starting signals and one up home for entering the platform, but there was no distant signal until the signalling was rationalized in

Right: The wonderful Eric Gray (*right*) one of Bere Alston's signalmen receives train staff from the driver of a train from Callington in 1960. He later became one of the last signalmen at Tavistock North, sadly becoming redundant in 1968 after which time he worked in Devonport Dockyard.

John T.R. Snell

Below: After 1968 when the Bere Alston to Okehampton section was closed the signalling was changed to allow trains to Gunnislake to run forward along the former main line in the Tavistock direction and then reverse onto the branch line. This was one of two new signals which indicated if trains were to cross back to the up main or down the branch. Confusingly the up direction had been to Waterloo; now it was in the other direction to Plymouth. The new signalling only lasted 2½ years and was seldom photographed over that period. Hence its inclusion.

Author

1968. It was a fine sight to see a branch train pulling towards Bere Alston from Calstock, a 1 in 40 gradient initially at 90 degrees to the station, until the final 200 yards when the line turned sharply round and up into its platform. From here the tank engine would uncouple, run around its train, with lots of points and ground signals being pulled in the process, before coupling up and making ready for the next trip down the branch. On a clear day the train could be seen and heard some 15 minutes after departure across the valley as it pulled up on the opposite, Cornish hillside from Calstock to Gunnislake, whistling at a series of unguarded level crossings.

After about an hour, a tall, strong looking cheerful man came singing his way along the platform and up into the box. This was the great Eric Gray who was to become such a good friend and who was to give me such an insight into the railway world.

Over the years I discovered that there is a code of conduct in gaining entrance to signal boxes which one must respect since they are out of bounds to all except railway employees. But many a good signalman is happy to allow the genuine enthusiast to come in and admire his little empire. Some you discover by word of mouth, are more than welcoming, while others you learn will never breach the rules and that has to be accepted. Some, if they see you with a camera, will invite you in. Others, if they are friendly, will often respond to a knock on the door and a polite enquiry. As with many things in life, common courtesy and good manners, can get you a long way. Oh, and a pretty girl by your side can also be a great help to receive an invitation to step inside! Sadly today, with health and safety such a strong factor in this, as in so many areas of life, getting into a signal box is perhaps not as easy as it once was. In those days I also had another card up my sleeve as seen at Ashwater and Mr Slade. Eric Gray also, on learning my name wanted to know if I was related to the ENT surgeon since he had operated on his throat. Since the operation had obviously been a success I was made more than welcome! Having a moderately well-known father who had operated on many hundreds of West Country ears and noses and throats for over 30 years did pay dividends!

Eric was for ever cheerful, often singing as he worked, with a wonderfully friendly energetic manner, especially when on the phone to colleagues down the line. 'Alston here', he would loudly proclaim as he picked up the phone in response to the Bere Alston bell code and 'lovely to here from you' was often the final rejoinder before replacing the receiver, usually adding as he did, 'Nice chap that!' But while he gave the impression of being somewhat happy-go-lucky, he was a professional through and through and hugely disciplined.

One of his particular habits was in his bell ringing. Signalmen who have been on the same line for some years, could tell who was on duty in the next box simply by the way they rang the bell code. Eric was a notoriously slow ringer and even in busy periods would never be rushed. There was another signalman up the line at Tavistock, who was quite the opposite, notoriously fast, and 3-pause-1 - permission for a train to enter section - could have been almost anything when he was in the next box up. Eric delighted on going even slower when this man was on, and on those occasions when he sat back in his chair and allowed me to take over, he would be for ever saying, 'Not so fast' as I, in my enthusiasm, beat out the variety of bell codes.

Another particular habit he insisted on following was in his use of metal collars on signal levers. By and large the semaphore signalling system combined with the block system, ensuring that only one train occupied any one section of track at any time, was incredibly safe. But there were some added safeguards which signalmen could use and the metal collars was one such. Thus, for example, if a train had arrived in a station and had to be kept waiting for a period of time, a collar could be placed on the home signal lever to protect the rear of the train, the collar ensuring that the signal could not be pulled. Not all signalman did this but Eric felt it was a good discipline to follow and more than once he would say to me, 'What have we forgotten?' when such a situation occurred.

In addition to all this Eric, like most good signalmen, insisted on a spotless box. The linoleum floor was regularly washed and the piece of carpet on top, was regularly shaken and vacuumed. The levers had to be shining and woe betide you should you ever consider pulling one without the duster!

In the final year of main line running, the Bere Alston train schedule was as follows. A casual glance might suggest an extremely good service; on closer inspection it can be noted that the service was totally biased for trains to Gunnislake. For passengers wanting to travel to stations beyond Bere Alston on the 'main line' to Tavistock, Okehampton etc., there was no through train from Plymouth until 1.45 pm, unless they had the desire to travel via Gunnislake! In this case a passenger leaving Plymouth at 7.00 am would have finally arrived at Tavistock, 17 miles away, an hour and a half later at 8.30 am. One can only feel that there was something nearing criminal contempt for passengers by the powers that be of the day.

Bere Alston

5.40 am	Up	Plymouth to Gunnislake
6.28 am	Down	Tavistock to Plymouth
6.28 am	Up	Gunnislake to Exeter
7.29 am	Up	Plymouth to Gunnislake
8.13 am	Down	Okehampton to Plymouth
8.21 am	Up	Gunnislake to Exeter
9.37 am	Up	Plymouth to Gunnislake
10.23 am	Up	Gunnislake to Exeter
10.25 am	Down	Okehampton to Plymouth
11.46 am	Down	Exeter to Plymouth
11.57 am	Up	Plymouth to Gunnislake
1.44 pm	Down	Gunnislake to Plymouth
1.45 pm	Up	Plymouth to Exeter
1.50 pm	Branch	departure to Gunnislake
2.49 pm	Branch	arrival from Gunnislake
2.59 pm	Down	Exeter to Plymouth
3.01 pm	Up	depart Bere Alston to Tavistock
4.35 pm	Down	arrival terminates from Tavistock
5.09 pm	Up	Plymouth to Okehampton
5.09 pm	Branch	departure to Gunnislake
5.58 pm	Down	Gunnislake to Plymouth
6.34 pm	Branch	departure to Gunnislake
6.35 pm	Up	Plymouth to Tavistock
7.06 pm	Down	Exeter to Plymouth
7.15 pm	Branch	arrival from Gunnislake
7.21 pm	Down	departure Bere Alston to Plymouth
7.56 pm	Up	Plymouth to Exeter
7.56 pm	Branch	departure to Gunnislake
8.49 pm	Down	Gunnislake to Plymouth
9.37 pm	Down	Exeter to Plymouth
10.01 pm	Up	arrival terminates from Plymouth
10.05 pm	Down	departure Bere Alston to Plymouth

When the line was tragically closed from here to Okehampton in 1968, one of the greatest mistakes ever made in the Beeching era, buffer stops were erected 200 yards up the line and the signalling on the up side changed. The up starter remained *in situ* but the up advanced starter and the down home were removed, as were all three stop signals off the down end of the branch platform. Since the eight trains a day now ran from Plymouth to Gunnislake, trains on arrival would stop in the former up main platform, then move forward past the signal box and starting signal to stop beyond a new signal facing in the Plymouth direction. The driver would then move to the other end of the train while the signalman changed the points for the branch. This new, lower quadrant signal of Western Region design had a direction indicator beneath it which could either display UP MAIN or BRANCH depending on how the points were set. The train then moved forward into the branch platform where it paused again for a moment or two before setting off down the branch. On return from Gunnislake the train usually passed through the branch platform without stopping and passed the second new signal, also lower quadrant, which allowed the train back again over the points and onto the main line.

In the May 1969 working timetable, four minutes were usually allowed for arrival and departure times at Bere Alston, and six minutes for the first train of the day. Departure times were as follows:

5.40 am to Gunnislake	2.35 pm to Plymouth
6.28 am to Plymouth	5.12 pm to Gunnislake
7.29am to Gunnislake	5.58 pm to Plymouth
8.14 am to Plymouth	6.37 pm to Gunnislake
9.39 am to Gunnislake	7.28 pm to Plymouth
10.28 am to Plymouth	8.27 pm to Gunnislake
11.54 am to Gunnislake	9.11 pm to Plymouth
12.43 pm to Plymouth	10.03 pm terminates from Plymouth
1.44 pm to Gunnislake	10.10 pm to Plymouth

Although double track still from St Budeaux to Bere Alston, no passenger trains passed each other under this timetable on any journey, although two evening trains passed each other between Dockyard Halt and Keyham at around 6.15 pm.

One little 'extra' was the occasional freight train which came up from Plymouth to Ernesettle sidings. which were situated between St Budeaux and Bere Ferrers. Access to these sidings was only from the former down line so the train from Plymouth had to come all the way up to Bere Alston, Bere Ferrers signal box having now closed, where the engine would run round the train before proceeding back down the line to Ernesettle. But it was good at least to see a freight train back in the station, if only to pass through.

All this was made slightly more complicated by the fact that the original up line was now the down line, since 'up' was always to London. Since the only way to London was now via Plymouth, the old down line was now the 'up'! The inscriptions on all the signal levers were changed and working levers reduced from 30 to some 15 with the other 15 now painted a redundant white.

One cannot but wonder how much all these changes cost. Obviously little or no forward planning had been done since within two years all was changed again and now with the whole line singled to virtually one even longer 'siding' from St Budeaux, all signalling was dismantled.

Finally, back to those earlier days of the 1960s. Eric knew all the guards and drivers of passing trains and there was a constant exchange of whistles and waves

Tavistock North looking in the up direction with the hills of Dartmoor in the background. The tall double-arm up starting signal can be seen by the signal box which is obscured from view.

Frank Quant Collection

from box to cab when he was on duty, as well as Eric's usual 'Nice chap that'! Depending on who the driver was Eric would often ask permission for me to travel back home in the cab, and occasionally, if a freight train, at the back in the open guard's van. Thus I came to know intimately every twist and turn of the six miles, 816 yards which followed, with views into Cornwall over the Tamar and Calstock viaduct on one side and across to Dartmoor on the other, through Shillamill tunnel, through conifer woods, over two fine viaducts, with the site of Sir Francis Drake's birthplace below, before the Tavistock up distant and the ½-mile long deep cutting which heralded the approach to the next station on the line, Tavistock North.

Tavistock North

Whereas the building of the GWR route through Tavistock had not been too difficult, the SR track had required to be blasted out of the hillside, and the station and track bed followed a shelf along the hillside, high up on the north side of the town with a huge eight-arched viaduct immediately beyond the down end of the platforms, a viaduct which appeared on almost every postcard of the heart of Tavistock, rising above the fine ancient parish church dedicated to St Eustatius and the spacious Bedford Square.

Like Tavistock South, I hope I do not cause offence by suggesting that certain aspects of the North station were not attractive. True the approach to the station via a winding road or a steep footpath was impressive. The exterior of the buildings on the down side, where the booking office and main buildings were situated were light and welcoming, facing high up in a southerly direction. But the two platforms were rather dark and a touch gloomy, partly because both platforms had canopied roofs extending over the platforms, facilities which were most welcome in the times of hard driving rain, but on sunny days cast dark shadows over the platform. Also the long building on the up side was one of the more boring examples of Southern Railway architecture, long, square and rather characterless. But like Tavistock South, it was a station demanding respect. It was after all, together with Okehampton, the most important stop between Plymouth and Exeter. Almost all trains paused here and in a few cases it was the only stop between Plymouth, or at least Devonport, and Okehampton. For some trains from Plymouth this was also a point of termination. And the compact goods yard on the up side, running well back close alongside the bank of the hillside, was a constant bustle of activity until sad closure in 1966.

If the station interior was not that attractive, the position of the station was quite superb perched as it was high above the town it served. In the down, Plymouth, direction the line curved gently away for some 200 yards over the great viaduct which loomed majestically over the houses of Bannerwell Street, with the short down starter betwixt the end of the platform and the bridge. At the far end of the bridge stood the taller down advanced starting signal with the squat little up home opposite it in an almost crouched position to enable drivers to see it as they approached Tavistock through the long dark cutting beyond with its trio of road bridges crossing over the top.

In the up direction towards Brentor, the line made a quarter mile 'S' bend curve up a 1 in 70 climb before disappearing past the up advanced starting signal, away under a field bridge and behind the imposing granite buildings of Kelly College, all this set against the tors of Dartmoor rising in the distance, with Cox Tor in particular dominance. On a fine summer's day few stations could have boasted a more lovely setting. Like Tavistock South, it was conveniently positioned for the town, although the climb from the town to the North station, while not very far, was extremely steep for the pedestrian with heavy shopping.

The 21-levered signal box at Tavistock was just off the end of the up platform, slightly elevated on a red brick base. Alongside stood a massive up starting signal with a repeater arm below. We've already met such as these on the North Cornwall line at Otterham and Wadebridge, built to enable the driver to see the top arm from a distance and the lower arm when close up, almost at cab eye level, especially when halted by the signal. On this line others were also still at Okehampton, North Tawton and Coleford Junction. At Tavistock there was the bonus of having the signal close to the box so that signalman and driver could exchange information as and when required, either from the window or from the steps of the box.

To my delight Eric Gray transferred from Bere Alston to Tavistock around 1963. Although his family lived in Bere Alston he had a wonderfully larger than life mother who lived in College Avenue and worked part time preparing the vegetables for lunch in the kitchen at Kelly College. Even at an advanced age she rode a bicycle through the town and had a precarious wave together with a smile for everyone. Eric was devoted to his mother and now working at Tavistock station was able to keep an eye on her, not least when her cycling excursions became something of a hazard to traffic!

Although I was already 'allowed' in the box at Tavistock thanks to station master Ronald Hooper, with Eric Gray installed I now had an even stronger footing as well as a wonderful bolthole to which I could escape from school, the already mentioned Kelly College, just up the line. The College stood back from the A38 Tavistock-Okehampton road, facing south over the River Tavy with the GWR line running close parallel to the river. The fine elevated buildings were built by Benedictus Marwood Kelly in 1885. Up behind the school was the Southern Region, at this point still running along the shelf in the hillside, the down distant signal for Tavistock being tucked away in a cutting above the school on the edge of Wilminstone viaduct.

I had quickly discovered the quickest way to the station was by climbing a gate at the back of the school, up a steep hill to the line, over a granite field bridge, and thence down through the well-tended allotment gardens to the east of the station. Apart from the final few yards over the goods sidings, no trespass was involved and within 15 minutes I had escaped from school and was in the safe confines of the signal box and probably drinking tea which on other occasions I seldom touched. But 'when in Rome' as they say , or in a signal box, one drank tea!

One event which I recall to this day with delight, involved the strict 'out of bounds' rule which applied to all Kelly pupils at that time. To go into Tavistock involved obtaining a signed 'exeat', meaning 'he may go', from the housemaster and this was allowed once each week. The boundary area for Tavistock was clearly marked out on a map in the school and the north side of this boundary went up to, and please note 'up to' the Southern Region railway line. On one occasion when I was in the signal box, the headmaster, John Melvin, alighted from a train and caught sight of me. This was a man who missed nothing I hasten to add! A few days later I was summoned to his study. To a junior boy John Melvin was an intimidating, quietly spoken man, with penetrating eyes, always immaculately dressed and who, when looking at you, gave the impression he knew everything about you and much more! To be summoned to his study was a major and deeply disturbing event, the more so since I was not in the house which he ran and usually my housemaster dealt with daily concerns. I later discovered that John Melvin was a very kind man, hugely cultivated, wise, scholarly and in fact by nature rather shy. But a professional headmaster to the fingertips and to a still fairly small boy, God-like!

Standing in front of his large desk, formidable in itself and with only his friendly springer spaniel for comfort who gazed at me with compassionate eyes, he asked me, rather quietly, if he had seen me standing in Tavistock North station signal box. What was I doing there? 'Visiting my friend Mr Gray', I had replied. Did I realize that public transport was out of bounds to pupils without permission. I ventured to reply as politely as I could that I was not actually *on* public transport, just watching it. This reply did not go down very well but he continued, 'But the railway station is out of bounds unless you have an exeat. Did you have one?' I replied, expecting the ground beneath my feet to swallow me up, that I did not since the exeat boundary went up to the railway but not over it. Thus since I was on the *up* platform and *not the down*, I was not in fact out of bounds. Somewhat stirred but still not shaken, I was marched from his study to where the map was pinned up on the school notice board. And there it was; a thick red line going up to the railway line but definitely not over it. I was right and it was the only time I ever got the better of John Melvin. He walked away not looking in the best of moods although I hope that behind closed doors he would have seen the funny side. I have to add in all honesty he might have asked if I had missed supper which was a punishable offence. Fortunately he didn't which was lucky for me since indeed I had! I must add in conclusion that in later life John Melvin became a supportive friend and a man for whom I had the greatest respect.

And so … back to the railway. I continued to spend many happy hours in the signal box usually under Eric's direction although other signalman were also kind to me.

Brentor signal box , the next up the line, closed in 1961, so by this time the block section ran from here to Lydford. Once or twice I visited the box late at night which was a good time since Tavistock did not have a 'closing switch' and if a few freight trains were running through the night as they did in the early 1960s, the box never closed and ran on signalmen running a 'three turn' system, the block sections in the late night being Devonport-Tavistock-Okehampton. Once the Callington branch had finished for the day, Bere Alston box closed and Tavistock was the only box left open between Okehampton and Devonport, even Meldon Junction having closed once the last North Cornwall train had passed.

Tavistock North in its latter days, despite the uncertainty of the future, remained a friendly and welcoming place to be thanks to the example and exuberant cheerfulness of station master Ronald Hooper, who ran a happy ship and was much respected. He always had that kind of expression on his face, which some people are endowed with, suggesting there was something rather amusing about every situation. In fact he took his job extremely seriously but never himself, and always had time for a kind word to everyone. He was also an avid amateur radio ham with a shed on the far side of the station car park with a huge radio aerial alongside. In 1965 when Tavistock North lost the status of having a station master, rather than take promotion elsewhere, Ronald decided to take on the job of booking clerk and remained in the station house until the station's closure, which he later bought, renaming it 'Beechings Folly'. As well as Eric Gray, Gordon Gauler was another rotund and jolly character in the signal box, while out on the platform there was a splendid porter called Harry McDonald who was full of bonhomie and talked to everyone. His broad accent did not always make it easy to understand what he was saying, but his enthusiasm for the job was unquestioned and everyone seemed to know him. In the Irwell Press book about this line, there are photographs of both Harry and Gordon (pp.71/72). In short the Tavistock staff made their station a great place at which to linger even in the worst of winter weather, and there was the charming and wise Frank Quant, the permanent way inspector who was never far away and whose avuncular presence was respected by everyone and who was always happy to lend me his beautifully bound copies of railway magazines.

Tavistock was well served by trains. In 1961 there were some 17 passenger services to and from Plymouth, half a dozen of which terminated and started from Tavistock. The 'Brighton' was always an important train of the day arriving around 11.45 am calling only at Devonport, Tavistock and Okehampton on the way to Exeter, with the return working arriving at Tavistock at 5.25 pm, but in this direction also calling at Bere Alston. But the crowning glory was the final train of the day which left London Waterloo at 7.00 pm, arriving at Tavistock at 11.45 pm. I recall spending a couple of nights in London with my mother in 1961, catching this train home on our last day. It was a beautiful clear night and having stopped at North Tawton and Okehampton the driver appeared to give the locomotive its head for the non-stop run to Tavistock. I remember the green light of the down distant at Lydford flashing past the window, followed by the points and signals of the station and one sensed the hand of a true professional on the brakes as the train gradually eased off speed from high above Kelly College and down the final familiar curve into Tavistock, arriving to find my father on the platform and the ever-present Ronald Hooper, who was delighted to inform us we were two minutes early! When not in the signal box he also allowed me to help with sweeping the platform or waiting room, sorting parcels, counting the money and sometimes letting the pigeons loose from the great wicker crates from the end of the platform, usually on a Saturday I recall.

Tavistock North marked, roughly, a halfway point between Plymouth and Okehampton, while Okehampton marked, roughly, the halfway point between Plymouth and Exeter, the whole journey being almost 60 miles. Between Tavistock and Okehampton were three small country stations, Brentor, Lydford and Bridestowe, and beyond Okehampton another three, Sampford Courtenay, North Tawton and Bow, after which the line joined forces with the North Devon line at Coleford Junction. These half dozen smaller stations were not as busy as stations south of Tavistock where half a dozen trains from Plymouth terminated and a number of the long distance trains rushed through them non-stop with local trains offering the service. At the start of the 1960s what made this line so exciting was the variety of traffic which passed along the line: express trains from Waterloo and Brighton, a variety of freight, some stopping at the smaller stations, others passing through, as well as the local stopping passenger trains. In the final couple of years all this variety had gone and a once grand main line, which also served local communities, was been reduced to a mere unloved branch line gradually awaiting its fate. Tavistock to Okehampton was severed for all passenger traffic on 6th May, 1968 although freight remained running through to Meldon Quarry. While the three stations beyond Tavistock suffered, in as much as they served remote areas where other transport was scarce, no location suffered more than poor old Tavistock which, having already lost its GWR branch line, now also lost its main line to Plymouth. Many others have written about the nightmare journeys by car that today face travellers driving into Plymouth in the early morning and returning at night. The short-sightedness of the decision to close the railway beggars belief. There is at the time of writing talk of the possibility of the track being relayed to a new station on the edge of Tavistock, but there are still many obstacles to be faced before this becomes a reality.

Tavistock to Coleford Junction

The shelf along the hillside on which the Southern line ran continued a couple of miles after Tavistock. After the down distant signal on the edge of Wilminstone viaduct, beyond which, as I remember it, were the remains of Wilminstone Quarry sidings. These closed in the mid-1950s although the old gate giving entrance to the sidings was still in place in the 1960s. Lever 21, last lever in Tavistock North signal box, controlled the electrical release to these sidings.

From just before Tavistock the line began a steady climb up to Sourton, just before Meldon Junction, but at milepost 212 there was a brief stretch downhill in order to allow the line to cross over the GWR line at Wringworthy. There were two good spots to watch trains go by near this point. One was as the A386 started its climb out of the valley towards Mary Tavy, just beyond the turn off to Peter Tavy. Halfway up this hill there was a place for cars to pull in and both railways could be seen curving their way around sharp bends before the crossover bridge. The second was from a side road which turned off by Downs Garage towards Brentor halfway up the hill in Mary Tavy. This road ran high above the railway as the two lines twisted and turned their way up the valley towards Brentor. I recall one afternoon when we had stopped the car on this moorland road, there, stationary in the middle of nowhere, close to the point where the railways crossed the river Burn was a short freight train on its way to Plymouth on the GWR line. Had it broken down, or were there sheep on the line? Not a bit. With time to spare, the driver had stopped and with his firemen both were spending a few minutes in search of mushrooms which could be found around here at the right time of year!

Until its final few years, **Brentor**, rather like Bere Ferrers, was not served by as many trains as some of the bigger stations. Like Bere Ferrers also it was only a short distance from the little village it served, with neat station buildings, clusters of rhododendrons, and a signal box off the down end of the down platform. I have just one memory of the daily train which terminated here at 5.20 pm each weekday from Plymouth before returning at 5.30 pm for the benefit of schoolchildren and commuters, the engine moving forward over the crossover points on the up side, then down through the down platform and back across the downside crossover points. With Lydford only a mile up the line it was hardly surprising that at most times the signal box was switched out and the signals left 'off'. Once this train had been withdrawn and the daily freight having stopped calling here in 1960, the box was closed in 1962. This was an attractive spot to watch passing trains as they swept around a gentle curve from the down direction, through the platform, under the road bridge leading up to the village, and up a long straight stretch to lonely Lydford, the outskirts of which could be seen in the far distance. With the line being so tragically reduced from its once important status, in the final year the sole-surviving local trains stopped at almost every station. In the case of Brentor this was:

6.50 am to Exeter	1.37 pm to Plymouth
7.48 am to Plymouth	2.07 pm to Exeter
8.43 am to Exeter	5.31 pm to Okehampton
9.58 am to Plymouth	6.44 pm to Plymouth
(10.43 am non-stop to Exeter)	7.20 pm to Exeter
11.24 am to Plymouth	9.35 pm to Plymouth

The working timetable has the instructions for both Brentor and Bridestowe, that the guard of the last train of the day must to extinguish the station lamps.

Brentor station looking up towards Lydford.   *Author*

Sad times. With the down line already removed demolition is taking place of what remains north of Brentor looking towards Lydford. The former GWR track ran parallel to the left of the Southern line.   *Author*

As at Tavistock, the line stretched up towards **Lydford** on a 1 in 75 gradient and I recall one journey when the three-coach diesel rail car had to stop just before the Lydford up distant, put on the brakes, draw breath and start again. As stated in a previous chapter the former GWR line was still running parallel at this point up to Lydford station with freight also running to Tavistock South until 1964. This was the same year Lydford lost its freight facilities and from then on the vast sidings in both directions and rusting remains of the GWR trackbed made Lydford a veritable elephant's graveyard. Trains came and went from the rather forlorn looking Southern Region platforms but there was a real sense of bereavement. Although the GWR and SR had at one time been such rivals, there was a sense that the poor old Southern line was in a state of mourning for its old neighbouring sparring partner.

After final closure Lydford's buildings were all dismantled and today it is hard to recall what this once magnificent rural junction looked like, unlike its two neighbours Brentor and Bridestowe where the station buildings have been beautifully preserved and enhanced. In its heyday, despite the remoteness of its setting, Lydford, with its four platforms and huge sidings covered the greatest area of any other station between Plymouth and Exeter.

Signalling at Lydford remained intact until closure with the impressive three-armed gantry supporting the down starting signal in the middle, the signal for down main sidings on the left and the signal to cross over the main line onto the WR rails on the right, although this arm was removed latterly. The down advanced starter was nearly 700 yards away from the box with Brentor's down distant signal beneath until its removal in 1962. In the up direction just beyond the road bridge, stood a quite unique pair of twin signals which acted as the up advanced starter. One of these was high up on the bank while the signal 'proper' was in the small cutting below. This latter position was totally out of sight to the driver of a non-stop train, hence the second signal up on the bank. To the end on a lovely summer's day, Lydford was an impressive place to be, surrounded by the moors and open countryside, although the diesel rail car units which quietly passed through in the final year hardly did justice to what had once been such a busy outpost.

A couple of miles further on, in a deep cutting, the train passed the village of Lydford itself. It was in fact almost as easy for Lydford residents to catch a train from **Bridestowe** as it was from Lydford, both being equidistant from the village. Here was another charming example of a rural outpost served by main line trains. Although the station buildings were similar in design to those at Lydford, the setting was far more pastoral with some beautiful lime trees on the approach road which I recall all too clearly since this was the road along which I first drove a car on my 18th birthday. On that day, as was often the case until the box closed in 1964, the box was switched out and all the signals were 'off' including the fine lower quadrant up starter. Freight finished here in 1961 and I only once visited the box when it was open when Gordon Gauler was on duty, later to move to Tavistock. This was an attractive little box with 17 levers. Unusually, although there was a crossover on the down side, there was no advanced starting signal in the down direction. The line curved away quickly towards Lydford, but from the up side there was a fine curving approach, rather as at Tavistock, with an impressive backdrop of Dartmoor tors behind towards which the line now curved its way up to the summit of the route a little before Meldon Junction, towards which the line had gradually climbed its way since leaving Tamerton Foliot.

From the relatively sheltered oasis at Bridestowe, the line was now once again open to all the elements of wind, rain, mist and snow from north, west and southerly directions. At 950 ft above sea level with the little village of Sourton to the left of up trains, it was hardly surprising that this was an area where snow could cause huge

Lydford's up advanced starting signals, a unique formation. The signal on the right is in effect a repeater signal enabling driver's to see if the signal was 'on' or 'off' from the station, the left-hand signal being totally obscured by a bridge. *Author*

The Plymouth to Brighton train approaches Lydford station in the summer of 1961. The sidings here were the most extensive on the line. The signals on the gantry controlled entrance to the sidings (*left*) the down main line starter (*centre*) and the crossover to the GWR line (*right*). The top of Brentor can be seen in the far distance. *Author*

problems. This was also the highest point on the Southern Railway although of course the little branch terminus on the GWR at Princetown would be wanting me at this point to remind readers that this was nothing compared to his 1,373 ft!

Almost a mile from **Meldon Junction** stood the up distant signal, lever number one from the box, at the mouth of what was known as Darkey's cutting. Sometime in 1964 I had been given an introduction to Mr Bill Mortimore who was one of the last signalmen at this very special location. Unlike a railway station, where an invitation into a signal box was relatively easy, unless you knew somebody, remoter places like Meldon or Coleford were more difficult at which to gain access. On my first visit I had taken my bicycle to Okehampton and ridden back to Meldon which Mr Mortimore had kindly allowed me to visit.

Meldon was very special. Some may have over-stated how remote it was. If you knew your local roads, it was not in fact that out of the way, But it was incredibly exposed to the already described elements of the area. Access was off a small byroad away from the main Tavistock-Okehampton road. A hundred yards or so on the up side of the box were some railway cottages and from here there was a footpath up along the track to the signal box.

I visited Meldon Junction half a dozen times thanks to Bill Mortimore, a man who loved his job and whom I was also met when on duty at the box at Dawlish. He was a man who liked a good view from his signal box! As at Dawlish, so too at Meldon, the views were stunning, running away over rolling fields towards the outskirts of Exmoor. Immediately ahead the North Cornwall Railway curved away over the half-mile embankment on its way towards Ashbury, Bude and Padstow, while to the right of the box loomed the excavations of Meldon Quarry, from which direction North Cornwall trains had usually started their journey at Okehampton, three miles away. In from the left curved the line from which we have journeyed in this chapter, up from Tavistock and Plymouth.

The box boasted 26-levers. On the main line there were three stop signals and a working distant in both directions with a second distant signal in the down direction beneath the home signal at Meldon Quarry, less than a mile away. For a down branch train approaching Meldon Junction the distant signals remained at caution with an outer and inner home signal on the approach to the junction. For up trains coming off the branch one home signal guarded the approach to the junction from Ashbury, with the Meldon Quarry fixed distant below it. The up starter on the main line was just out of sight from the box round the corner on the edge of the impressive Meldon viaduct.

Steps led up into the box on the up side, a box which was in fact always warm, despite its exposed position. Signalmen here knew how to make sure of that. Although apparently out in the wilds, Meldon Quarry signal box was just around the next corner and Okehampton not too far beyond. With the single line to North Cornwall as well as the main line to Plymouth there were plenty of trains to attend to, the North Cornwall line also requiring the signalman to descend from his box to deliver or collect the token to and from Ashbury, not always the most pleasant of tasks when the winds were strong. Thus on a weekday in the summer of 1963 when traffic was still considerable, the trains passing Meldon were, as near as I can discern as follows:

1.47 am	Up	Light engine	Laira to Exeter
2.32 am	Up	Freight	Plymouth to Yeoford
3.50 am	Up	Freight	Plymouth to Exmouth Junction
4.35 am	Down	Freight	Yeoford to Tavistock North
4.51 am	Down	Mail and freight	Okehampton to Bude

5.15 am	Down	Freight	Nine Elms to Plymouth
5.54 am	Down	Freight	Exeter to Launceston
6.13 am	Down	Passenger and newspapers	Exeter to Plymouth
6.39 am	Down	Passenger	Okehampton to Padstow
7.14 am	Down	Passenger	Okehampton to Plymouth
7.31 am	Up	Passenger	Plymouth to Salisbury
7.31 am	Down	Freight	to Bude
7.48 am	Down	Freight	Okehampton to Lydford
8.03 am	Down	Freight	Basingstoke to Plymouth
8.47 am	Up	Passenger	Plymouth to Exeter
8.55 am	Down	Passenger	Exeter to Plymouth
9.13 am	Up	Passenger	Launceston to Okehampton
9.14 am	Down	Freight	Okehampton to Plymouth
9.28 am	Up	Passenger	Plymouth to Waterloo
9.55 am	Down	Passenger	Exeter to Plymouth
10.04 am	Down	Passenger	To Padstow and Bude
10.53 am	Up	Passenger	Padstow to Exeter
11.10 am	Up	Passenger	Plymouth to Okehampton
11.23 am	Up	Passenger	Padstow to Waterloo
11.40 am	Down	Freight	To Wadebridge
12.05 pm	Up	Passenger	Plymouth to Brighton
1.05 pm	Up	Passenger	Plymouth to Waterloo
1.12 pm	Down	Passenger	Exeter to Plymouth
1.20 pm	Up	Freight	Bude to Okehampton
1.26 pm	Down	Passenger	To Bude
2.20 pm	Up	Freight	Plymouth to Yeoford
2.20 pm	Down	Passenger	Waterloo to Plymouth
3.09 pm	Up	Passenger	Padstow to Okehampton
3.16 pm	Down	Passenger	Waterloo to Padstow
3.24 pm	Up	Passenger	Plymouth to Exeter
3.24 pm	Down	Passenger	Okehampton to Plymouth
3.43 pm	Down	Passenger	Okehampton to Wadebridge
3.55 pm	Up	Passenger	Plymouth to Exeter
4.30 pm	Up	Passenger	Bude to Okehampton
4.32 pm	Down	Passenger	Okehampton to Bude
4.58 pm	Up	Passenger	Plymouth to Waterloo
5.08 pm	Down	Passenger	Brighton to Plymouth
5.23 pm	Up	Freight	Lydford to Okehampton
5.49 pm	Up	Passenger	Padstow to Exeter
5.52 pm	Down	Passenger	Waterloo to Plymouth
5.59 pm	Down	Passenger	Okehampton to Bude/Wadebridge
6.11 pm	Up	Passenger	Plymouth to Eastleigh
6.28 pm	Up	Freight	Bude to Exmouth Junction
7.12 pm	Up	Freight	Plymouth to Feltham
7.32 pm	Up	Freight	Wadebridge to Okehampton
7.38 pm	Down	Passenger	Waterloo to Plymouth
7.53 pm	Down	Passenger	To Launceston and Bude
8.25 pm	Up	Passenger	Padstow to Okehampton
8.39 pm	Up	Passenger	Plymouth to Exeter
8.53 pm	Up	Light engine	Halwill to Okehampton
9.07 pm	Up	Freight	Wadebridge to Exeter
9.23 pm	Down	Passenger	Exeter to Plymouth
9.40 pm	Down	Freight	Exeter to Tavistock Junction

10.46 pm *	Up	Empty coaches	Tavistock to Okehampton
11.25 pm	Down	Passenger	Waterloo to Plymouth
11.32 pm	Up	Freight	Plymouth to Salisbury

It seems extraordinary that within five years this once proud and magnificent line was reduced to a mere local service, and for stations such as Tavistock and Okehampton such a totally inadequate one.

On 24th April, 1966, six months before the closure of the North Cornwall line, the double track line over the magnificent Meldon viaduct was reduced to a single track. This resulted in all trains both from Ashbury and from the main line, Lydford direction, pausing to pick up a token at Meldon Junction for the three-quarter mile journey to Meldon Quarry where the signalman was ready to retrieve it. All distant signals were now fixed at caution and Meldon Junction's up starter at the head of the bridge (*see rear cover, top photograph*) was removed. Once the North Cornwall line closed the single line practice over the viaduct continued until May 1968 when the main line was severed and Meldon Junction Box closed. In its final year, trains passing Meldon Junction, now devoid of the branch, were as follows:

Meldon Junction 1967-1968

7.07 am	Up	Passenger	Gunnislake to Exeter
7.32 am	Down	Passenger	Okehampton to Plymouth
9.00 am	Up	Passenger	Gunnislake to Exeter
9.43 am	Down	Passenger	Exeter to Plymouth
10.55 am	Up	Passenger	Gunnislake to Exeter
11.08 am	Down	Passenger	Exeter to Plymouth
2.21 pm	Down	Passenger	Exeter to Plymouth
2.25 pm	Up	Passenger	Plymouth to Exeter
5.42 pm	Up	Passenger	Plymouth to Okehampton
6.27 pm	Down	Passenger	Exeter to Plymouth
8.40 pm	Up	Passenger	Plymouth to Exeter
8.58 pm	Down	Passenger	Exeter to Plymouth

Once again, how were the mighty fallen.

Over the much photographed Meldon viaduct were the sidings and signal box for **Meldon Quarry.** The box here survived two more years after its nearby junction neighbour although trains no longer crossed the bridge on the down side. Unlike the junction box, Meldon Quarry signal box faced eastwards away from the stormy weather; however the daily blastings from the quarry necessitated that the windows of the box be, reinforced by iron grills. Although Gerry Masters was often at this box I sadly never visited it until after closure, on a special train in 1980 which went on to visit the line from Barnstaple to Meeth Sidings. By this time however the signal box was still standing but void of all levers and equipment. Today, thanks to the hard work of inspired preservationists, it is still possible to travel from Okehampton on certain days to Meldon Quarry to which ballast trains also continue to journey. The rebuilt platform on the up side was not entirely original since for many years the tiny one coach-length 'Quarry Halt' was of service to quarry workers. The times of trains which stopped here were never published in the public timetables although they were clearly marked in the unpublished timetables.

The line from here to Okehampton was something like the Tavistock line in reverse, clinging as it did to the side of the hillside above the valley which led the road below to Okehampton's ancient town. Unlike Tavistock, however, the railway

* Fridays only.

Meldon Quarry looking towards Okehampton, showing the unadvertised Quarry Halt. The engine shed and signal box are visible in the distance.   *Author's Collection*

Okehampton station looking towards Exeter. 'N' class 2-6-0 No. 31844 waits in the bay platform with a train for Bude.   *Roger Joanes*

at this point and the station at **Okehampton** faced north rather than south; and with the hillside over and above it, this was always a rather sombre station on the line. If the pedestrian climb up to Tavistock North was steep, the climb up to Okehampton's station was thrice as long and as steep.. The main buildings and signal box were both on the up platform with a somewhat dull structure for passengers on the down side. On the down side too was the extra bay platform from which trains for North Cornwall bided their time for connections to come and go before their departure down the line. Compared with other signal boxes on the line, Okehampton's last signal box on the down end of the up platform was more modern, brick-built in 1936 and on platform level. Sidings stretched out in both directions and it was an important point at which freight was sorted from all destinations, both from the main line and from North Cornwall.

When the line was closed from here to Bere Alston, Okehampton remained the penultimate digit for the withered arm, but many already felt that the writing was on the wall. The line remained double track from Coleford Junction and with a train service as follows:

4.51 am	Arrival from Exeter
7.20 am	Depart to Exeter
9.14 am	Arrival from Exeter
9.20 am	Depart to Exeter
10.59 am	Arrival from Exeter
11.12 am	Depart to Exeter
1.32 pm	Down to Meldon Quarry ballast empties
2.22 pm	Arrival from Exeter
2.35 pm	Depart to Exeter
3.10 pm	Ballast from Meldon Quarry to Westbury
4.27 pm	Arrival from Exeter
4.40 pm	Depart to Exeter
6.03 pm	Down to Meldon Quarry ballast empties
6.24 pm	Arrival from Exeter
6.30 pm	Depart to Exeter
7.09 pm	Ballast from Meldon Quarry to Salisbury
8.39 pm	Arrival from Exeter
8.53 pm	Depart to Exeter

In October 1971 the line was singled from Crediton although the signal box at Okehampton limped on until a year later when, on 5th June, 1972, all passenger services were withdrawn, yet another tragic amputation of the Southern network. One month later, with only ballast trains now rumbling through the increasingly decaying station, the signal box was also closed.

As from Tavistock to Okehampton, so from Okehampton to Coleford Junction there were three small stations serving scattered rural communities, Sampford Courtenay, North Tawton and Bow. On leaving Okehampton the line dropped down for a quarter of a mile before making a huge left-hand curve to the east of Okehampton, the Okehampton bypass running close to the line at this point.

Sampford Courtenay was reached after some four miles. Architecturally, this was something of a poor relation on the line. Although the terminus for some five years when the line originally opened, and enjoying huge importance under the name of Okehampton Road as the local railhead, once the line was extended the little station sunk into relative obscurity. The single-storey building on the up platform lacked

Lonely little Sampford Courtenay station looking towards Exeter before the line was singled in 1971.   *Author*

North Tawton station with its long straight section, looking towards Okehampton.   *Author*

the grand design of most stations on the line and was more reminiscent of Dunsland Cross on the Bude branch. There was, however, an attractive station master's house set back from the station above the down side with steps leading up to it from the platform. There was a signal box on the down end of the up platform with five short sidings, one of which ran alongside a small goods shed with buffer stops close to the wooden entrance gateway. The box closed in 1964 although latterly mainly switched out with the block section usually running from Okehampton to North Tawton or Coleford Junction. Sampford Courtenay village was some two miles away and the main Okehampton to Crediton road crossed the line over a bridge on the up side continuing the long curve which had run through the platform and beyond on the Okehampton side. Few passengers used the station and only half a dozen trains stopped here in either direction until the final couple of years when, as just a local railway, all trains called. My first visit to this station was in the 1950s, when we must have been driving home to Plymouth via one of my father's 'pretty routes' for which he was renowned. It was getting dark and it was slightly misty. We were on the up platform. Nobody else was at the station, either employee or passenger but there was activity in the signal box and bells were ringing. I knew something was imminent although my father was less convinced! However, after some 10 minutes of my vanishing into the shadows of the waiting room, finally an up express thundered around the bend from Okehampton and through the platform. Even dad was impressed!

About a mile further on, at around milepost 192, there was the start of a four mile section of straight track along which stood **North Tawton** station. No station on the line had as clear a view of trains in each direction as could be found here. In the down direction the line dropped down initially on a 1 in 80 gradient after which it could be seen climbing up at 1 in 77 past the distant signal (the only coloured light distant signal I recall anywhere in the early 1960s between St Budeaux and Cowley Bridge), marking the start of the long climb up to Sourton beyond Meldon Junction. In the up direction the line continued the 1 in 80 climb up to bridge 590, Halse bridge, at which point it dipped out of view dropping away towards Bow again at 1 in 80. North Tawton, with its graceful architecture, was a delightful station from which to view passing trains. The down starter was another of those fine tall signals with a repeater arm below, the top arm according to George Reeve's book being 40 feet in height. Again this double signal enabled the driver of a non-stop train to see more clearly if the signal was 'on' or 'off', although the distant signal beyond Halse bridge would in fact have given him some sort of a clue. The attractive signal box, set at platform level on the up side had 18 levers. Despite the fact that there was considerable freight traffic here until 1965 there were no advanced starting signals in either direction despite the two crossovers. There were four unused levers in the box, two of which, Nos. 4 and 15, could have been used as advanced starters but I can find no evidence they ever were. My old latin teacher at Kelly College, Lesley Stoddard, was aware of my interest in railways and in his mind the long straight sections on railway at this point had been due to the fact that there had been a Roman settlement near North Tawton, hence the straight trackbed.

The views of the countryside from trains around this point were beautiful and typical of mid-Devon agricultural scenery. Only shortly before **Bow** did the four mile straight section come to an end as the line curved to the left and into Bow station. As at North Tawton, the station was some 1½ miles away from the village it served and like North Tawton the main building, here on the down side, was a handsome structure. Also as at North Tawton, there was a small awning over the

A railcar approaches Coleford Junction signal box in 1970 ....   *Author*

..... before taking the sharp right-hand curve up towards Bow and Okehampton. A far cry from the days when the 'Atlantic Coast Express' rushed by. The Barnstaple line goes away on the right becoming single track at the next station, Copplestone.   *Author*

A solitary railcar pulls away from Bow on its way from Okehampton to Exeter in 1970.
Author

booking office door onto the platform. As at Sampford Courtenay, many long distance trains rushed past this small station leaving only a handful to stop here, until the final years when, as just a local line, all trains stopped. A bus service from the village to Crediton and Exeter, however, made life for passengers rather more convenient and the railway suffered as a result. The signal box was off the end of the down platform and was, as at Sampford Courtenay, often switched out. Rather more exposed to the elements than the box at North Tawton, the wooden facing below the windows had been replaced by brick. Freight finished here in 1961 and the box was closed one week before that at Sampford Courtenay on 26th January, 1964 although it remained *in situ* for several years afterwards. In both directions there was a fine view of approaching trains; from the down side a sweeping curve around past the siding and advanced starting signal. In the up direction there was a straight section for almost 1,000 yards before the line curved away past the down distant, just visible from the up platform. Up trains from Bow rattled down the hill towards Coleford Junction and I always enjoyed this part of the journey.

Coleford Junction was similar in some ways to Meldon Junction giving access to a branch line but without any station. The setting however was far more verdant with the charming little hamlets, Colebrook and Coleford close by, adorned with thatched cottages, streams and meadows, and a delightful village pub complete with a famous parrot! Unlike Meldon, however, the 'branch' line to Barnstaple had the straight run through the junction while the main line approach from the down direction was around a sharp 20 chain curve, necessitating a 40 mph speed limit. Coming down from Bow, some drivers, having enjoyed considerable speeds from Okehampton, would brake fiercely as they passed the up distant signal over a mile away, followed by a lower quadrant outer home signal over 700 yards away and finally, as the train curved under Mill Hill bridge and into sight of the signal box, the tall inner home signal with a repeater arm below, 300 yards from the box. Because of the blind approach on the up main line, there was a track circuit indicator in the box which informed the signalman when an up was train approaching from 250 yards before the up outer home signal. The delightful, if slightly cramped, 13-lever signal box was without electricity or water but it had a picturesque setting and I was lucky to have visited it on two or three occasions. There were no starting signals in any direction beyond the box, unlike at Meldon Junction, but all four distant signals were working signals, since the branch from Barnstaple was by this time double track from Copplestone, the next box down the branch line, so there was no token exchange here.

There was long straight section coming down from Yeoford with a double-armed gantry signal at the approach to the junction, the main line home signal being slightly higher than the Barnstaple line, as was traditional, indicating the more important route. Just out of sight around the bend towards Yeoford was another gantry with two split arm distant signals, again one for the main line and one for Barnstaple, with Yeoford's advanced starting signal above the latter. To signal a train from Barnstaple, the signalman had to pull levers Nos. 11 and 12, the up branch home and distant. Unusually the lever at the far end of the box, No. 13, was a black point lever, controlling a crossover on the up side of the box for any train working in the 'wrong' direction. At night, if all trains to and from Barnstaple had been dispatched, the signal box could be switched out although often it was only for a very few hours. Latterly, however, the long hours of signalmen on duty at this box were slightly less demanding than in earlier years, although with normally only two turns working shifts, even in the summer of 1968, after the main line had closed beyond Okehampton, Coleford Junction could still be a busy place. However, the line to Barnstaple and Ilfracombe had very much become the dominating route:

3.27 am	Down	Parcels and freight, Exeter to Barnstaple
4.25 am	Down	Passenger and newspapers, Exeter to Ilfracombe
4.36 am	Down	Passenger and newspapers, Exeter to Okehampton
4.52 am	Down	Freight and milk empties, Exeter to Barnstaple
6.12 am	Down	Freight and milk empties, Exeter to Barnstaple
7.28 am	Up	Passenger, Barnstaple to Exeter
7.41 am	Up	Passenger, Okehampton to Exeter
8.48 am	Down	Passenger, Exeter to Okehampton
9.10 am	Down	Passenger, Paignton to Ilfracombe
9.38 am	Up	Passenger, Okehampton to Exeter
9.49 am	Up	Passenger, Ilfracombe to Exeter
10.33 am	Down	Passenger, Exeter to Okehampton
11.33 am	Up	Passenger, Okehampton to Exeter
11.41 am	Down	Passenger, Exeter to Barnstaple
12.25 pm	Up	Passenger, Ilfracombe to Exeter
1.02 pm	Down	Ballast Empties, Salisbury to Meldon
1.43 pm	Down	Passenger, Exeter to Ilfracombe
1.56 pm	Down	Passenger, Exeter to Okehampton
2.25 pm	Up	Passenger, Barnstaple to Exeter
2.49 pm	Down	Light engine, Exeter to Torrington
2.57 pm	Up	Passenger, Okehampton to Exeter
3.25 pm	Up	Ballast, Meldon to Westbury
3.50 pm	Up	Freight, Barnstaple to Exeter
4.01 pm	Down	Passenger, Exeter to Okehampton
4.17 pm	Down	Passenger, Exeter to Ilfracombe
4.55 pm	Up	Passenger, Ilfracombe to Exeter
5.02 pm	Up	Passenger, Okehampton to Exeter
5.20 pm	Down	Ballast empties, Salisbury to Meldon
5.58 pm	Down	Passenger, Exeter to Okehampton
6.11 pm	Down	Passenger, Exeter to Ilfracombe
6.52 pm	Up	Passenger, Okehampton to Exeter
7.15 pm	Up	Milk, Torrington to Exeter
7.25 pm	Up	Ballast, Meldon to Salisbury
7.54 pm	Up	Passenger, Ilfracombe to Exeter
8.13 pm	Down	Passenger, Exeter to Okehampton

8.15 pm	Up	Milk/freight, Torrington/Barnstaple to Exeter
8.46 pm	Down	Passenger, Exeter to Barnstaple
9.15 pm	Up	Passenger, Okehampton to Exeter
9.27 pm	Up	Passenger, Ilfracombe to Exeter
10.38 pm	Up	Freight, Torrington to Exeter

I find it impossible to believe that this delightful junction box, which, having been built in 1877 did not quite make its centenary, has now been closed for 42 years. It still seems only like yesterday I was standing at the top of those steps watching down trains travel along the straight approach from around the corner from Yeoford. In the final years, however, there was an almost insulting contrast between the one coach unit which seven times a day sauntered by on its way to Okehampton, and those great locomotives which had steamed past with coaches bound for a multitude of west country destinations, less than 10 years before.

Today no sign remains of the points, signals and signal box which guided trains over onwards from this important knuckle of the 'withered arm'. Today two single lines run parallel from Crediton, and trains for Barnstaple at this point rattle straight on by while the weekday ballast trains squeal their way around the tight curve up towards Bow and on to Meldon Quarry.

Following its closure in 1972, Okehampton station slumped into rusting non-entity and was a tragically sad and lonely sight. But all is not quite lost thanks to enthusiastic folk who were determined not to let this be the last word. Today at summer weekends, trains once again come from Exeter encouraging passengers to explore by foot, bicycle or bus the delights of Dartmoor. The station has been repainted. The up platform boasts new signs, together with an extensive gift shop, a café and proud volunteers. Sampford Courtenay has been modestly restored so that trains can stop once more in the former up platform and, from Okehampton, diesel engines pull coaches down to Meldon Quarry where visitors can alight and cross by foot over the massive viaduct.

New alignment of the track at North Tawton has meant that there is now no sign of any platform here, but at Bow where the station house still retains its former handsome architecture, trains continue to rattle through the old down platform. Perhaps one day they will also stop here again?

Should the line to Tavistock from Bere Alston be reinstated, and many are hopeful about this, then the other dream to relay track further on to Meldon again will be rekindled. In some ways it makes some sense since before 1968 this was the alternative route for trains heading up the Paddington line when the sea wall at Dawlish was awash with waves during stormy spring tides. Who knows what the safe future of that sea wall is going to be, sad though that would be for Teignmouth, Dawlish, Dawlish Warren and Starcross should that line ever be forced to close.

But being realistic, the six miles to Tavistock may be one thing, however, the 20 miles to Meldon is quite another, requiring unimaginable finance over difficult terrain that has several large viaducts and where station properties and other areas of track bed are now in the hands of private landowners. It would be only a very distant dream and sadly not one I can see becoming reality in my lifetime. So I must be content with the memories of the days when I lingered so often along the fine Southern route through Tavistock and try not to be too uncharitable for those responsible for one of Beeching's biggest blunders.

The first train of the morning prepares to leave for Bridport on the last day of service (with wrong destination displayed), 3rd May, 1975. *Author*

The interior of Maiden Newton signal box. Latterly there were just 20 levers. When the line was double track throughout there had been 56. *Author*

Chapter Seven

Into Dorset

The year 1966 was one of huge change both for myself but rather more importantly for the railways. For me, it was the year when I finished school. There were a number of options as to what I might do but unfortunately it was the year when my childhood asthma had returned for a brief period and our doctor advised that before anything like university happened I should try and sort this out. By chance the Old Malthouse School at Langton Matravers, near Swanage in Dorset, was looking for a student teacher who could help with French, Music and English which were subjects I had studied latterly at school. The headmaster, Victor Haggard, nephew of the author Ryder Haggard, invited me to go for an interview and thus in July 1966 I set off by train to Dorset from Tavistock North, which was still thankfully to be up and working for two more years.

My parents, like so many of their generation, were generally very content to lead a fairly insular life insomuch as travel was concerned, not least because by this time my father was just over seventy. So they were happy to spend most of their time and their holidays in Devon, Cornwall and just occasionally Somerset. Dorset was therefore something of new territory for me although I did have some knowledge of the Exeter to Salisbury line. Thus the journey from Tavistock to Wareham in July 1966 was something of an adventure.

The year was also a traumatic one for railways since it was by now that the effects of the crippling Beeching report, some three years old, were really starting to be felt. This fact was brought home to me more clearly than on any other occasion over this journey. For on that July day, as I travelled beyond Exeter towards Salisbury, I found myself passing through nine stations which, although still *in situ*, had been closed less than four months previously: Pinhoe, Broad Clyst, Seaton Junction, Chard Junction, Milborne Port, Semley, Dinton, Wilton South but above all, tragically, Templecombe which had closed on the same day as the famous and still lamented Somerset & Dorset line. Some milk traffic was clearly still being handled at Seaton Junction but as we rattled through on the up fast line, despite the impressive signal box and fine array of signals, the platforms were poignantly empty and with no little branch train waiting on the down island platform to whisk passengers away down to seaside Seaton. Axminster, three miles on, was still functioning but here too no familiar branch train was waiting in the up bay platform for passengers to lonely Combpyne or bustling Lyme Regis. A year later both boxes at Seaton Junction and Axminster would also have been swept away.

The particular tragic picture of Beeching legislation, and the one which still remains forever fixed in my mind was shortly after passing Sherborne and the recently closed and charming rural station at Milborne Port. As we came down the gradient towards Templecombe the train slowed to a snail's pace. The radical and, as it was to prove hugely mistaken singling of the Exeter-Salisbury line did not start until the following year, so I do not know the reason for the slowing of the train. But I recall very clearly how we crawled through Templecombe (a station which I had never visited but knew so well by repute and from pictures in magazines), and seeing this once busy and important station silent and empty, rusting, and neglected. This unnerving scene of demise continued as we crossed the bridge under which the Somerset & Dorset line crossed our own, with its array of empty sheds and disused

A diesel railcar curves in towards Maiden Newton. A down train is already signalled from Yeovil Pen Mill on the main line. *Author*

Maiden Newton's up branch fixed distant signal with wooden arm and post. *Author*

tracks. Of course there was to be a happy scenario here when the station reopened in 1983 and looking very different. But on this day I simply recall a picture of a desperate and tragic bereavement and feeling terribly sad. I suppose most railway-orientated people of my generation have some conscious or sub-conscious picture of what the Beeching cuts meant to them, but passing through Templecombe on that journey, and at that respectful funereal pace, brought home to me what it was going to mean to so many who had relied upon this vital network.

A few years later, in 1972, I was to find myself in Gillingham as a curate until 1976, and the Salisbury-Exeter line was thereby to become a familiar friend; even more so when I moved to Sherborne for 10 years from 1983, and I shall return here later.

Although by July 1966 steam had largely vanished, it still existed on the Waterloo to Weymouth line much to my delight, as well as on the branch line to Swanage. I had rather hoped I could have changed at Wareham, where an enticing little train was waiting in the down bay platform, and been picked up at Swanage station. However a charming school secretary called Angela was waiting for me at Wareham on this perfect July day, and we set off to Langton Matravers via Corfe Castle where I caught brief sight for the first time of that chocolate box of a crossing station which today has been so lovingly restored to its former glory.

The Hardy-esque village of Langton Matravers is perched high up on the hill above Swanage and its beautiful old houses and warm Purbeck stone give it the most perfect of Dorset settings, and also, as it turned out for me, a healthy place for somebody with asthma! Below in the valley the little branch line tank engines whistled happily as they made their way to and from the seaside terminus situated perfectly right in the middle of the town.

Thus I came to Dorset and started to discover the railway network of this wonderful county in which I was to live for the next 27 years, less three years in Salisbury. Sadly, between that July interview and September of 1966, steam came to an end on the Swanage branch and although the main line at Wareham was still to echo to the sound of steam for a little longer, the distinctive throttle-sound of Southern Region diesel-electric units with their goose-like 'honk' was what now resonated up from the valley below Langton Matravers. But much better that than nothing!

The Bridport Branch

Maiden Newton (0m. 0ch.) - Toller Porcorum (2m. 44ch.) - Powerstock (5m. 62ch.) - Bradpole Crossing - Bridport (9m. 21ch.) - East Street (9m. 54ch.) - West Bay (11m. 19ch.)

By 1966 the lines to Swanage and to Bridport were the only two remaining branch lines in Dorset. Until 1952 another delightful branch line had meandered its way across the nearby Jurassic landscape to Abbotsbury via Upwey and Portesham, the track bed of which can still be clearly seen today, and what a tourist attraction that might have become for such a village steeped in history, with its matchless swannery, sub-tropical gardens and Chesil Beach, had the closure not been so premature. Dr Beeching cannot be blamed for this. Nor indeed could he be blamed for the extraordinarily mindless closure of the Swanage branch in 1972 since this line was not even included in his report. However, there was of course to be a happy ending to this line with its later resurrection thanks to the terrier-like tenacity of visionary supporters.

The verdant pastures around Toller Porcorum. Church, pub and station were all close together. The station building was later removed to Littlehempston on the South Devon Railway.

Author

One solitary passenger waits on Powerstock station for an approaching up train summer 1973.

Author

Bridport on the other hand had been listed for closure in 1965 but was destined to cling on magnificently to life for another 10 years. By 1967 when I first visited the line, the nine mile branch had been reduced to a simple single line and run as just 'one engine in steam', as it was called, although 'steam' had finished on the line a few years previously (nowadays referred to as 'one train only' working). In other words, it was worked as one very long 'siding' with just one train at a time along its length.

As on the Exeter to Salisbury line, here too it was a time of unrest and change in the area since notice for closure had been issued and the still double-tracked line from Castle Cary to Weymouth which passed through **Maiden Newton**, the junction for Bridport, was due to be reduced to a single line from Castle Cary to Dorchester, with crossing loops at Yeovil Pen Mill and Maiden Newton. At the time, however, Maiden Newton was still a busy and attractive rural junction with a mixture of lower and upper quadrant signals, a fine 56-lever signal box and an impressive canopy over the bay platform for Bridport off the up side. Despite the reduction in both staff and facilities, this was still a beautiful little line on which to travel with an adequate train service of nine trains a day to the very end and a line which retained the true epitome of a real rural branch line.

On that first visit the Maiden Newton end of the branch was still fully signalled with starting and advanced starting signals together with an outer and inner home, the outer home being way out of sight 845 yards from the box. The line ran out of the station parallel to the main line in the up direction for 200 yards before curving away to the left under two road bridges and continuing to curve over a fine embankment towards the end of which was the outer home signal. The cutting which separated the branch and the main line was a superb place for photographing trains and I spent many happy hours lingering here. A little further on a fine wooden up fixed distant signal, one of the two signals to remain to the end, stood up on the edge of a cutting as trains rattled away westwards towards the first of the two single-platformed intermediate stations of **Toller Porcorum** with its sister village of Toller Fratrum nearby. Toller was the most delightful of stations, an integral part of the tiny village with church, pub and station all huddled close together. The station faced south over an attractive small field and was of typical GWR variety, constructed of wood and with a stone base. Standing midway along a long straight stretch of line, this was an idyllic point at which to watch the trains pass by. By the time I visited the station it had been an unmanned halt for over a year and the small freight loop had disappeared some years previously, although an incongruous sign for the goods yard still remained on the south side of the track pronouncing that this entrance was 'TO GOODS DEPOT ONLY'. The rooms and windows of the station were boarded up although various fine station signs, cream lettering with green background, still proudly advertised 'BOOKING OFFICE AND WAITING ROOM' and 'LADIES WAITING ROOM', reflecting the services which even a tiny station had, until recently, provided.

Between Toller and the second intermediate station at **Powerstock,** was a steep drop of 1 in 50 down through Witherstone cutting, a somewhat remote and lonely spot, which had been known to cause problems for up trains in wet and wintry weather, and not least the final steam train special in January 1967, when the train struggled to a halt at this point and help had to be summoned in the shape of a diesel. Oh the shame of it!

Powerstock station was totally different in contrast to Toller, somewhat remote and out in the wilds. It was also some way from the village after which it was named, the hamlet of Nettlecombe being in fact where the station was sited. The station

With only a month before closure, a single car dmu drops down towards Bradpole crossing.

Author

'Is this the train for Yetminster?', a little lady asks the guard of a Bridport-bound train as he opens the gate for the driver at Bradpole crossing. The guard is not allowed to let her board the train at the crossing. But there is a happy ending... *see text*.

Author

building was constructed of stone; it was cottage-like and housed the station master until it too was unstaffed in 1966. A couple of sidings had crept around the back of the building coming off from the up side with a small loading platform. But by the time of my first visit these were no longer in use. In the down direction the line went into a short cutting before dropping down the gradient for a mile or so of beautiful open countryside and a gift for photographers.

The views from the train from here over these next few miles were also magnificent with rolling hillsides and finely cultivated fields. The second signal which remained to the end was the fixed distant signal for **Bradpole Crossing**. By 1967 it was the job of the guard to descend at this point and open the gates although previously a crossing keeper had always been on duty here, together with a three-lever ground frame controlling the two working distant signals and a gate lock. The up distant for the crossing was situated beneath the up advanced starting signal at Bridport.

On one subsequent journey to Bridport, I recall the guard opening the gates while a little old lady, smartly dressed in a blue overcoat, complete with handbag and umbrella, and who had been waiting at the crossing, asked him if this was the train for Yetminster. Unwilling to risk an accident in getting her up onto the train, he told her to wait there and he would see what he could do. At Bridport, with time enough to spare before the return journey, the kind guard nipped into the station and persuaded a member of staff who happened to be there on the duty to get in his car and bring the lady back to Bridport, which he duly did. Great service!

Bradpole Crossing was less than a mile from **Bridport**, the approach to which was over a long straight section before a sharp right curve into the platform. By now Bridport was a shadow of its former self with the down platform bereft of rails and a solitary buffer stop just beyond the end of the one remaining former up platform. The signal box, together with the down loop, had been closed in 1965. Beyond the buffer stop the old track bed to West Bay stretched away into the distance with the armless signal post of the former down advanced starting signal still pathetically *in situ*, as were the gates across the main road at the former station of **East Street**. Passenger trains on the original two miles, almost, to **West Bay** had stopped as far back as 1930. The hopes for the growth of this charming resort had not come to fruition although time would tell that in future years West Bay would be expanding hugely and what a blessing the line might have been today. Freight, however, continued to West Bay until 1962 with an occasional enthusiasts' special as late as 1964. The track was removed the following year. Happily, the station at West Bay has now been beautifully restored with a couple of coaches located on a length of rail and a slightly unconvincing starting signal. Alas the connection to Bridport is now a thing of the past. The whole chronology of the rise and fall of the complete line is clearly set out on page 215 of Brian Jackson and Mike Tattershall's very fine definitive book of the branch published by Oakwood Press (see Bibliography).

Despite the cut backs at Bridport, in 1967 life very much went on here with one friendly porter on duty and a strong sense that here was a station which was still very much up for business, with the doors of the station welcomingly open and the fine canopy over the old up platform still offering good protection from the rain which blew in from the sea. On a later return journey that day the train was noisily well patronized with a jovial guard who seemed to know most of his customers, and who was far more concerned to shower joyful bonhomie upon the travellers than to be too worried about their tickets. Wonderful! A branch line at its very best.

During the 1970-1971 season of the line, my notebook reminds me that weekday trains in and out of Bridport were as shown below, The dozen trains each way of the

With weeds encroaching both the track and platform, a train from Maiden Newton waits at Bridport for the return journey in 1974 less than one year from closure. *Author*

With a crowded up platform ahead and two trains already in the passing loop, the penultimate train from Bridport arrives at Maiden Newton on its final day. *Author*

1950s and 1960s had latterly been reduced to nine, with the later trains at nine or ten o'clock having been cut back. Nonetheless there remained an adequate service. In the final year this was similar to the 1970 service with some slight variation as indicated below:

Bridport trains

	1970	1975			1970	1975
Arr.	7.37 am	7.34 am		Dep.	7.43 am	7.37 am
Arr.	8.37	8.27		Dep.	9.38	10.05
Arr.	11.22	10.57		Dep.	11.55	11.35
Arr.	12.46 pm	12.39 pm		Dep.	12.50 pm	12.42 pm
Arr.	1.42	1.29		Dep.	2.17	1.55
Arr.	3.07	2.47		Dep.	4.10	4.05
Arr.	5.02	4.57		Dep.	5.45	5.50
Arr.	6.40	6.42		Dep.	7.30	7.40
Arr.	8.27	8.34		Dep.	8.30	8.38

Despite the tenacity to hold on to life, it was not to last. On 3rd May, 1975 the final trains to Bridport ran over the line. I was a curate in Gillingham by this time and had arranged, several weeks previously, with my boss, the Archdeacon of Dorset and vicar of Gillingham, the Venerable Ted Seager, to have this day off.

I arrived at Maiden Newton at around 6.30 am in plenty of time to see the first branch train of the day with no less than four coaches, appear slowly out of the early morning haze, having come down the gradient from the Yeovil direction. To be precise the 'four coaches' consisted of a single car unit and a three-car diesel-multiple-unit (dmu) joined together.

By now Maiden Newton was a crossing loop. In 1968 the large double-track lay-out had reduced the 56-levered signal box to a mere 20. Distant signals were now 'fixed at caution', one up siding alone remained and only a home and starting signal in each direction on the main line. One solitary ground signal at the foot of the down home, lever No. 16, was the sole working signal which controlled trains off the main line onto the branch. A three-levered ground frame at the end of the branch platform, released by lever No. 12 from the signal box, controlled the points from the main line into the bay platform. Once on the actual branch line, there were no working signals at all between Maiden Newton and Bridport after 1968, only the two fixed distants. In fact the fixed distant for Bridport was still *in situ* alongside Bradpole Crossing but, alas, armless!

Back to 3rd May, 1975. Having come to a halt at the down home signal, the train waited while the ground frame was put into action, the points changed and the ground signal pulled off. One of the Maiden Newton relief signalmen, Bill Love, a delightful and warm-hearted man who lived at Chard Junction, told me that a six-coach train had been originally been planned for the last day, but the powers that be having realised the crossover into the branch platform now only just allowed a four-coach train, the six coaches had had to be reduced. As it was the leading coach of the train was still off the platform and very close to the edge of the crossover points.

The 3rd of May started as a clear if slightly chilly day, but as time progressed it became warmer and brighter. The normal final timetable of nine trains was increased to 11 with an extra train from Bridport at 2.50 pm and 5.00 pm. A small handful travelled on that first down train but as the day went on numbers quickly increased and by the time of the final trains it was standing room only. Powerstock retained its somewhat quieter, and usual remote rural ambience for most of the day, whilst at Toller a number of locals made this day something for a social gathering on the platform, with one older couple sitting on deck chairs throughout to ensure that no souvenir hunters made off with things which were not theirs!

During the day I visited most of the familiar locations on the line. The weather was kind and the countryside beautiful. On the down side of the road bridge at Toller a fine flowering cherry tree gave a misleading impression by its magnificent blossom that new life was in the air. That may have been true for the countryside but sadly for the railway the season was late autumnal.

I travelled on the penultimate train from Bridport where I had left my car and then back on the final down train from Maiden Newton. The former train was packed and no seats were free but I was lucky enough to get a place by an open window and watched the sun setting behind the village as we pulled away from Toller Porcorum. Curving around the approach into Maiden Newton, a down dmu on the main line ran in alongside us from the Yeovil direction while a diesel-hauled up train was already waiting in the up loop as we slowed past the 10 mph sign into the bay platform. This was as crowded as the train itself and a friendly police officer was at the end of the platform to ensure safety although with a gentle and understanding smile that indicated there was no need for over officiousness on such an occasion.

The two trains on the main line set off in their opposite directions and then the final down branch train departed around 8.15 pm by which time the light was fading. Toller and Powerstock were shrouded in darkness, punctuated by many torch-lit well-wishers. On arrival back at Bridport a vast crowd awaited us on the platform and indeed off it! But there was little time for lingering since the timetable only allowed the last train of the day a four minute turnaround. Cameras flashed as we waited for the inevitable detonators to salute the final departure up the line. People cheered and shouted, as the train pulled away and the familiar red light on the end of the train disappeared away into the darkness. A minute or two later, hoots from the distant train indicated that Bradpole Crossing had been reached where the guard would be opening, closing and locking the gates for the last time. Within a few minutes many people had walked away while a few lingered on the darkened platform. The atmosphere changed. The strange euphoria of the past slightly false celebratory hour now turned a touch sour, like an old wine that had outlived its time, as the reality hit home that it was all over.

At a little after 9.00 pm I set off on the drive back to my flat at Gillingham, rather glad that I had no company with whom to make polite conversation, while it slowly sunk in that I had witnessed the last departure of the final branch line in Dorset.

Does a closed railway, which has both been loved and been of immeasurable service to so many thousands over so many years, have a soul? I don't know. Perhaps it is even blasphemous for a priest to suggest this; at the time of the Reformation I might well have been burnt at the stake for thinking such a thing! And yes I am aware, before anyone says it, that railways and the Reformation are not exactly historical bedfellows!

But as I celebrated Holy Communion in the tiny village church of Milton-on-Stour at 8 am next morning on Sunday 4th May, 1975, I have to admit that the eternal memory of the wonderful little branch line to Bridport was not far from my mind as I offered the intercessions.

Chapter Eight

Branch Line Perfection
Devon's final fling: Torrington to Halwill

Torrington (0m. 0ch.) - Watergate Halt (1m. 58ch.) - Yarde Halt (4m. 42ch.) - Dunsbear Halt (5m. 50ch.) - Peters Marland Clay Works (5m. 72ch.) - Petrockstow (7m. 68ch.) - Meeth Clay Works (9m. 55ch.) - Meeth Halt (10m. 46ch.) - Hatherleigh (12m. 55ch.) - Hole (17m. 40ch.) - Halwill Junction (20m. 47ch.)

Familiar as I am used with both writing and speaking in public, I have never written a book before and when meeting my publisher for the first time over dinner, I confessed the most difficult thing seemed to be not what to put in but what to leave out and how to finish. 'Just write what you want to write', she said, 'No more and no less'. It was an obvious but enormously helpful answer because I felt at once absolved of certain locations I felt inadequate in writing about, but at the same time encouraged to write about railways along whose lines I felt more confident. So away with anxious soul-searching and on into an unspoilt area of Devon through which ran the ultimate epitome of the perfect branch line, sadly now gone to that great terminus in the sky.

Now some may say that I lack ambition, but if I could have had any job on the railway network, on reflection it would have had to be that of station master of Hatherleigh in mid-Devon which included the care of Hole to the south-west together with Meeth Halt, where it all began in Chapter One, and Petrockstow, both to the north.

The Halwill Junction to Torrington line was the last to be built in Devon, as late as 1925, although half of the line had been built on a 3 ft gauge mineral railway running from Torrington to the Marland Brick and Clay Works which dated from 1880.

Until 1925 **Torrington** was simply a normal, busy country terminus for trains from Barnstaple dealing with considerable freight as well as huge numbers of travellers. Indeed as late as the early 1960s and up towards closure the station was still bustling with eager customers. Yet in 1965 all passenger trains vanished. It seemed crazy then and even more so today when the narrow North Devon roads to the coast are so crowded.

After 1925 when the new line to Halwill was built, Torrington was changed into what looked like a normal rural crossing station. In practice it was a dual, head-on terminus with trains terminating from the south and others from the north. But over the period of a few hours an interested observer would soon have spotted activity in the up direction towards Barnstaple was always far busier than that in the Halwill direction. Even it its last year there were nine trains each day to Barnstaple only two to Halwill with one extra morning train to Petrockstow.

Torrington station was on a steep mile downhill from its town. For a heavily-armed shopper without a car, the climb back up the town 200 ft higher up was demanding. The only compensation was a series of wonderful views. Looking back lay the whole layout of the station with trains to and from Barnstaple disappearing and emerging under a bridge beyond the signal box and away into the distance, while in the steep valley immediately below, trains from Halwill curved out of the woods of the Langtree valley, over the Torridge via a steel viaduct, whistling past the fine lower quadrant up home signal and curving sharply into Torrington station under the main A386 Torrington to Bideford road.

This arrival was at a prescribed 10 mph since the approach into the station was on a blind curve and with no passenger footbridge at Torrington and a foot crossing at

123

Ivatt class '2' 2-6-2T No. 41295 has arrived from Barnstaple at Torrington and stands in the down platform in April 1960. The author is on the platform in shorts.   *Roger Joanes*

The last train for Halwill at Torrington on 27th February, 1965.   *Roger Joanes*

the Halwill end it was little wonder drivers were required to whistle continuously for 200 yards on their approach according to the Rule Book.

Although Torrington's 'face on' double terminus was not immediately obvious to a casual passer by, the contrast between the line to Halwill and that to Barnstaple was distinctively obvious as will be shown. Opened some 50 years earlier, the busy line northwards featured three well-built intermediate stations, each with crossing loops on an attractive route along the banks of the Taw-Torridge estuary. There was a magnificent two mile run out of Barnstaple with an array of fine signals stretching into the far distance including the somewhat battered fixed up distant almost a mile away.

Fremington station with its tall impressive signal box and complex of sidings off the up side was where rail and shipping worked closely side by side, the last station master acquiring the added title of quay superintendent. Coal and clay were the chief assets handled in huge quantities. Large amounts of clay were still being handled here right up to the quay's closure in 1969, four years after the last passengers. Passenger numbers here, however, were never large since access to the station was some distance from the village and it was far easier to go by bus to Barnstaple, the bus going straight through the main village.

The midway station was **Instow,** perfectly situated for the village with, on a hot summer's day, something of a Riviera touch. The view across the estuary to Westward Ho! and Appledore, the beach just a stone's throw away, the level crossing and charming signal box with the line curving away in the distance along the banks of the estuary towards Bideford, all made this one of the most attractive stations in Devon comparable with main line Dawlish on the south coast. On one occasion I ventured up the steps of the box to find it empty. A moment later came running down the street along the sea front with a large cornet ice-cream in his hand which he had purchased from the kiosk a couple of hundred yards away. 'One of the perks of being in Instow box', he informed me!

Thanks to a group of enthusiasts, the grade two listed signal box has been saved for posterity with a couple of signals, a short length of track and level crossing gates. No trains alas but should these reappear again one day, Instow will be more than ready to receive them.

Bideford station squeezed itself slightly uncomfortably onto a narrow shelf on the eastern side of the town with the main goods yard some half a mile back in the up direction, the station itself having very limited accommodation for extensive sidings. The station, with large canopies over both platforms was impressive and with a typical Southern Railway stone-based signal box on the down end of the up platform. As at Instow the signal box here too has been restored with a length of track, some rolling stock and both platforms well-preserved.

Despite the awkward access, the station was always well-patronized and there remains nearly 50 years on, frustration that such a large North Devon town and important holiday resort should have lost its railway. The frustration, however, has always been mingled with a degree of optimism since it would still be possible to relay the nine miles from Barnstaple. This is not some rose-tinted hope since the Tarka trail along which the whole distance runs means that the relaying of track would not be a difficult one … and if to Bideford then why not to Torrington?

All this is by way of an aperitif to the main course of this chapter. So far there have been 14 miles of well-proportioned, solidly built branch line with no gradients to mention, gentle curves, traditional signal boxes and gated level crossings. Beyond Torrington all this changes to the much slower pace of a 'Light Railway' with four

Right: Still standing preserved for posterity. The up starter and signal box at Instow.

Author

Below: Another of view of the last train over the Torrington-Halwill section, this time at Bideford on 27th February, 1965.

Roger Joanes

simply constructed halts, steep gradients, sharp curves, a multitude of ungated level crossings, and three charming, small manned crossing stations, each signalled but instead of sturdily-built signal boxes, here were seven-levered ground frames open to all the elements, situated at the end of the platform.

Here was the total epitome of the really rural branch line where time stood still, where there was no rush and everybody seemed to know everybody and strangers were something of a surprise unless armed with the tell-tale of a camera which suggested that this was another railway-crazed fanatic, a breed that may be odd and yet harmless and generally very sociable! Passenger-wise the line was never going to make money and were there ever to be a profit this would only be from its freight service; once these went the result of closure was inevitable. None the less along these lines came 40 years of rural railway perfection.

The timetable changed a little but latterly there was a basic pattern which only varied slightly. There were two through trains a day to and from Halwill Junction, nearly always of one-coach with an extra early morning train to Dunsbear Halt (according to the timetable) for the workmen at Peters Marland but which always went on to Petrockstow. From here there were various 'as required' possibilities whereby the train might return again to Dunsbear Halt or even go through to Hatherleigh and back depending on what was needed. This first train left Torrington around 6.25 am and after whatever was required from Petrockstow would be back at Torrington by around 8.30 am in time for the first down passenger train to Halwill which latterly departed Torrington at 8.55 am. This returned from Halwill shortly before midday.

For a number of years this crossed with the down freight at Petrockstow about 11.15 am, the freight having left Torrington at 10.30 am. There was all the time in the world for this freight to make its way to Halwill, one timetable allowing it $3\frac{1}{4}$ hours arriving at Halwill a little before two o'clock.

Latterly however the daily freight departed from Torrington sometime after 12 noon once the first up passenger train had returned. The stop and start times in practice were allowed huge latitude but in theory the plan ran as follows. The train ran to Marland sidings where after 10 minutes it continued for a short time at Petrockstow. After 15 minutes at the Meeth clay sidings the daily freight passed through Meeth Halt with an allowed 15 minutes at Hatherleigh and just five minutes at Hole arriving at Halwill a little after 2.30 pm. Half an hour later the return journey started with six minutes designated at Hole, 14 at Hatherleigh and a few minutes at Meeth Halt, 'If required'! With 15 more minutes at Meeth clay sidings it was back at Petrockstow around 4.20 pm. Here the train was to change its status from 'freight' to a 'mixed' train, picking up a single carriage from the Petrockstow siding for workers at the end of their day's work. The second Halwill-bound train of the day left Torrington around 4.00 pm and would cross this now 'mixed' train at Petrockstow, the really busy moment of the day, about 4.30 pm after which up and down trains would continue on their separate ways, the up arriving back at Torrington at 5.15 pm and the other at Halwill at 5.20 pm. This now left the line clear for the last movement of the day which left Halwill at 6.20 pm arriving back at Torrington around 7.40 pm. In the last year of the line both up trains continued on to Barnstaple. This was the basic pattern of the day although flexible, with allowances for extra freight traffic to the clay quarries when needed. Passenger train times also varied slightly on Saturdays.

Journeying down the line trains left Torrington curving sharply away over the River Torridge and up into Langtree woods with tall evergreens reaching high into the sky as the train twisted its way to the first tiny halt at **Watergate**, nearly two miles from Torrington. If small be beautiful then in the railway world this was it, the

The author's parents on the platform at Watergate, Devon's smallest station, in the summer of 1959.   *Author*

Less than a mile beyond Dunsbear Halt the clay line to Peters Marland curves off to the left of the main branch line.   *Author*

smallest station in Devon amidst an almost alpine-valley setting with a fine forestry area and the nearby river just a few yards from the platform. Here one could almost expect morris dancers or some musical chorus to appear through the trees. The station offered nothing other than a notice board, the station's name and two lampless lamp posts. But with, in season, a fine display of rhododendrons around the little platform here was a wonderful watery tranquillity which made waiting for the so very infrequent train a real pleasure. Only one coach could fit onto the platform but since that was the norm for most trains this caused no problem to anyone. Few passengers used this remote halt apart from an occasional forester or workers on their way to the clay works, although very few of these used Watergate.

On the Halwill side of the platform was the first of the many unguarded crossings, this carrying a minor road from Torrington to Holsworthy. 5 mph was the regulated speed combined with some continuous whistling which echoed up the secluded and generally quiet valley. Until 1960 there was a short siding coming off in the down direction beyond the crossing used by a local farmer. From this point began the steep 1 in 45 climb to Yarde, and when cycling along the track here one realises just how steep that climb was! For the small passenger trains this was no problem but for a long line of clay wagons, even when empty this was a demanding haul, not helped by the obligatory 5 mph speed restriction at Vinney Copse Crossing on the way up on a fairly sharp curve and still clearly visible today on the Tarka Trail.

Shortly before Yarde, the summit was reached, a stone today indicating this location. This was followed by a sharp left-hand curve through a cutting and at the top of a long straight descent, **Yarde Halt** appeared on the down side. This was one notch up on Watergate in that it provided passengers with a small and very basic waiting shelter off the down side of the platform made of prefabricated concrete. This station, however, was not nearly as attractive as Watergate facing southwards towards the back of a row of terraced cottages which somewhat gloomily dominated the tiny halt. Despite its size, records indicate more people used Yarde than any other intermediate stop on the line largely of course because of the Marland Clay Co. workmen who lived conveniently opposite in the cottages.

Just beyond the station, dropping down a gradient which now increases to 1 in 40, the train crossed its third unguarded crossing which heavily loaded clay trains could have done without when travelling in the up direction. However, on the one occasion I actually saw, by chance, an elderly gentleman was standing with a walking stick by the crossing. This he waved with great accustomed gusto at the approaching train which subsequently rumbled over the crossing at considerably more than 5 mph, accompanied by much whistling and waving from the engine and crew for whom the gentleman was an obviously well-known figure and this an accustomed ceremony. Once the train had past he explained with much enthusiasm that he had worked on the railway for a number of years and now living in one of the cottages he often saw up freight and clay trains over the crossing so that they did not have to reduce too much speed on the steep climb. Totally illegal of course but what a help this must have been for drivers and what a great branch line tradition.

After passing through lonely Willeswell Moor the train turned sharply into the third halt at **Dunsbear.** Like Watergate Dunsbear had also had a solitary siding coming in from the up side used by farmers and occasional clay traffic. The platform was twice the size of Yarde or Watergate and boasted two waiting rooms, one wooden and one stone-built, these providing protection for the large number of workers from the clay works who came and went from this station. Dunsbear had opened with the line in 1925 while Yarde and Watergate appeared one year later. At

Trains passing at Petrockstow. Ivatt 2-6-2T No. 41297 is on the right, waiting to leave with a train for Halwill, 20th April, 1960. A mixed train stands in the other loop. Note the 7-lever open ground frame behind the 'Whistle' board. *Roger Joanes*

A train for Torrington at Petrockstow on 15th September, 1958. Note the milk churn being handled by railway staff. *Roger Joanes*

almost six miles from Torrington trains were allowed a generous 25 minutes to reach this point. Over another unguarded crossing on the down side of the platform, the line curved gently away to the right straightening up just under a mile further on where the clay line branched off to the left controlled by one solitary point lever which, like the other sidings would have been unlocked by the single line tablet. Once over these points the empty clay trains under the shunter's control would have entered into one of the loops where the locomotive would have uncoupled before moving forward to collect the loaded wagons in preparation for the return journey.

John Nicholas' fine book about the Torrington lines (see Bibliography) goes into great detail about the working of this network of sidings and for further reading on this topic I would encourage any reader to look here.

Passing these sidings in the down direction, trains skirt alongside the Peters Marland clayworks and over another crossing. On another mile and eight miles from Torrington, now on a rising gradient, the home signal for **Petrockstow** comes in view just before yet another unguarded crossing heralding the entrance to the crossing loop, the first of the three on the line.

Everything so far on the journey had come under the jurisdiction of Torrington. Petrockstow and as far as Hole came under the care of the station master of Hatherleigh. Until the line's closure to passengers in 1965 and indeed for two years after Petrockstow was a manned station. In his book John Nicholas speaks warmly of Fred Cooper whom I remember and whose entire railway career was here at Petrockstow from 1925 until 1967 by which time only clay trains were running. In February of that year the signalling and goods yard were dismantled and Mr Cooper retired.

For me and Petrockstow it was true love at first sight, well for me at least! The only problem was I felt slightly guilty about taking the detour here which meant if we stopped at Petrockstow we didn't go by Meeth Halt. However, if there was one station anywhere on the whole network which I could today bring back to life I think it would have to be Petrockstow. Here was an absolute gem, even if there were signals without a signal box! The station was less than a mile down the hill from the attractive Devonshire village it served. There were two platforms, the small main building being on the up side with a short wooden canopy extending from the roof. There was no shelter at all on the down platform just a short bench underneath the station sign and yet another fine display of rhododendron bushes. The lack of facilities was no problem since prospective passengers could always find shelter on the up side and cross the line at the train's arrival, there never being any hurry to rush away.

The approach from Torrington was via a gentle quarter-mile curve, trains always approaching very slowly because of the unguarded crossing restriction. In the down direction trains appeared through a magnificent avenue of tall trees which threw dark shadows across the line creating a picture of an almost magical mystery. If only Petrockstow were there today what a setting it would create for the 'Hogwart Express', far better than … I must not be rude about a certain station on the North Yorkshire Moors Railway! There was an almost fairytale quality about the scene, the whole station on the down side and in the down direction being embraced by forestry that might have jumped out of the pages of *Hansel and Gretel*, but perhaps without the wicked witch!

Two home signals guarded the approach to the loop. The up starter was close to the edge of the platform while the down starter somewhat further off, this remaining deliciously lower quadrant until its sad execution in 1967. The seven-lever ground frame controlling all these was off the down end of the up platform and was identical in format as at Hole and Hatherleigh further down the line:

Lever No. 1 - Down home signal; No. 2 - Down starting signal; No. 3 - Up loop points; No. 4 - Points to sidings; No. 5 - Down loop points; No. 6 - Up starting signal; No. 7 - Up home signal

Within the sidings hand-operated points at the head of the sidings gave access to whichever siding was to be used.

The two-roomed station building housed the public waiting room and booking office while the other room from which tickets were sold housed the two tablet instruments, one for the section to Hatherleigh the other to Torrington. So far as I can recall, while signals and points were interlocked in the usual way, the actual tablet instruments were not interlocked with the signals. Signals for a down train could be pulled off 30 minutes before a train was due unless crossing with an up train.

Although Petrockstow's sale of tickets was higher than at Hole or Hatherleigh, even here numbers in later years of daily passengers could be counted on one hand. Over the years it was coal, animal food, fertilisers, timber and cattle which were the main commodities handled at the station, as elsewhere on the line, and the sidings were often full. Even in the 1960s there was considerable movement with a single coach often being left in the siding for the afternoon up train back to Torrington, with the sidings also used for the storage of clay traffic. Although the loops at all three crossing stations could contain over 20 loaded wagons, in practice the tank engines were only allowed 16 on the return journey to Torrington. Thus any extras would be shunted into the sidings and half a dozen or so then attached to an up train thereby changing its status from 'passenger' to 'mixed'. Not all traffic went back up to Torrington. I note that clay destined for Fowey would be sent via Halwill Junction and Wadebridge thus bringing a little more life to the much quieter southern section of the line.

Petrockstow was almost halfway along the line and was by far the busiest on this quiet, slow moving railway. Considerable latitude was allowed for the comings and goings of clay traffic for the obvious reason that passenger trains were so few. After the comings and goings between 7.00 am and 8.00 am of the early morning train which terminated here but which had time to go to Hatherleigh if required, there was an 1½ hour of peace before the first through down train at around 9.30 am. This returned from Halwill as the first through up train about 11.15 am. For many years this crossed with the down freight but latterly the freight left Torrington once the up train had returned there getting to Petrockstow sometime after 12.30 pm. The freight would then make its way southwards when shunting was finished returning again sometime before or just after 4.00 pm allowing time to change from 'freight' to 'mixed'. Now it would wait in the up platform for the second down train of the day which appeared about 4.30 pm. The up train now went on its way some 10 minutes later after which the line went quiet until the final up train came through at about 7.00 pm.

Petrockstow now as well as Meeth became regular stopping places on our twice-or thrice-yearly journeys to North Devon and we were always welcomed by whoever was on duty in a way that made the arrival at Petrockstow something of a tradition. The welcome included an over-friendly ginger tom who always insisted on wrapping itself around my father's legs and finding his way into the car while he was eating his picnic lunch. Sadly for all his many qualities Dad did not like cats but, as so often happens, the cat never seemed aware of this and never gave up the affection!

So enthralled was I by Petrockstow that in the spring of 1961 I persuaded my parents to take two nights at a farmhouse B&B in the village. The delightful farmer's wife lent me her bicycle and I recall setting off down the hill around 7 am amidst quite a heavy early morning valley mist to watch to first train of the day. The train had just arrived and was shedding its load in the siding before moving back into up platform. The best was yet to come. The light engine had to go to Meeth clay sidings and from there to Hatherleigh and back. 'Would I like to go on the engine?' ... those magic words. Well there must be a God! We set off from the up platform and away towards Hatherleigh. Such was the mist that the tops of the trees were hidden from sight. There were five of us in the cab so it was quite cosy ands the only reason I seem to recall for the journey was to drop one person off at the Meeth clay sidings and another at Hatherleigh. No sooner had we got up to speed than we were slowing for the Meeth clayworks and although it was almost impossible to see much ahead the driver obviously knew every twist and curve of the journey coming to a slow halt opposite the clay works which had suddenly emerged out of the mist. We remained on the main running line with the loop into the clay works on our right. One man plus the driver descended and set off a few yards down the line to where another man was waiting. It was the perfect setting for some great spy thriller, the driver reappearing with a battered old file which had to be delivered to the station master at Hatherleigh. Within a minute or two we were off again and over the points on the down side of the loop and past the point where the line would terminate after 1965.

The next ¾ mile was a climb up towards dear old **Meeth Halt.** Through the mist first the site of the old siding came into view followed by the curving face of the platform on the down side and then ahead the crossing over the main Hatherleigh-Torrington road. Regulations here as at other crossings required drivers to whistle for 100 yards before these crossings but on this occasion, possibly because of the poor visibility we almost came to a halt at the down end of the platform before moving forward very slowly with just a couple of short whistle blasts. Having passed through the cutting we were now descending at a great pace at the point on the journey where the track changes from south-east to south-west. Had visibility been better the Torridge would have been appearing below us by this time. Although **Hatherleigh** was graced with an up distant signal in this down direction there was none such and it wasn't until the home signal came into sight that the driver gradually slowed the speed which I suspect had been just a touch over the required 25 mph! The signal was 'on' but we moved forward without stopping into the up platform. We all clambered out and into the booking office where three or four linesmen were sitting with mugs of tea. The welcome was hearty and tea was being served by the station master himself. The whole atmosphere gave off a sense of cheerful bonhomie and happy comradeship which as a 14 year old I hugely appreciated. With no particular hurry the round tablet was removed from the leather pouch in which it had travelled on our engine and replaced in the machine, with 2-1 being punched out to Petrockstow indicating 'Train out of Section'. This was followed by 2-3 to Petrockstow, the bell code asking permission for a light engine to enter the section. With the tablet duly retrieved and replaced in the hooped pouch and with the blessed sacrament of railway tea duly consumed we were ready for the return run. The station master, the much respected Mr Morgan, suggested I should pull off the starting signal. I didn't need to be asked twice and off I went up the up platform and down the sloping edge to where the levers stood, the points already set for the up road. With the up starter being the closest signal to the ground frame lever six moved across all too easily. With a miniscule toot of farewell the engine was off and away and with the mist starting to lift slightly it was back to Petrockstow and breakfast.

In most respects Hatherleigh was very similar to Petrockstow apart from the ground frame and sidings being on the up side of the up platform, Petrockstow's being on the down side. In addition Hatherleigh boasted two water columns. As at Petrockstow and Hole the main buildings were on the up platform with no protection on the down

Ivatt class '2' 2-6-2T No. 41297 takes water at Hatherleigh on its way to Halwill in April 1960.
Roger Joanes

The morning train from Halwill at Hatherleigh on the last day, 27th February, 1965. The dmu bears a special headboard.   *Roger Joanes*

side. Although the line south of Petrockstow was considerably quieter than the north end, until 1955 on Tuesday market days, an extra engine would come here with the first down train and spent the whole day shunting wagons of livestock which were taken up to Halwill returning with empty wagons and then back again until the work was complete. Earlier timetables also indicate that the early morning train from Torrington to Petrockstow continued on Tuesdays up to Hatherleigh where it had a 10 minute turn round before returning to Petrockstow and Torrington.

Here was another attractive crossing station with lovely views of trains approaching from the Torrington direction along a straight section before curving into the platform. In the down direction trains went straight ahead through a deep cutting with a road bridge crossing the cutting a few yards further on from the up home signal.

Although the largest town on the route by far, Hatherleigh from its start sadly never generated much passenger traffic, receipts from its freight always generating far more than that of its passengers. The station also suffered having been built 1½ miles from the town down a narrow lane. In addition there were only two trains a day and the journey very slow. The greatest drawback, however, was the fact that line terminated at Halwill and it was towards Okehampton not Halwill that Hatherleigh people gravitated. A journey to Okehampton via Halwill was 24 slow miles whereas the direct journey by road was, and is, a mere seven miles. No wonder the poor line was so badly patronized. Had the sheep and cattle traffic not been curtailed in 1955 possibly things could have lasted longer, but with public goods facilities also withdrawn in 1964 it was obvious there was no way the line could continue. But of course it is easy to be wise with the benefit of hindsight.

Although some distance from its town, trains running through Hatherleigh were still more than capable of making their presence felt as they whistled over a series of nearby unguarded crossings passing through some beautiful fields and farmlands, climbing their way on ruling gradients of 1 in 50 all the way to the highest point of the line at Halwill Junction during which time the line rose 400 feet. To the right of passing trains were a series of tiny communities and the slightly larger village of Highhampton not far from the line. But it was not after any of these that the penultimate station was named. After a steep cutting and under a bridge whose track seemed to go to nowhere, the train curved into the strangely named station of **Hole**. All literature points out the fact that this station should have been called after its nearest community of any size, Black Torrington, the actual hamlet of Hole being closer to Dunsland Cross on the Bude line. However, it was felt that to call this station 'Black Torrington' might have been confusing for the travelling public so Hole it was. Despite being close to the main Hatherleigh-Holsworthy road, access to this station always seemed difficult to locate and even today I still shoot past the bumpy unadvertised lane which led unlikely travellers along the half-mile to this well-hidden station.

Hole did not enjoy the warm setting of a Petrockstow or a Hatherleigh but its peculiar attraction lay in its remoteness and lack of activity. Again the buildings were in similar design to the other two crossing stations with ground frame and sidings at the down end of the up platform as at Petrockstow.

With the limited number of trains and with the limited amount of finance for a light railway in 1925 I cannot quite understand why it was necessary to build a crossing loop here since trains were never, so far as I can tell, booked to cross here.

As already stated, in latter years the basic pattern was three trains each way a day, two passenger and one freight, and since Hole was the last station to open around 9.30 am and first to close around 6.45 pm, the whole day was easily covered by one person on duty. The first down train of the day came through a little after 10 am returning from Halwill

Railcar No. W55000 waits to leave Hole station with a down passenger train for Halwill on 13th Fenruary, 1965.   *Roger Joanes*

Hole station building as it is today, looking along the former up platform. Standing at the down end of the up platform is Greg Brown's 1926 Norwegian coach.   *Author*

about 10.45 am. The daily freight arrived anytime after 2.15 pm and returned from Halwill about 3.10 pm, each freight train being allowed some five minutes or so at Hole although it practice this could be either a good deal more or rather less time than was prescribed by officialdom. The second down train of the day arrived around 5 pm returning with the final up train around 6.30 pm. Once the train had passed Hatherleigh, the patient Hole porter-signalman would have been setting off home around 6.45 pm. Of course there had been the extra clay trains going south from time to time but once public freight stopped the man on duty would have been alone from 10.45 am until 5 pm without a train in sight. It must have been as lonely as any lighthouse keeper. Indeed I remember arriving here on one early autumn day in 1964 to find the up platform adorned with a coloured deck chair and a pile of paperback novels!

Behind the up platform the cattle dock and pens alongside the two sidings indicated that this had been the principal goods traffic, and as at Hatherleigh when the demands had justified, a light engine sometimes came down from Torrington with loaded trains then being sent on to Halwill. Once again it was cattle and freight rather than passengers which were the mainstay at Hole. In addition a somewhat austere warehouse depot for agricultural use stood behind the sidings which had in its day brought much extra traffic in the form of manure and fertiliser. The 1950 *Official Handbook of Stations* ticks all six boxes of station accommodation under the initials G, P, F, L, H and C' for Hole, Hatherleigh and Petrockstow:

G   Goods traffic
P   Passenger, parcels and miscellaneous traffic
F   Furniture vans, carriages, motor cars, portable engines, and machines, on wheels
L   Livestock
H   Horse boxes and prize cattle vans
C   Carriages and motor cars by passenger or parcels train

A proud boast indeed.

After Hole, in the down direction there was a long straight run before trains curved away into the far distance for the final climb to **Halwill Junction** amidst wide, wild open countryside. The fixed distant signal for Halwill was a mile from the final buffer stops, the down home being a generous 682 yards out.

As the driver took the final, long, gentle curve between these two signals, ahead he would have seen the line coming in on his right from Bude, and as he slowed towards the home signal these two lines ran parallel together into this great rural junction with the other line from Padstow coming in sharply on the right, a further 200 yards on.

These two mid-morning trains, the one from Torrington and the other from Bude, often rolled in from the north together while within minutes trains from Padstow and Okehampton would complete this quartet of activity, so typical of Halwill's contrasting character of rural peace and 15 minute non-stop activity.

While the Torrington line and its somewhat meagre platform was totally independent from the rest of the network, there were crossover points to the main line which were used when required, especially by freight traffic. Once the tablet from Hole had arrived in the box, it was the fireman who would make his way to one of the two ground frames which enabled the engine to run around its single coach to prepare for the return journey, allowing the signalman to deal with the comings and goings in the other three directions and be oblivious to what might have been described as the poor relation! The morning train from Torrington had some 15 minutes between arrival and departure while the late afternoon arrival was graced with about an hour. The daily freight arriving sometime in the middle of the day varied in its arrival and departure time, the only criterion being that it were back at Petrockstow around 4pm in time for it to cross with the second down train of the day.

There were 42 levers in the Halwill signal box but only two or three were ever needed for the normal arrival and departure of Torrington trains. Lever No. 40 was for the up starting signal for Torrington and 42 for its down home. Lever No. 43 controlled the ground signal which brought trains across from the branch onto the main line.

On 27th February, 1965 at 6.38 pm the last passenger train left Halwill for Torrington, a sad moment for it marked not only the end of this line but the start of the complete decline of the 'Withered Arm' with trains from Torrington to Barnstaple ceasing the following October and the lines to Bude and Wadebridge a year later.

For Meeth, Hatherleigh and Hole 1965 really was the end, with Hole for a while being preserved as a nature conservation area before being turned into a private residence similar to Hatherleigh. The track bed can still be discerned at certain places on this southern section of the line. Between Meeth and Hatherleigh a very bumpy pot-holed road leads off the main road to discover the course of the track, carefully hidden away.

However, south of Hatherleigh a considerable section of the old trackbed has been made accessible to the public for walking or cycling and this is well worth a visit since the terrain throughout is unchanged since the trains once passed. Getting closer to and beyond Hole, however, the track bed has become totally overgrown. A delightful couple, Mr and Mrs Brown, who run a camping site now inhabit Hole station and were kind enough to allow me to visit them in 2012. Their home is now the former station building on the up platform and houses a wonderful little collection of memorabilia here as well as a Norwegian railway carriage of 1926 vintage at the down end of the platform.

From Meeth northwards the Tarka Trail has allowed memories of this memorable line to be clearly preserved. Torrington's up platform, with its tiny section of track alongside the platform remains almost as it ever was. Where rails have vanished a thousand cyclists, and as many walkers, have continued to follow in the tracks of those long-gone trains. The trees are taller, the hedgerows less well tended, but still visible beneath ever encroaching foliage, the platforms at Watergate, Yarde, Dunsbear and Petrockstow continue to remind the passing rider that here 'once upon a time we were always there, faithfully serving those folk who trod the narrow pathways to our tiny platforms, day after day come rain come sunshine, waiting for infrequent trains to stop and take them on their way to a thousand destinations'. Still too can be seen those vulnerable locations where gateless crossings required 100 yards of whistling as trains approached and clattered across and away, disturbing for a few moments the silence of the Devon landscape.

But for me the strangest thing, and the most evocative, is that of all the intermediate stations that still remain, the most intact is the one where it all started and where the crumbs of my mother's pasties fell onto the track bed as we waited and waited for a train to come; the station where above all others that first seed was sown, at Meeth Halt. And even today when trains no longer come, I loiter and remember, while time stands still.

Footnote: The Tarka Valley Railway. Since writing this chapter tremendous strides have been made at Torrington station where the up platform has been wonderfully preserved. The short length of original track which remained has now been lengthened to the end of the platform and an extension of the line along the valley is planned in manageable sections. The first phase is to lay some 270 metres of track towards Beam Weir with a couple of trailing sidings. It is still early days but the station owner's enthusiasm is infectious and it will be exciting to watch things develop. A rich wealth of memorabilia can be found inside the building where there is also a restaurant and extremely good beer!

Chapter Nine

South western extremities
... in branch line Cornwall

A Cornish preamble

Despite the nostalgia and the eight previous chapters of tripping down many a memory lane, this may have left a sad taste in the mouth as we have savoured the glories of the past. So for the rest of this book I shall be mainly looking to the present and future, for let us not forget there still remain wonderful rural places where trains run in the West Country. I start in Cornwall where there is so much still to enjoy, and then creep slowly eastwards. So loiter on and lift up your hearts!

As already noted elsewhere, during the 1960s the former Southern Railway network in Cornwall was almost obliterated, and apart from the now truncated Callington branch which still just makes it into Cornwall as far as Calstock and Gunnislake, nothing else remains. Having said that I was delighted to note recently a replica Southern Railway green sign at restored Boscarne Junction on the Bodmin Steam Railway where once upon a time Great Western and Southern trains regularly rubbed axles.

The Great Western network had its casualties but not to so great an extent. No longer do trains curve away from the branch island platform at **Chacewater** en route for **Newquay** serving the seaside resorts of St Agnes and Perranporth. There were once 10 intermediate stations on this 18 mile branch whose hasty closure, with only two weeks' final notice, caused a huge Parliamentary row, although, alas, to no change of outcome. There were three crossing loops on the line including the delightfully named and lonely outpost of 'Shepherds', where until 1952 freight trains veered off to the iron mines at Treamble.

The seven little halts along the way also had wonderfully evocative names such as Goonbell, Goonhavern, and Trewerry and Trerice, all perfect examples of simple yet effective and attractive GWR halts. And to have a wander down memory lane with stations such as these I turn your attention to Kevin Robertson's delightful two volumes, *Great Western Railway Halts* (see Bibliography). Indeed the second volume gives pride of place to another halt on the branch, Mount Hawke Halt, by placing it on the front cover. Perranporth Beach Halt did not open until 1931 to serve the tourist traffic and was at times one of the busiest stations on the line, being better situated for town and beach than the main station with its fine island platform and crossing loop.

Another branch line casualty reaching towards the south coast was the eight mile branch to **Helston** with its three intermediate stations at Praze, Nancegollan and Truthall Halt. Sadly, as sometimes happens with a branch line closure, the two main line junction stations in both these cases were also to close soon after. The same occurred for example at South Brent and Stoke Canon in Devon with the closure of the Kingsbridge and Exe valley lines. The Chacewater to Newquay branch closed in February 1963 and the Helston branch in November 1962. Chacewater itself lasted another 20 months closing on 5th October, 1964 with Gwinear Road closing on the same day having survived almost two years after its branch closure. Bearing in mind its remote location this was hardly surprising. Chacewater's closure came as more of a surprise since it was well-patronized and is reputed to have been the busiest passenger station to be closed on the Cornish main line. Today only an informed eye can spot the few tell-tale landmarks which hint at the fact there was a station at either of these locations as main line trains obliviously clatter past. Again one should

Like so many counties Cornwall lost many stations such as Perranporth Beach Halt, seen here looking towards Newquay. However, the platform was later moved to 'The Dell' on the Falmouth branch seen here looking in the down direction towards Falmouth Docks.

(Both) Author

also point out that although Lord Beeching may be held responsible for the massacre of the former Southern Railway routes, the closure of these two branch lines, cannot be laid at his door since these were implemented before his report came into force.

Apart from the usual track bed scars and surviving bridges, a few tangible reminders of the lines remain. Perranporth Beach Halt's platform was later resurrected on the Falmouth branch in 1970 at the newly opened 'The Dell' station, still in use today.

Even more positively a small section of the track between Trewerry and Trerice and Mitchell and Newlyn halts has been re-laid as 'The Lappa Steam Valley Railway', and although the 15 inch gauge is not quite the same as in the old days, it is well worth a visit. As one journeys along the countryside, it is not too difficult to be carried back to the days when the likes of Prairie tanks rattled along this rural domain.

Meanwhile on the Helston branch slow but steady progress has been made on restoring a small section of track around former Truthall Halt, seven miles from the main line and some two miles from Helston.

Finally one must pay tribute to those who have restored several miles along the **Bodmin branch** from the now renamed Bodmin Parkway through Bodmin General and down to Boscarne Junction. This is a wonderful reversal of fate with plans for greater expansion and it is really exciting to see a branch line train simmering in Bodmin's bay platform as main line trains come and go, just as it was in former days.

But since the point of this part of the book is to find present day living spots where it is still possible to linger on rural railways which are still on the main network, all this is by way of preamble. So, back to the present.

Despite all the closures, in the case of Cornwall of some 50 stations, over 30 still live on. So far as signal boxes are concerned not one of the 18 former Southern Railway boxes now remain. Wadebridge's two boxes just made it into 1967 together with the tiny box high up on the hill at Gunnislake. However, nine former GWR boxes are still in operation, seven of which are dominated largely with 'proper' semaphore signals: Liskeard, Lostwithiel, Par, St Blazey, Goonbarrow Junction, Truro and St Erth. Roskear Junction and Penzance have coloured light signals, the latter now controlling the areas formerly covered by Long Rock and Ponsandane boxes along the glorious seaside wall approach to the terminus with St Michael's Mount as its eternal backdrop. Lostwithiel now also controls the single line section over Largin viaduct which once had its own box, and the Truro box which was formerly Truro East now controls the area once supervised by Truro West and Penwithers Junction where the Falmouth branch leaves the main line. In recent times Truro has the added responsibility of the reinstated passing point at Penryn on the Falmouth branch, as explained in a later section.

Over and above all this, five delightful passenger branch lines still remain open, each generally offering at least a very adequate service, and at best a very generous one. The St Erth to Ives branch runs up to the north coast at almost the far end of Cornwall. The Newquay branch is unique in England in that it touches both sides of its county running from the north to the south coast at Par. Running south are the branches to Falmouth from Truro, and Looe from Liskeard. The somewhat downgraded line to Gunnislake starts from Plymouth in Devon but finishes in Cornwall. To these I must add, for reasons that I shall explain, the branch from Lostwithiel to Fowey which remains intact but only for clay traffic, now ending just a few hundred yards from its original terminus, at Carne Point.

All of these lines provide good places for much rural lingering!

St Erth retains much of its original features including its signal box and semaphore signals. Here the down branch home has been pulled off to allow a train to move from the main line to the branch. *Author*

The minimalist platform at St Ives is not much to look at. But the position above the beach is delightful and it has a very good train service. *Author*

The St Ives branch

St Erth - Lelant Saltings (819yds) - Lelant (1m. 8ch.) - Carbis Bay (3m.) - St Ives (4m. 24ch.)

If the well known saying 'Small is beautiful' be true, then confirmation of this in railway terms must be made evident in Cornwall's shortest branch line; not only is it the shortest, the Fowey branch being just a touch longer, but it is the branch line considered by many to be the most beautiful. Many an advertisement for West Country rail travel has, as often as not, been accompanied by a picture of a small train wending its way against the luxurious backdrop of the Atlantic Ocean crashing onto the white sands of Carbis Bay or Porth Kidney Sands.

The main line starting point at **St Erth** is in itself a remaining jewel of GWR excellence. The down platform is adorned with palm trees and well-tended flower beds while on the up side the well-canopied platform gives access down a couple of steps to the bay platform where the branch train is usually waiting for main line connections. Semaphore signals still abound with the exception of the main line distants, the up advanced starter and the branch inner home, but all these are way outside the platform areas so they do not intrude upon the eye. A fine footbridge connects the two main line platforms while a traditional GWR signal box stands at the throat of the junction from the main line onto the branch.

Most trains for St Ives currently start from the branch bay platform; the first and last trains of the day plus a couple of others cross over onto the main line and rattle their way along the six miles to the buffer stops at Penzance.

Curving away to the left out of the branch platform, past the rear of the signal box and over the points towards the out-of-sight advanced starting signal, the line disappears momentarily into an austere cutting under the main Truro-Penzance main road bridge before emerging the other side, usually to stop again after less than a mile at **Lelant Saltings**. This attractively positioned, long curving concrete single platform is but a mere 30 plus years young having been built in 1978. Although less than half a mile from its much older sister station named simply 'Lelant', its purpose was to provide much needed parking facilities for the vast number of people who flock to St Ives and who often, in past years, found parking in the narrow streets of St Ives a huge frustration. The view from this little halt over the western reaches of the Hayle estuary is utterly delightful with a rich variety of wildlife grubbing away for food on the mud flats between the ingoing and outgoings of the daily tides. Between trains this is a tranquil spot at which to pause, especially towards the end of the day as the light starts to fade and birds serenade each other with a varied cacophony of sounds. This tranquillity is only disturbed by the sudden unexpected metallic 'clank' of St Erth's outer home signal, over half a mile out from the box, situated at the up end of the platform, as it drops to 'off' indicating that the branch train is on its return journey from St Ives.

Less than half a mile around the corner is the other **Lelant** station, 90 years older than Lelant Saltings. The attractive station building still stands recognisable although converted to private ownership. Again there is a delightful view over the estuary with main line trains visible in the distance on their way between Hayle and St Erth.

Beyond Lelant the line curves to the north, climbing steadily up the hillside towards **Carbis Bay** as the view changes dramatically from sleepy estuary to vibrant and glorious seascape with sand dunes and white sandy beaches down below the ascending line.

A train has just arrived at St Ives and after a very minutes will return back to St Erth. Porthminster beach is to the left of the picture, December 2009.   *Author*

As at St Ives, no longer does Carbis Bay have any GWR architectural beauty to complement the view. A dull, soul-less glass-encased waiting shelter squats boringly on the platform. Gone too is the unusual attractive booking office which once stood proudly above the station by the path which led down to the halt. But being objective, for the traveller who simply wants to enjoy the trip and the view, perhaps this is of little import; for whatever has been lost on the railway, the views remain changeless, as does the final glorious mile towards St Ives as the line hugs the cliff face via two viaducts, although the fine stately tall wooden fixed distant signal for St Ives station, once easily visible from Carbis Bay has long gone. Gone too is the familiar outer home signal for St Ives marking the approach to the station where many a train was briefly halted before squeezing its way under a tight little footbridge, which still remains, and thence towards the terminus.

Once upon a time **St Ives** station was a modeller's delight with its long curving platform designed for through trains from Paddington, a run-round loop, engine shed, signal box, and compact goods yard all of which embraced from above the perimeters of Porthminster beach just a few yards beneath. As one writer described it 'St Ives station was almost the perfect setting on which to stage a play'. Gradually, however, the cutbacks came. Fish and mineral traffic, once so much a part of the line, gradually came to an end and freight ceased altogether in 1964. The previous year had also seen an end to through coaches off the 'Cornish Rivera Express' and by 1965 the signal box and run-round facilities had all been swept away.

For six years however the fine station building, so reminiscent of Great Western architecture remained *in situ* while the line's future became more and more uncertain. Flanders & Swann's tear-jerking song *Redundant* includes 'St Erth to St Ives' in its musical list of stations which Lord Beeching had in his 'grim-reaperish' eye. However, in this case, as also with the Looe branch, closure never came thanks to Harold Wilson's Minister of Transport, Barbara Castle, who refused closure on the grounds of social need and poor road access.

So sadly, in 1971 the fine station buildings were demolished to make way for a new car park and the line cut back a couple of hundred yards to just north of Porthminster viaduct. The new bare concrete platform is an appalling unimaginative insult to a town famous for its quaint architecture, as well as its being one of the busiest stations in Cornwall with 28 trains arriving each day in the 2012/13 timetable.

This said it remains a remarkable and beautiful line whose future looks secure. The fact that it is so short is also of course the reason it is able to sustain such a remarkable train service and, unlike the Newquay branch for example, one never has to wait for very long before a train appears.

From an appreciative railway point of view St Erth remains the unspoilt gem of a rural junction which has changed little over the years. And although St Ives station itself is utterly boring, the view looking down from the road above as trains come and go is not without appeal. But for pure branch line tranquillity it is Lelant Saltings which, although modern, for me has a particular charm as the train from St Ives 'S' bends its way towards the platform while a flight of disturbed oyster catchers take off with indignant cries across the waters of the changeless dozy Hayle estuary.

Above: Three trains converge at Penwithers Junction in July 1961, the 9.12 am Newquay to Truro via Chacewater, the Newham goods to Truro and a dmu in the distance making its way to Falmouth.
Peter W. Gray

Right: A train for Truro waits to depart from Falmouth in the spring of 2010.
Author

Truro to Falmouth

Falmouth - Penwithers Junction - Perranwell - Penryn - Penmere Platform - Falmouth

Until 1964, Helston had the distinction of being the most southerly station in England. After that this title moved eastward to Falmouth although possibly with the revival of track laying on the former Helston branch perhaps this will change again.

I first visited the Falmouth branch around 1960 with my mother whose family had lived here, some of whom are laid to rest in the local cemetery. In those days I recall a branch line which buzzed with activity, 12 miles long with crossing loops at Perranwell and Penryn, a busy and impressive two-platformed terminus at Falmouth, and a small halt 1½ miles towards the end of the line at Penmere. None of this was ever threatened by Beeching.

The main line into Cornwall from Plymouth was indeed a main line but there was a rural charm about it, and being me I always preferred the trains which stopped at those small stations such as St Germans, Menheniot, Lostwithiel, and once upon a time even quiet little Probus and Ladock a few miles before Truro. On stepping off a down train at **Truro** the branch connection was already waiting in the bay platform, hard against the station's dark boundary wall.

Unlike any other Cornish branch line the first mile was over main line tracks. (I hasten to add that the Gunnislake branch started in Devon not Cornwall for those who may spot a flaw in that first sentence!) There was always a slight delay before departure as the main line down train pulled out and cleared the section to Penwithers Junction a mile away before the bay platform down starter could be pulled off. Around the curve from Truro station, into Penwithers tunnel and out towards the junction of the same name where the main line turned sharply westwards towards Chacewater and away from the branch which charged straight ahead past the signal box and onto the single line to Falmouth. Well, perhaps not quite 'charge' since the driver had to slow while the signalman descended from his box, set at a slight angle to the branch, to give him the token to Perranwell. From the main road bridge, high above the tunnel there was a magnificent view of trains passing this point, the branch going ahead past a series of signals, the main line going off to the right and the freight only line coming in opposite the box from the left from Newham Wharf back on the banks of the Fal in Truro. That great West Country photographer Peter Gray captured what is one my favourite railway photographs of all time at this point with three trains all converging at this rural junction (*see photograph, above left*).

From this point to Penryn the Falmouth branch displays rural Cornwall at its most lush, over fine viaducts, through sharply rolling, wooded countryside, the views from the train of villages and valleys show off the county at its best. The first station, **Perranwell,** was really the only village station on the line, Penryn and Penmere both being suburbs of Falmouth. Here was a charming crossing loop on a sharp curve with three stop signals in each direction and a strangely tall signal box which straddled the goods yard on the down side. I recall a large station cat which I met more than once, who lived at the station and who, lying in the middle of the platform would move for nobody other than to roll over for a tummy-tickle. Genial staff, an idyllic village close at hand and an impressive approach of up trains coming up from Falmouth made this a delightful place to pause for a while. More viaducts and more fine views followed until **Penryn**, four miles on. This was not as attractive a station as Perranwell but its position was impressive, set high above the town it served and with fine views of the River Fal in the distance. The ornate main station building was oddly set apart from the main station platform.

On into the suburbs of Falmouth and into the well-patronized single platform of **Penmere** on the down side with a single siding, in earlier days, on the far side. Finally the line twists and curves its way through cuttings and glimpses of comfortable streets and houses into **Falmouth** station itself, a large and somewhat austere two-platformed station with a complex of sidings some of which continued off the far side of the down platform down to Falmouth Docks with its own railway system. The station was, if somewhat dark, none the less impressive with its Brunel style granite structure above which ran an extensive overall roof. I recall in those days how trains terminated in the down platform and once passengers had alighted the train would shunt across to the up platform ready for the next departure. The signal box diagram, however, shows that both platforms were arranged to cope with both arrivals and departures. The view from the station was over a dark twisting 's' bend with a succession of points, passing the 41-lever signal box and away through the trees of leafy Falmouth. That was how I first recall it.

But as happened elsewhere and as future visits were to show, there was a gradual reduction of everything. Falmouth signal box was the first casualty in 1966 followed closely by Perranwell, its 21-lever box closing in the same year with only the down platform now in use. Penryn's goods yard remained active until 1971 when it too, together with its signal box, was closed also leaving just the down platform in use. Thus the line became yet another one single line from Penwithers Junction although this lovely box too was swept away, the junction thereafter controlled from Truro and today its is almost impossible to see where the box once stood.

Today as one steps out of a down train at Truro, one might be led to believe that all is as it ever was for the branch line starting signal is still there beckoning the branch line train out of its bay platform but beyond that it is multiple aspect coloured light signals that guard the junction. Perranwell still remains a sleepy little village halt but without, of course, any staff to greet you and the old up platform lost beneath 50 years-worth, or nearly, of unchecked overgrowth.

Penryn had the reputation, like Bugle, of one time being the worst kept station in Cornwall. But with increased traffic it has received a new status and a new lease of life with its crossing loop restored. Unusually, although economically, instead of restoring the old up platform, the down platform has been lengthened and the loop, coming in from the up direction comes into the platform half way along it via points on the down side. Thus in practice up trains arrive first and proceed to the far up side of the platform. The down train then runs in alongside it before crossing over the points behind the up train and into the down end of the platform, The two trains then continue their journey away from each other in opposite directions. All this is controlled from Truro signal box and the majority of the current 29 trains each way on weekdays now cross here.

Little Penmere Platform has a delightful garden area at its entrance lovingly tended by local residents making this arguably the most attractive station on the line. In 1970 a new terminus station called 'The Dell' and later renamed 'Falmouth Town' was opened half a mile north of the original and a few hundred yards closer to the shopping centre, the structure having been procured, as already stated, from Perranporth Beach Halt. It is a fairly characterless structure which was to have marked a new end of the line. However, since the station was on a steep gradient, safety regulations would not allow a driver to walk from his cab at one end to the other. In practice therefore trains had to continue forward to the old, now closed station before returning to The Dell. So ridiculous was this that after five years the original station was reopened in 1975.

The once well-equipped station at Falmouth, latterly renamed Falmouth Docks, on my last visit looked like a stripped fish, with all that is left being one long single platform with a meagre backbone of a corrugated metal umbrella covered roof overhead. However, a rusting set of sidings still remain with a bramble-covered track still leading off down towards the docks with vague rumours there might be life here again. To quote the much-used motto of the resurrected narrow gauge railway at Woody Bay in North Devon: 'Perchance it only sleepeth', well let's hope.

There is much to commend this branch line but try as I may I find it a touch soulless. Of course it is the busiest branch in Cornwall, the new loop at Penryn has enabled it to be even busier; there is a half-hourly service in each direction allowing 29 trains both to and from. There remain the fine viaducts and lovely views, but there is something about the line that suggests some lack of warmth. Those who admire the line must forgive my odd prejudice.

So where would I linger? Probably at the pretty gardens alongside Penmere Platform although Perranwell is also an attractive spot on a lovely summer day.

Par to Newquay

Par - St Blazey (36ch.) - Middleway Crossing - St Blazey Bridge Crossing (1m. 7ch.) - Luxulyan (4m. 12ch.) - Goonbarrow Junction (5m. 54ch.) - Bugle (6m. 17ch.) - Roche (8m. 54ch.) - Tregoss Moor Crossing (10m. 47ch.) - St Dennis Junction (12m. 35ch.) - St Columb Road (14m. 25ch.) - Halloon Crossing - Cosworth Crossing - Quintrel Downs Platform (18m. 30ch.) - Chapel Crossing - Trencreek Crossing - Tolcarn Junction (20m. 0ch.) - Newquay (20m. 65ch.)

The Par to Newquay branch remains both the longest (20¾ miles) and probably the most exciting of the Cornish branches. Like the Falmouth branch, Dr Beeching was wise enough not to include the line itself in his list for closures although bizarrely all five of the intermediate stations were on the dreaded list to be given the chop. As it happened all remain open.

Unlike the relative simplicity of the back and forth of the St Erth to St Ives branch, this line was, at least on my first encounter in the late 1950s, far too much to for my little brain take in. There was so much! Four of the five stations were crossing loops with six further boxes at St Blazey, St Blazey Bridge, Goonbarrow Junction, Tregoss Moor, St Dennis Junction and Tolcarn Junction. In addition there were a further six manned crossings on the journey which were not block posts.

The various freight lines running off at Goonbarrow and St Dennis Junctions kept the line busy with china clay traffic, and although the St Dennis link was gradually closed down over the years, Goonbarrow still remains very much alive and active.

The line starts from **Par**, an open and airy station which has always struck me as a happy, smiling place which has changed little over the years with the sound of the south coast sea not far away. The main buildings, usually with somebody on duty, are on the down side while the branch platform for Newquay trains is over the bridge on the far side of the up platform. On the down end of the same up platform sits a long wooden signal box which controls the multitude of semaphore signals still gloriously scattered around, not least a delightful short double-armed gantry signal at the foot of the signal box with the 'branch starter' on the right and the 'branch starter to down main' on the left. Nobody really likes photos of themselves very

A train from Newquay approaches Middleway Crossing near journey's end at Par in the summer 2010.

Author

The author with Tilly (Till Eulenspiegel) by one of his favourite spots, the down branch starting signal at Par with the left-hand arm for the main line, the right for Newquay.

Author

much but there is one photo taken of me by this signal, slightly over-dressed in a summer suit for some reason, with my very faithful springer spaniel, Till Eulenspiegel (Tilly for short!), loitering patiently alongside, and this is a photo I wouldn't mind being remembered by. Tilly incidentally appears in several photographs of the 1980s and early 1990s. More recently a Jack Russell, Gigi, is visible from time to time. I digress!

The journey to Newquay takes around an hour, give or take a few minutes depending on trains crossing, so this is really is branch line where you can sit back and relax for a while! Traversing the very heart of the china clay world of Cornwall, this line has often been described as somewhat bleak and unattractive. That may be true around the Bugle-Roche area but in fact there is no branch line which offers such a vast variety of contrasts as does the Newquay branch.

Leaving Par the line takes a sharp semi-circle, almost like a homing pigeon searching for its bearings before finding its correct direction. The initial mile through **St Blazey** is double track, this being a busy centre for marshalling freight. The one or two-coach dmu often has to pause at the St Blazey home signal before proceeding, having only set of from Par a couple of minutes previously.

For signalling enthusiasts like myself, there is nowhere in Cornwall where so many semaphore signals still reign supreme. Down trains to Newquay pass seven stop signals within the first two miles controlled by Par and St Blazey, the last of the these being the former down home at St Blazey Bridge but now controlled by St Blazey 911 yds away, the signal being worked by an electric motor.

Amazingly the ancient platforms which once formed St Blazey's station still remain, with the fine signal box on the up end of the down platform, amazing that is, since the station itself closed in 1925! Until not so long ago it was still relatively easy to gain access to the down platform to watch trains pass. However, modern security has made this less easy unless one catches the eye of a friendly signalman on duty. There is usually not long to wait before there is some activity taking place here since it is very much a hub of the china clay workings and John Vaughan's wonderful book about the line gives enormous information of both the passenger and freight workings, both past and present (see Bibliography).

As the double track curves into single, it crosses the main road at **Middleway Crossing,** now controlled from St Blazey box but which until 1981 had its own ground frame with manually operated single-width crossing gates. The point rods and signal wires stretched rather strangely out of the box and over the River Par in order to gain access to the tracks as can be seen in John Vaughan's book. He is also not the first to point out what a fine vantage point this is from which to watch passing trains, with a fine uninterrupted straight stretch in the down direction and good view of trains curving away past signals in the up. More photographic arenas are on offer via various footpaths which run back in the Par direction alongside the old Par canal.

Not only does the branch offer a huge variety of scenery but there is still a rich variety of motive power which varies from the depth of winter as a sparsely patronized diesel railcar makes its daily round of seven trips up and down the line, to packed through trains from London and further north in the height of summer Saturdays. In addition heavily loaded china clay trains thunder up and down the 1 in 40 gradients of the Luxulyan valley as far as Goonbarrow Junction.

A mile on is **St Blazey Bridge Crossing** which had a small ground level signal box until 1973 when automatic barriers were put in controlled from St Blazey box. The former St Blazey Bridge down home signal is now the section signal for St Blazey to Goonbarrow Junction. The former St Blazey Bridge up outer home signal was done

Luxulyan, and a perfect village halt set in the middle of its community looking towards Newquay. *Author*

Goonbarrow Junction, the last remaining crossing loop on the branch with sidings going off on the down side. The fixed distant signal for Bugle had been below Goonbarrow's down starting signal, seen here *Author*

away with when the box closed but its inner home was replaced by a colour light signal and is now St Blazey's outer home at 1,406 yards from the box. The distant signal is an amazing 3,993 yards from St Blazey, tucked far away as the line descends through the Luxulyan woods.

Inland Cornwall is not as well known for its countryside as neighbouring Devon, but these woods are magically unspoilt with towering trees, gushing small streams and narrow lanes. Up through this luxurious terrain climbs the branch line passing under the impressive Treffry viaduct, 98 ft high and 216 yds long, a memorial to the original tramway which ran from Par to Bugle. At the top of an almost three mile climb the line makes a sharp left turn and squeezes itself through the short Luxulyan tunnel before passing under a small road bridge and into the picturesque village of **Luxulyan**. The now single platform station is at the start of a mile long straight stretch in the down direction. There is nothing to suggest that this was once an impressive long island platform with sidings and a large signal box. Today there is a simple white-painted waiting shed behind which is a small car park. The station at the heart of its village and just over the bridge, but a stone's throw away, is a large welcoming pub called the Kings Arms which is well worth a visit. More than once over the years I have left the car here and travelled the round trip to Newquay, back to Par and thence back to Luxulyan. Although diminished in size Luxulyan still has real character and has the feel of a proper, old fashioned village halt. A good place to linger. Out of season six trains call on Saturdays and three on Sundays although on summer Saturdays, strangely, no trains call.

At the end of the long straight section away from the station, the line curves away to the left and then another long stretch through wild, uncultivated countryside with the towers of china clay coming ever closer. When describing the Newquay branch the only words possible in that description at certain places is that the line 'squeezes its way' … and no more so than on the upside approach to **Goonbarrow Junction** where for half a mile wall and hedge are so close that it is hard to believe that lengthy passenger trains from such as Dundee or Manchester can possibly make there way along here.

Although there is a fine view from a minor road bridge to the south of Goonbarrow as trains make there way towards this narrow cutting, photographing at Goonbarrow itself can be difficult. The road to the box is through china clay property and although I have driven down here a number of times, always unchallenged, I suspect I may have done so illegally. Much to my delight, however, a few years ago I discovered a tiny, seldom used footpath off the road on the up side, thanks to a local map. Having almost given up hope of finding a way through shoulder-height bracken, I was finally rewarded with the discovery of a stile giving access across the tracks just a few yards short of the down home signal which guards the entrance to the long loop. As well as the heavy china clay trains which start their long descent from here back to St Blazey and the main line at Par, it is here that the long distance summer Saturday passenger trains pass one another, Goonbarrow now being the only crossing point on the line and there is, in my opinion no better place to observe this than from this remote stile. From a point of photographic view, it is better to do this earlier in the day rather than later because of the sun. That said others might well argue that as good a place is from the bridge at Bugle, but we have yet to reach this point.

A plethora of white clay-coated sidings branch off from the down side of the loop and from Mondays to Fridays there is still much movement in and out of here interspersed with the gentle passings of the passenger train on its way to Newquay.

With the tokens exchanged by the signalman and driver the line from here to Newquay is now just one 15 mile long stretch of 'siding' or 'one engine in steam' as some still say. Once upon a time there were seven block posts between here and Newquay; now there are none, just as in similar vein the same has happened from Eggesford to Barnstaple as noted in Chapter Ten.

I am no prophet, but with the apparent increase of use of the Newquay branch one cannot help but wonder if a loop might one day be re-instated at St Columb Road or St Dennis Junction since the slightest delay on summer Saturdays inevitably means a knock-on effect for all later trains when one also has to allow for the 'turn-round' time at Newquay of all long distance trains. Further time is lost at Goonbarrow if the down train arrives before the up train since the signalman has a very long walk around the down train to reach the driver of the 'up'. Furthermore with the possibility of Newquay passenger trains using the line up through Burngullow rather than up the Luxulyan valley, the future holds a number of possibilities and options. Watch this space!

With two stop signals in each direction, home and starter, Goonbarrow's down starting signal is the last semaphore on the line until the train returns towards the up home. From here **Bugle** is a straight half mile run. Until 1964 the line from Goonbarrow to Bugle was double track with a third line at Bugle running parallel to the down line. This was the short branch line to Carbis Wharf which remained *in situ* until 1992. The three lines necessitated a large, heavy-gated crossing. The fine 41-lever signal box alongside was ignominiously reduced to a ground frame with latterly only a couple of levers in use after the major cutbacks on the line, one being the gate lock and the up distant signal; the down distant remained fixed at caution beneath Goonbarrow's up starter. The old wooden station building on Bugle's

Bugle station looking towards Par. The line on the right ran to Carbis Wharf which closed in 1989.   *Author*

unstaffed platform gradually fell into total disrepair until is was mercifully put out of its misery and was removed. The *Western Morning News* carried an article pronouncing Bugle as Cornwall's worst kept station since at one point there was no waiting facility, no station sign, no lighting and no timetable on the platform.

Today, all these modest facilities have been restored with Bugle being the only station where all trains are booked to stop. As already mentioned, there is a good view from the road bridge on the down side of trains coming and going from Goonbarrow Junction with the up home clearly visible in the far distance. Traces still remain of the old trackbed running past the station towards Carbis Wharf.

The 2½ mile climb from Bugle to Roche is via a mixture of agricultural and rough scrubland with the china clay industries still never far away on the skyline. The tiny single-platformed station of **Roche** on the down side of the line, surrounded by shrubs and small trees, is totally unrecognisable from the place it was back in the 1960s. Then there was a crossing loop with extensive sidings off the up side. Unlike Luxulyan or Bugle, Roche serves several scattered communities but is poorly patronized. Originally called 'Holywell' after a nearby well dedicated to St Roche, the station was renamed Victoria before finally ending up as Roche in 1904. Access to the platform is via a foot crossing from the car park on the down side. From here the line curves away into a long curving cutting and a series of bridges emerging finally onto the extraordinary landscape of lonely Tregoss Moor.

I say 'lonely' which is only part true since during the summer months it was far from that, this being the notorious A30 bottleneck where cars would find themselves bumper to bumper on their way to north Cornwall's seaside resorts while trains ran cheerily by running parallel to the road. Today the new bypass has totally alleviated all this much to everyone's relief. Coming away from Roche, the final minor road bridge over the line still provides a wonderful vantage point for watching up trains from some two miles away as they wend their way from St Dennis Junction, then along the mile long stretch of Tregoss Moor before curving up and over the A30 and into the cutting leading towards Roche.

There is a unique kind of beauty here which in winter might described as 'stark' and in summer 'dramatic'. Halfway across **Tregoss Moor** the remote and now unstaffed crossing named after the moor, marks the halfway point of the line. A small signal box once guarded the crossing which also marked the start of a two mile double track section to St Dennis Junction. After the line was singled in 1965 the box was reduced to a ground frame with all signals removed and a crossing keeper on hand simply to open and shut the gates. Gates and keeper were later dismissed when the crossing was automated in 1973 with flashing nights and audio warnings. The crossing keeper's house remains as a prominent feature in the middle of this extraordinary landscape.

Sitting in the front of a dmu over the next couple of miles and allowing the imagination to run wild, one might expect Indiana Jones to emerge from the unusual wilderness struggling with a boa constrictor or James Bond being fired at by South American drug dealers such is the unusual terrain at this point, the result of disused areas of one time china clay land. At 12 miles from Par trains always slowed to enter the long twisting approach for **St Dennis Junction**. After the closure of Tregoss Moor box St Dennis became a crossing loop. At times when freight traffic abounded here the signalman had his work cut out with endless shunting of trains coming to and from clay centres with lovely names such as Melangoose, Drinnick Mill, Retew and Parkandillack. Trains coming from Par would go beyond the signal box towards the Newquay direction and back into the long sidings at St Dennis where engines could run around their trains. The track work here was quite complicated but fortunately for the signalman, once inside the sidings and run-round loop, shunting of trains could be done from various ground frames rather than from the signal box. Some of these trains were of considerable length and thus on the main line there were three starting signals in the down direction to enable trains to move forward in that direction.

Standing on the A30 road bridge at St Dennis on the down side, there was a fine view of the clay lines and sidings stretching away into the distance while passenger trains curved sharply around from the left to the signal box where the signalman would be ready to exchange tokens. As the years went by of course the freight grew less and less and fewer and fewer trains crossed at St Dennis. However, the crossing loop continued in use until 1986 with only the occasional train crossing here on summer Saturdays. Once closed the sidings remained *in situ* for a while, controlled by a small ground frame. But the site soon became desolate and overgrown and today there is little sign of this once special place.

After the long expanses over the Tregoss Moor, the terrain and the track changed to some sharp curves through and around a much more 'tamed' and lush agricultural landscape. **St Columb Road** was two miles from its town. A lovely station in its day with, again, a crossing loop and sidings off the down side. A modern glass waiting room now stands on the former up platform, not very attractive. The crossing loop could easily be replaced here should occasion call for it one day.

Trains from here to Newquay still negotiate five small level crossings, all of which were once manned by people who lived in cottages alongside. The first of these was a few hundred yards on the down side of St Columb Road known as **Halloon Crossing**, the crossing keeper being provided with a hut and warning bells to advise him of approaching trains. This crossing had never been provided with signals, its protection being St Columb's fixed up distant and down advanced starting signals. However for some strange reason in the 1970s when many cutbacks were starting to take place, a working distant and home signal were provided in each direction, although these were short-lived.

Coswarth Crossing is a mile or so further on, originally protected by two fixed distant signals. A working down distant would have been more sensible here since the approach from the up side is on a blind curve and there were several occasion when drivers, assuming the gates were closed to road traffic, came around the sharp bend to discover they were not! In the summer this is delightfully tranquil spot and the former crossing keeper's cottage is still plainly visible.

By this time there is a sense that the sea is not far away with glimpses of caravans and holiday parks with their colourful chalets and well laid-out gardens. After a short tunnel and a bridge carrying the A392 road there is another tight squeeze between walls and hedges before the third level crossing at **Quintrel Downs Platform** 18 miles from Par. This pretty little station had its resident crossing keeper who lived in the cottage alongside not only opening and closing the gates and pulling the two working distant signals; she also tended the flower beds and garden alongside making this a delightful of a perfect GWR rural halt. As at Halloon Crossing, working home signals were erected in the 1970s but these again were short lived disappearing in 1981 when all were swept away to be replaced by an automated crossing.

Until 1981 another working distant signal was visible off the end of the down side, marking the approach to the fourth manned level crossing known as **Chapel.** A mile beyond this and with Newquay clearly visible in the distance, was **Trencreek Crossing**, this protected by two home signals and two fixed distants. Both these last two crossings had tiny little garden shed type boxes, the first cream and the second black, both poised a couple of feet up on top of their garden wall, wonderful rural reminders of a bygone age.

The line had many level crossings with crossing keepers. This is Chapel Crossing protected by two working distant signals. The tiny ground frame box is perched precariously next to the house and above the track as was Trencreek Crossing a little further towards Newquay.   *Author*

Until 1964, one year after the Newquay to Chacewater line was closed, Trencreek marked the approach to the huge complex of **Tolcarn Junction**, less than a mile from the terminus at Newquay. Originally this had been a triangular junction with trains from both Newquay and Par able to veer off down the line to Perranporth and Chacewater but since in practice only trains from Newquay went down to Chacewater the southern link was discarded. With Newquay at times bursting to capacity, Tolcarn Junction was the place engines could come and turn thus easing up space at Newquay. Another problem at the Newquay end was the fact that the final bridge into the station was single track. A second track was therefore put in place at the start of World War II although not brought into use until 1946.

When Tolcarn closed in 1964 the whole area went into fast decline. In time a housing and industrial estate gradually took over the site and for a number of years one lonely fixed distant signal for the approach to Newquay, placed on an original Tolcarn Junction signal post, was all that remained of this once incredibly busy railway location.

The last of three long distance trains arrives at Newquay on a summer Saturday in August 1987 while the local train waits for the up home signal to clear. After this year the signal box was to close and Newquay reduced to just one platform. *Author*

The guard rings Goonbarrow Junction in December 2006 to let him know the midday train is about to return up the line. The railcar stands in the one remaining slightly truncated platform. *Author*

The double track remained over the viaduct until Newquay box closed with a double-armed home signal on the south end of the bridge close by two advanced starting signals, entrance and exit from Newquay being bi-directional on both lines.
Newquay station had platforms which accommodated trains with up to 14 coaches and which made the small dmu workings look even smaller! Even in the 1980s this delightful seaside terminus could be bustling with activity in the summer months. On a beautiful early August morning in 1987 I managed to fulfil a long cherished ambition of being at Newquay to capture the three long distance trains arrive within close succession. One by one the long trains arrived, passengers disembarked, locomotives ran round their trains and coaches were moved across to make way for the next arrival, and leaving platform one clear for the modest little local train to come and go but, rather like my Jack Russell in the company of much bigger dogs, undaunted and perfectly equal to the task! The charming signalman on duty, whom I had met on the previous day, was a touch uncertain as to whether to invite me into the box since the Area Manager was on the platform. I realised I had just walked past him. On retracing my steps I found him talking to a colleague. 'Good morning Peter', I ventured to say. A slight pause and then, 'Good heavens Robert. What on earth are you doing here?' 'Hoping to go into the signal box', I replied. 'Of course you may', and calling up to the signalman, 'It's alright John. Robert is my cousin!' What it is to have friends in high places! The kind favour resulted in a wonderful set of photographs which I treasure but which will never be repeated.

During the weekdays of the 1980s Newquay signal box was a very quiet location. But on those summer Saturday mornings it was all levers go. It was not to last for this was the last summer of those early morning trains and indeed the last year of Newquay signal box which closed two months later in October. Its subsequent vandalism and collapse as the result of a fire was a sad end for this fine GWR structure which for years had heralded trains from near and far into Cornwall's longest platforms serving the county's busiest holiday traffic.

Today trains still make their way across the magnificent viaduct as they approach Newquay station but now only one platform remains, the former platform two, and this has been truncated with only a meagre small glass waiting room. But at least the line lives on and at times there is still considerable bustle in the summer months and there is a tourist centre at the end of the platform.

In the 2011 summer timetable, long distance trains were still coming to Newquay although, because of the lack of run-round facilities and with the long section all the way from Goonbarrow Junction, arrival times are spread throughout the day. In practice the shortest time for a train leaving Newquay and for the next to arrive from Goonbarrow is 1 hour and 20 minutes. Were St Dennis still open the time would 40 minutes.

Saturdays

8.27 am	Arrival from Plymouth	3.25 pm	Departure to Manchester
9.27 am	Departure to Dundee	4.52 pm	Arrival from Paddington
10.55 am	Arrival from Plymouth	5.18 pm	Departure to Paddington
11.22 am	Departure to Paddington	6.45 pm	Arrival from Dundee
12.44 pm	Arrival from Paddington	7.55 pm	Departure to Plymouth
1.14 pm	Departure to Paddington	9.10 pm	Arrival from Par
2.36 pm	Arrival from Manchester	9.21 pm	Departure to Plymouth

With the exception of the first and last trains of the day all of the above cross at Goonbarrow Junction and as can be see from the arrival and departure times, plenty

The 4.40 pm from Liskeard at Terras Crossing on 11th July, 1959.

of time is generally allowed for the turnaround of the long distance trains, a figurative term of course since there are no turnaround facilities. Thus time for disembarking, train cleaning, time off for the drivers, and re-embarking. The only disadvantage for local folk is that on summer Saturdays none of these trains stop at intermediate stations. Summer weekdays now bring six trains to and from Newquay with one through train to Paddington in the summer. In July and August there are six trains on Sundays including one to Edinburgh and three trains the rest of the year. Even in the winter months the train service has improved from what it once was. There was a time when there was definite feeling that services were being run down. This no longer appears to be the case.

As already mentioned, way back in the late 1980s there was talk of re-routing the line for passenger services via Burngullow and thereby ending passenger services at Luxulyan, Bugle and Roche. But this discussion seems to have died down for the moment and the line's future appears secure thanks to the Devon and Cornwall Rail Partnership's promotion of the line renaming it the 'Atlantic Coast Line' although the thought of the 'Atlantic Coast Express', proud flagship (or should that be flag train?) of the Southern Railway having ever been allowed on GWR lines seems a touch unlikely!

Of all the branch lines in Cornwall there is so much more which could be said about both the route and its offshoots and I can only urge people to read John Vaughan's two wonderful books *Newquay and its Branches* together with *Rails to Newquay* (see Bibliography) which leave not a sleeper unturned.

Of course the cut-backs have been huge and those faceless 15 miles from beyond Goonbarrow which once brought employment to so many good people of Cornwall makes sad reading. But no further cutbacks can really now be made and the optimist may well be tempted to feel that things from now on can only get better and grow. A second platform again at Newquay, a restored loop at St Columb or St Dennis? And with all its variety it remains a great line on which to linger, although to miss a train can mean quite a long one!

For me the favourite spots? … Par remains a good place, Middleway Crossing, Luxulyan, on the footpath the up side of Goonbarrow and, on a fine day, at the up end of Tregoss Moor.

Liskeard to Looe

Liskeard - Coombe Junction Halt (2m. 5ch.) - St Keyne (Wishing Well) Halt (3m. 64ch.) - Causland Halt (5m. 9ch.) - Sandplace Halt (6m. 39ch.) - Looe (8m. 51ch.)

So what exactly is a branch line in 2013? If you had only one chance to demonstrate an answer to this question to somebody who knew nothing about railways, let alone branch lines, and you hoped to initiate, educate and captivate your questioner, where would you take them? Go back 50 years and I think I would have had to take them back to the already described Torrington-Halwill line. But in 2013 I look for a line that is rural and complete in itself; not too short so that the atmosphere has a chance to settle in but not too long as to bore, and it would have to be a line that has not lost too much under modernization.

Of course I've given the game away already by asking this question at the start of a chapter about the line to Looe! For surely, if ever a line still epitomized the truly rural branch line, this must be it with its ancient history and with some 10 miles of

A diesel railcar arrives at the branch platform at Liskeard in 2011.   *Author*

An afternoon train to Looe departs from Coombe Junction Halt in 1975 when the signal box was still in operation. The line on the right continues to Moorswater.   *Author*

scenery almost totally unchanged by time. The line to Looe ticks all the boxes. Well not quite since all boxes of the signalling variety on the branch have gone. The branch box at Liskeard together with the other two at Coombe Junction and Looe itself are now just memories. There is still a little clay traffic at the top end of the line but none between Coombe and Looe. As at St Ives the Looe terminus has been vastly shortened and sidings removed. That said the line remains much as it ever was with its four halts virtually unchanged. I have retained the 'Halt' after each station for old time's sake since I recall as a child, before I had ever travelled on the line, being fascinated by noticing in the timetable a line where every intermediate station was a 'Halt'.

As we have already noted, the line was due to close as a result of the Beeching report but like the St Ives branch closure was stopped by Barbara Castle in 1968, in particular on the grounds of poor road access. The ancient history and ongoing charm of the line has inevitably resulted in a number of fine books being produced about the line together with numerous articles in various magazines. The origins go as far back as 1846 when copper ore and granite were moved from high up on Bodmin Moor to Looe by tramway as far as Moorswater, 300ft below Liskeard, and then from Moorswater to Looe by canal along which the railway was later to be built, opening in 1879. Amazingly, another 22 years were to follow before a connecting line was built to climb its way up to Liskeard on the main line.

The branch platform at **Liskeard** is largely unspoilt despite there no longer being a small signal box just off the end of the platform and no more run-round loop. But the building is as it ever was, situated arrogantly and independently at 90 degrees to the main line, access to which is by a short path and a two minute walk for the Paddington-bound trains but rather longer over a bridge for access to down trains bound for Truro and Penzance. There are a few remaining sidings off the branch line and from these there is rail access to the main line via a very sharp curve and a crossover opposite the main line signal box. This box is the last manually operated signal box on the line before the Plymouth panel takes over near St Germans, two stations up the line. There are no through passenger trains to Looe but the first and last trains of the day, Plymouth, use this access line as do the china clay trains to and from Moorswater when they are running, with their wagons screeching wildly like a flock of frightened birds as they slowly take the sharp curve onto the main line. If there are passengers on board the final train of the day they are supposed to be deposited on the branch platform. But if no passengers are on board the train will stop at the points and then proceed onto the link to the main line.

All this said by way of introduction, it is the journey itself which makes the line so utterly captivating. Travelling briefly north-east out of the still lengthy platform before crossing the points which are now controlled by a small open lever ground frame, the line performs a complete 180 degree turn to finish running south-west and then under the main line viaduct at whose level the train started only a few minutes previously. Falling at 1 in 40 with lush fields rising up on the left, the line now descends into wooded countryside dropping down to **Coombe Junction** with the line to Looe gradually coming into view, running in below to the left of the train.

Until 1980 the most delightful small GWR junction box stood by the hand-operated level crossing where the line from Liskeard joins the line from Looe. Latterly this controlled an outer and inner home signal for both routes and a two-armed starting signal near the end of the tiny platform, the arm on the left for Liskeard and the one on the right for Looe. From the box running northwards, one line ran directly into the platform and buffer stops while a second line running parallel to the first continued under a road bridge and onwards to Moorswater, the original birthplace of the line where spasmodic china clay traffic still runs. In the days of steam trains engines uncoupled and crossed over onto the Moorswater line in order to run around their coaches. After dmus took over, the run-round loop became redundant. Once the box closed the two parallel lines were reduced to the one running through the halt and thence on to Moorswater. Two ground frames were then erected, the one by the junction and the other beyond the platform towards Moorswater. Points are always left set for the Liskeard direction leaving it clear for trains to Moorswater.

Thus in practice, today trains run down from Liskeard crossing the junction points before running forward the 100 yds northwards to Coombe Halt if booked to stop there. Once upon a time all trains ran into this little platform and it was said that if you missed the train at Liskeard, with a brisk pace you could run down the hill and catch it here. Today only two trains a day in each direction are booked to call here, the station being seldom used for passengers and more often by passing lovers in need of shelter from the rain in this romantic setting! So if a train is not booked to call here, the dmu just moves over the junction points, stops over the level crossing while the driver moves from the north facing cab to the south facing. The guard descends, changes the points and the train moves forward in the Looe direction. He then resets the points for the Liskeard direction thus locking the train in with the key token and thereby enabling a freight train to descend from Liskeard for Moorswater should it be necessary. The guard re-ascends and it's off again to Looe!

The train sets off along a short straight section while the line to Liskeard now climbs up to the left above it, before curving gently to the right and away down the verdant river valley towards Looe and at a gentle 25 mph pace. The slow 'clickety-click' (or is it clunkety-clunk?) rhythm of the train can be quite soporiphic. In the summer the hedgerows and tall trees are heavy with leaves which block the views, but there is an occasional glimpse of stream, little cottages with tidy and not so tidy gardens, a wandering very free range chicken or two and with sloping fields on either side which reach up to the sky in this rich and totally unspoilt and gently naturally untidy valley.

Nearly four miles from Liskeard with the stream on the left, the train slows down for **St Keyne (Wishing Well) Halt**, passing first under a solid square ivy-clad road bridge with the station just beyond on the up side. St Keyne, like Causland and Sandplace are all request stops and with no passengers waiting or alighting, the train often simply glides slowly past and on its way, the driver not accelerating too much to avoid passing any of these stops too early allowing just eight generous minutes from Coombe to St Keyne or slightly less if not booked to stop there, four minutes from St Keyne to Causland and three from Causland to Sandplace. If a train is going to stop anywhere it is most likely to be St Keyne which is the most used station on the line. And should a train pause here for a moment, it may be that a passenger will look up from his book or open his eyes from his dreaming at the sound of a fairground organ playing. No, he is not still dreaming for there alongside the little halt is a unique mechanical organ museum which has become a huge tourist attraction over the years. A few cottages also stand nearby the station although St Keyne village is about a mile away. At the back of the station is a large gate with parking space for a couple of cars. The platform is wide and roomy and here, as at the other halts, brick-built waiting shelters have quite tastefully replaced the original wooden ones with even the suggestion of flowers in stone containers alongside. The station is sometimes given the fuller name of St Keyne Wishing Well Halt after a nearby ancient well which was home to St Keyne, a virtuous lady whose father was King Brechan of Wales. This 15th century monarch is believed to have had 26 children, 15 of which became saints! The mystic powers of the well stem from a blessing St Keyne placed upon the waters whereby whichever of a newly-wed couple drank from the well first would wear the trousers in the marriage.

> The quality that man or wife,
> Whose chance or choice attains,
> First of the sacred stream to drink,
> Thereby the mastery gains.

Frankly this does not strike me as having been a very saintly thing to do! Many superstitions, however, arose from this belief although disaster befell one bride who in her eagerness to be first to drink the water got out of the train on the wrong side, fell and broke her neck! All this added to the superstitions which surrounded the area and not least the belief that a veiled bride haunts the station. I have yet to see her, however.

Moving away from St Keyne on a short straight section, the line curves away into an even remoter wooded section curving sharply to the left after 1½ miles into **Causland Halt.** And here we really must pause for a short while for this station is an absolute gem and very much one of an endangered species.

The setting is quite idyllic with a narrow lane running just behind the station with just about room for one car in front of a similar white gate as at St Keyne giving access to the tiny halt which, like St Keyne is on the up side although unlike St Keyne is on a curve. The station faces over the same clear-running stream which was once part of the original canal. Sitting on a this isolated platform without a soul or a house in view, this quietly chattering stream is as often as not one's soul companion together with hovering butterflies in the summer and a host of wild flowers which thankfully have usually escaped the annual passing of the weed killer train.

Across the line is a gate into a steeply sloping field and a perfect picnic place once one has negotiated an initial soggy few feet before the land rises. Both here and elsewhere wooden-sleepered crossing places once made easy access for lovely vantage points, and high up in the field, looking back down on the station was one such spot. Sadly, more recently, some bureaucratic cad has decided these crossing points are undesirable and safety hazards, and such access is now less easy. So now the picnic may have to be on the platform but when all is said and done that's pretty good!

When the line first opened in 1879, Causland was in fact the only intermediate station, Coombe and St Keyne not appearing until 20 years later when the branch was joined to the GWR main line. It is also the remotest. There are in fact a scattering of houses nearby and some comfortable holiday chalets at Badham Farm. I have spent a few days here on two occasions, both in January and I cannot speak too highly of this location. Here is perfect peace in a comfortable warm chalet overlooking a large pond, in the company of Muscovy ducks, beautiful woodlands and the branch line to Looe a stone's throw below, just a few hundred years south of Causland Halt. If you want to 'get away from it all', go to Badhams Farm. Seldom have I discovered anywhere where two or three days can restore one's equilibrium ... and nobody has paid me to say that! Trewidland village is way up a nearby hill. But the station itself is truly a time warp and how it has survived is quite extraordinary. Not that I for one moment am complaining!

Tranquil little Causland Halt basks in summer sunshine in 1991 with its stream running alongside.   *Author*

An afternoon up train passes the tranquil setting of Badhams Farm in January 2012 where charming holiday chalets offer away from it all peace and quiet.   *Author*

All this said the station is still used and on my last visit to the line, five passengers carrying shopping from Looe alighted from a late afternoon train, to disappear up the lane and to be swallowed up into the leafy countryside.

I would like to loiter here even longer but the train moves on towards Looe curving away from Causland and very quickly, the train is passing below Badhams Farm and the holiday chalets. Between Causland and Sandplace the hedges and trees become so dense in this already dark valley area that at times, even in the summer, it is hard for the sun to penetrate. A few more curves and three little road bridges, and the little station of **Sandplace** comes into view, this time on the down side and again like Causland built on a tight curve.

Opened a couple of years after Causland and having lived up to its name as the place where sand from the building industry was loaded into trucks from a small siding, the remains of which are now overgrown, hence 'Sand-place', the station is close to a cluster of houses and cottages together with a small but extremely comfortable hotel. A larger road here joins the one which has accompanied us down the valley, as the train now sets off on its final two mile run towards Looe.

Within ¼ mile of curving away from Sandplace, there is an extraordinary change of scenery. From the close-knit valley with its secret gardens and moss-covered bridges shaded by towering trees, the views now open up over untamed marsh and reed-covered sandbanks as the inland streams gather themselves together and flow towards the Looe estuary which suddenly and magnificently comes into view.

A mile from Looe and there is a sharp turn to the left as the train slows and halts, then 'whistles' as instructed before crossing very slowly over the unguarded **Terras Crossing**. Until 1975 a crossing keeper was housed here in order to open and shut the gates and to operate the two distant signals. Although the keeper's house was minute it must have had one of the most impressive views of any such job anywhere with its panoramic view over the causeway and stretching away all the way down to Looe. From here could be observed the dramatic ebb and flow of the tides with vast mud banks at low tide cut deeply in two by the out-flowing river with everything totally submerged when the tide was high, even occasionally the causeway road itself with particularly intrusive spring tides. When a steam train returned over two weekends in the autumn of 2010 it was hardly surprising to discover this was the most popular vantage point for photographers with cars parked all the way up the hill on the west side of the road across the river.

Exciting though this was, equally beautiful was to be at this same point on the morning after the steam trains, a Monday, as the sun rose reflecting the amazing autumn colours in the water while a host of river and sea birds rummaged for their breakfast on the reedy mud banks. This magical, misty stillness was only briefly disturbed by the single coach train of the early morning unfussily making its morning journey, a few feet from the water's edge on its way to Looe, its honking whistle echoing up and down the valley as it made the customary pause before proceeding over the crossing.

In the days when a crossing keeper would have been on duty, as he shut the gates behind a down train, and with time to spare before its return, he might well have watched the train curving off to the left and then back to the right, hugging the shoreline on one side while the road, largely hidden by trees, ran parallel on the other side. He might well have paused to see the train pass his own squat little up distant signal and pass the tall wooden fixed distant signal for Looe until the train vanished around the final bend into Looe station.

An afternoon train passes Sandplace in 1997.   *Author*

A railcar makes its way up the estuary from Looe in the summer of 2010.   *Author*

Although not inconveniently placed, the station at **Looe** has always been on the edge of the town; to be precise on the edge of East Looe, West Looe being on the other side of the road bridge over the river. Despite the wonderful panoramic views along the final mile of the line, passengers on the platform have no warning of a train's arrival, the final curve into the station being totally blind. To truly appreciate Looe station, both in older days and now, one needs to stand on the west side of the town where an almost mile and a half vista is available of the coming and going of trains.

The modest terminus is beautifully situated, as modern branch line termini go, marginally better than some with some waiting facilities and well-positioned posters to cheer the platform. However, it was unfortunate that unlike any of the other branch line termini, when the station was reduced in size, the result was that now only a two-coach train can fit into the platform and unless the police station next door is ever knocked down there is not much chance of any change here.

Until 1979 the line continued to fan out on the down side of the station into a series of sidings alongside the quay, providing not only a large area for the sorting of freight trains and with a convenient location for the handling of fish traffic, but also facilities for an engine to run around its train in readiness for the return journey.

Reputed to be the smallest signal box on the network inside which even one was almost a crowd, Looe's 8-lever frame was situated just off the down end of the platform. The up starting signal at the up end of the platform, just before the sharp curve, appeared in numerous pictures of the station and was Looe's only working signal on the up side, its forlorn post remaining *in situ* for a while long after the arm was removed. Only one passenger train at a time was ever between Coombe Junction at Looe at any one time so far as I can tell, but if a freight train were at Looe, this could be safely shunted away on the down side beyond the two small bracketed signals which graced the entrance to the sidings.

Gradually the sidings were cut back and were finally removed after the demise of freight and after the introduction of the dmus. After this the fine old GWR station was replaced by today's shortened platform and the modern edifice. I gather that sometimes on busy summer days a member of staff appears on duty at the station although I have never seen this and possibly by now this has also stopped. The view, however, from the platform across the river and harbour waters remains delightfully unchanged as trains arrive, bide their time and then quickly disappear again around the corner.

Not that trains do much biding of time here these days. With a train service which has increased considerably over the years the recent weekday pattern has been:

Arrive: 06.36, 07.45, 09.04, 10.29, 11.46,* 12.46, 13.50, 14.56,* 16.12, 17.12, 18.32, 19.49
Depart: 06.37, 07.46, 09.09, 10.32, 11.47,* 12.47, 13.51,*14.57, 16.13,* 17.15, 18.33, 19.52

* Booked to run non-stop along the branch

Trains vary slightly in running time from a little under ½ hour to a little over, depending on the stopping schedule. The only slight drawback to what is arguably an excellent service is that with many trains only allowed a one minute turnaround, one can sometimes perceive an understandable pressure upon the train crew to hurry the departure in order to keep up to time and a sense of being rushed is not in the tradition of the good old branch line. That said I have always found the vast majority of staff courteous and only to happy to stop to chat once the train is under

Bere Ferrers in 2012 beautifully restored with Pinhoe signal box at the down end of the platform looking towards Bere Alston. *Author*

A train from Gunnislake arrives at Bere Alston in January 2012 . Having changed the points the train will continue back out towards Plymouth. The line on the left continues a couple of hundred yards towards buffer stops along the track bed which once continued to Exeter. The former up platform remains *in situ*. *Author*

way again. An extra evening train runs on summer Saturdays arriving at Looe at 20.50 and leaving again at 21.12. There are eight trains on summer Sundays.

So this enchanting little branch line looks safe for the future. Occasional mishaps do occur over the final two miles when the line is prone to flooding in very stormy weather. But otherwise the little trains continue to rattle up and down the valley with an occasional freight train struggling gallantly up the 1 in 40 from Moorswater to Liskeard. Here is a real branch line which is essentially unspoilt and it remains a real favourite of mine.

A Southern remnant – Plymouth to Gunnislake (Callington)

Plymouth - Devonport - Dockyard Halt - Keyham - St Budeaux Victoria Road - Bere Ferrers - Bere Alston - Calstock - Gunnislake - (Chilsworthy - Latchley - Luckett - Callington)

This somewhat unusual and beautiful line only just squeezes its way into this section because of its last three Cornish miles, although when it ran its full length to Callington it had eight miles from the Devon boundary into Cornwall. The line is unusual because it is a hybrid cross of a former main line and part of a once longer branch line. The first part of this line has already been partially described in Chapter Six of this book going back to the days when the Southern line ran from Plymouth to Waterloo via Tavistock and Okehampton. As already noted this wonderful line was amputated in 1968 between Bere Alston and Okehampton. Dr Beeching's original plan had been to close the whole line from Plymouth together, obviously, with the adjoining Callington branch. But it was Calstock's graceful viaduct which saved the day being the only immediate access across the Tamar from Devon and thus a reprieve was granted from Bere Alston to Gunnislake. This in turn secured also a happy salvation from Plymouth to Bere Alston.

The line starts, contrastingly with its later rural wanderings, at the heart of very urban **Plymouth**. Branch trains today normally sets off from one or other of the two bay platforms at the down end of Plymouth station, the first three miles of the line following the main line to Penzance through suburban **Devonport, Dockyard Halt** and **Keyham** before curving over the wartime spur into **St Budeaux Victoria Road** just a few yards across the road from St Budeaux Ferry Road on the main line.

In 1970 the double track from St Budeaux to Bere Alston was singled and was run as 'one engine in steam' from St Budeaux to Gunnislake. Since this date all trains must by necessity stop at St Budeaux where the driver procures the single line staff from a locked cabinet on the platform, this effectively locking the train into the section. On the return journey the staff is replaced enabling the Plymouth signalman to switch signal and points for the train to regain access to the main line. On the singling of the line, the Bere Alston signal box was closed and a new access was created onto the branch from the Plymouth end with the result that thereafter only the former down platform was used with a two-lever ground frame off the end of the platform, now worked by the guard, consisting of one point lever and one point lock.

I well recall visiting **Bere Alston** very shortly after the changes had been made and being utterly aghast at seeing lifeless and armless signal posts lying prostrate on the ground and this once so busy station totally devoid of staff. But strangely enough since that moment, time has stood still at Bere Alston with the main platform totally unchanged from 50 years ago. The former, now trackless, up platform is still *in situ* with the waiting room intact if boarded up, and the leverless signal box still standing. Thus if one day tracks are relayed to Tavistock, and a quick nip to Google suggests that plans for this are still alive with even a proposed timetable, perhaps Bere Alston's old up platform will once again be in use.

For the moment, 18 times a day, nine trains bound for Gunnislake and nine returning to Plymouth, pause for a few minutes while there is a flurry of activity as passengers ascend and descend. The guard walks to the end of the platform, key in hand changing the points for the reversed journey, and while the two-coach train idles quietly under the same old canopied roof of the station as of days past, the driver changes ends just as at Coombe Junction on the Looe branch.

A quick glace to see all is well along the platform, and the train is off again across the points and down the hill to Calstock or around the sharp left-hand curve and immediately out of sight on the way to **Bere Ferrers** and Plymouth.

At a little less than three miles along the line and on a 1 in 52 gradient, this charming, once main line, station has gracefully grown into its new status as a branch line halt. The original up platform has been swallowed up by overgrowth although the station owner Chris Grove, something of a local legend, has re-established the 'Bere Ferrers' sign for all to see on the up side. The fine Victorian station building has been beautifully preserved with station approach and car park as they ever were. Although privately owned the station drips both outwardly and inwardly with memorabilia of a bygone era, together with Pinhoe's former signal box, two working home signals and a couple of ground signals tucked neatly against the station wall. Not only is the signal box complete with levers and instruments, but thanks to the wonders of computerisation an imaginary train can be signalled from Exmouth Junction to Honiton with signals, levers, level crossing and bell codes all set in motion as it once had been in Pinhoe box. Mr Grove is rightly proud of this magnificent piece of modern preservation as well as the track and rolling stock he has assembled on the former sidings, complete with dining car, sleeping accommodation and compartments stuffed full of memories of the past. At my last visit the turntable was being repositioned in order to build a small engine shed. The site may be small but every inch is being used.

Bere Ferrers remains therefore not just the delightful country station it ever was but one which has readjusted to a new era of its life and a place where there is plenty to look at between trains. The recent weekday train service has been as follows:

Up	Down
06.15 (SX)	05.18 non-stop (SX)
07.56	06.57
10.10	09.11
12.10	11.11
14.10	13.11
16.10	15.11
17.54	16.55
19.38	18.40
22.46	21.48

Key: SX - Saturdays excepted

Returning to the original branch, from Bere Alston the line drops rapidly away at 1 in 40 towards the Tamar Valley. Here as at so many other railway locations trees and shrubs have grown considerably taller than when, once upon a time, they would have been pruned back. And the one time views of branch trains climbing up to Bere

Alston are not as impressive as once they were, but views from the train are as lovely as ever as the line drops down over farm crossings and through lush fields as views of the Tamar gradually come into view. Then through the trees and over an embankment there is a quick glimpse of the houses of Cornish **Calstock** and the jewel in the crown of the line, the 120 ft high Calstock viaduct with its 12 slender 60 ft spans, a bridge described by John Betjeman as 'deliciously feminine'! Another embankment hides it from view for a moment or two, a sharp curve and then the track straightens up for the straight run across the top with the sharp curving edge of Calstock's platform just visible at the far end. Until 1968 when the tiny signal box closed, two fine lower quadrant LSWR signals guarded the approach to Calstock, one at each end of the viaduct, signals which are evident in many older photographs of the station and viaduct. The view of the Tamar and of Calstock village and quay is quite magnificent from both sides of the train and with the 15 mph speed restriction over the bridge there is time to savour the same.

Calstock station, curving back on itself as if its back might break, has a somewhat disappointing setting after what has gone before, facing as it does into the high rock face opposite. Access from the quay requires a steep climb up the hill for the pedestrian. Although there has always been just the single platform here, passenger trains could cross with a freight train if required since a non-platformed loop was provided. Wagons standing in the siding were often the recipients of a multitude of local market gardening produce which abound in abundance around this area, including strawberries to die for! Even after the loop and sidings were removed one solitary wagon remained here for a while for the same, slightly infrequent, purpose. The old station building which had grown tired and dilapidated now consists of a modern concrete shelter with a sloping roof, not far from the up end of platform which is just a few feet from the start of the viaduct. Compared with the old station in its latter days, I have to admit that the current station is almost an improvement and does appear cared for.

At the down end the line curves sharply away vanishing immediately from view around a sharp embankment beyond which once stood the only signal in the up direction. From here the line emerges to climb at 1 in 40 with small market gardens on each side, some of which nowadays appear somewhat unloved. Looking back to the right there is a fine view of the northern side of the viaduct and the steeply sloping fields on the Devon side. The next mile is a series of climbing twists and turns and something of a challenge for the driver in slippery wet weather. This is made even less easy by a compulsory stop before the unguarded Okletor road crossing followed by another deep rock cutting as the climb continues. Emerging towards the top with the tower of Calstock church appearing on the left, the view which opens on to the right of the train is quite stunning falling down towards Morwellham Quay below with the hills of Dartmoor in the far distance beyond the pine-covered hills which slope up from the Tamar. The landscape here is also a continual reminder that this is a world of abandoned mines which once produced tin, copper and arsenic, and which were the origins of the line itself. Like the Looe branch, so the Callington line was built primarily for the transport of such minerals. It was not until 1908 that the line finally became a fully fledged branch line joined to the main line at Bere Alston as a light railway. Indeed it remains the last survivor of the famous Colonel Stephen's light railway. A mile from Gunnislake as the gradient starts to ease at last is another compulsory stop at Sandways open crossing where the road from Gunnislake crosses the line on its way down to Calstock ... a considerably shorter route than that taken by the train!

A photograph taken from the Calstock quay, of a double-headed train, preparing to pull its load of freight up the steep incline towards Bere Alston in 1962. *Author*

An afternoon up train in 1962 crosses over Calstock viaduct from Cornwall to Devon. The down outer home signal stands on the 'wrong side' on the bank. Signals at Calstock guarded the entrance to the station but not the exit. *Author*

Finally, just over 14 miles from Plymouth the line comes to a halt at **Gunnislake** situated at the top of the town's steep hill on the Tavistock-Callington-Liskeard road. Until 1966 this was a crossing loop with an attractive island platform and with another five miles to travel on to Callington, a journey I had first made some 12 years previously with my mother to visit her Godmother. I recall little of the journey or the visit apart from a smiling spaniel with an array of medals won at dog shows around his neck and a warning that I could stroke the dog but must not touch the medals as he didn't like it! My mother and I had had to catch a bus from the station into Callington since despite it being called 'Callington' it was situated outside the town at Kelly Bray. But I do recall an impressively intimate little country terminus with a small signal box at the end of the platform and with a fine roof covering the whole station making the interior rather dark. I also recall the three little single-platformed stations with evocative names, Chilsworthy, Latchley and Luckett, all with wonderful views northwards as far as the eye could see, Luckett being slightly superior since there was a porter on duty here. The trackbed can still be clearly seen although there is no sign of the terminus which has been swallowed up under housing development.

After the section to Callington closed the loop was retained for a while with trains arriving on the down side and then returning from the up. The line in fact still continued enticingly out of sight towards Callington for a couple of hundred yards, although a little investigation soon stumbled upon an emphatic buffer stop! The almost alpine view from Gunnislake was one of the most spectacular anyone could possibly imagine although facing north-easterly, highly exposed in winter. But then the rot set in. With the closure of the signal box in 1968 the station became unmanned and only the up side of the island platform was retained. The station buildings became tatty, uncared for and unsafe until they were pulled down to be replaced by a single, very exposed, modern shelter. The car park became a dreadful mess. Finally in 1994 after some years of debate the old station was closed and for four months the line terminated at Calstock while a new station was built 100 yards closer to Bere Alston. The reason for this was to enable the low bridge over the main road to be demolished and the height restriction on vehicles being lifted. The new station is clean and serviceable with a neat car park alongside. It is as they say, 'satisfactory' although without much character. But perhaps character is something that comes with age and at least it is there! This new station stands on what was originally the site of coal sidings with the original track on a rising gradient up towards the old station. A 60 ft drop was required for the creation of this new platform so that this new terminus would be safe on a level plateau. Contractors had perhaps learnt their lesson for the mistake made at 'The Dell' on the Falmouth branch! (see earlier section of this chapter).

The train service today is as good as it has ever been although as on the Looe branch there is little time these days to linger for the return journey. In recent years a Sunday service has been reintroduced. At one time there had been a huge gap in weekday afternoons when a slot had been allowed for freight trains to run into Ernesettle sidings on the down side of St Budeaux. When these ceased British Rail was persuaded to provide a more balanced timetable. Thus trains on normal weekdays were recently as follows at Gunnislake:

Arrive: 05.50, 07.27, 09.26, 11.40, 13.41, 15.40, 17.24, 19.09, 22.17
Depart: 05.51, 07.31, 09.29, 11.45, 13.45, 15.45, 17.29, 19.13, 22.21

The original island platform as it was at Gunnislake in 1958 looking towards Callington.
Roger Joanes

The author's son Ben, and wife Susie, shelter from a summer shower on Calstock platform in July 1997. *Author*

With fractional time changes, the Saturday services are similar less the first train of the day which does not run, its main function being to serve early morning workers for Plymouth and the dockyard.

But however good the service, the 'one train only' system limits what is possible. We've already seen this from Goonbarrow to Newquay and the same applies from Eggesford to Barnstaple as illustrated in the next chapter. In all such cases no second train can run until the first train has been to the end of the line and returned to where it entered the single line section; in the case of the Gunnislake branch that means back to St Budeaux. At best a train requires 80 minutes to make it back to the main line which in the height of summer and at the rush hour could surely offer something better. Had the second platform been retained at Bere Alston could not a system have been implemented such as at Bourne End where a train for Marlow and a second from Bourne End to Maidenhead can run concurrently at busy periods? Well, it's a thought.

Whatever its future, this remains a wonderful line on which to travel. It is a line which survives not just as a vital link to Plymouth for workers and shoppers, but thanks to good advertising it also survives as a fine tourist attraction for the beautiful Tamar valley, especially for Calstock where round trips may be made by boat to and from Plymouth. It is an absolute gem and there are superb lingering points almost everywhere from Bere Ferrers to Gunnislake, not least in the fields on the Devon side of the Calstock viaduct. An A1* picnic spot for a glass of wine and a proper pasty!

... and lest we forget – Lostwithiel to Fowey

Lostwithiel - Golant Halt (3m. 57ch.) - Carne Point (4m. 60 ch.) - Fowey (5m. 31ch.)

I felt it unfair and unkind to end this chapter without including the branch line to Fowey. Sadly the line is no longer open to passengers having been closed as a result of the Beeching report in January 1965. But it is still open for china clay traffic and local residents still feel some justifiable frustration that if it can run for freight, why not for passenger traffic. Thus I include it with the others.

In passenger days it was a touch longer than the St Ives branch, and just as that line is a fine advertisement for the dramatic Atlantic Ocean of the North Cornish coast, so too the Fowey branch would be a complementary advertisement for those quiet, romantic estuaries which are so much a part of south Cornwall.

Travelling time was usually 15 minutes, nine to the one intermediate station of Golant, and then six to Fowey. **Lostwithiel** on the main line, and the junction for the branch, still remains a fine location to watch the considerable traffic to flow by both freight and passenger. Semaphore signals still abound and the fine signal box on the up end of the down platform is open 24 hours a day, controlling a level crossing. Like Totnes, it has just had a preservation order placed on it. It is the only signal box that cannot switch out between the Plymouth panel and Truro. It also controls the single line section between Bodmin and Liskeard over Largin viaduct, since the small and inaccessible Largin signal box closed on 16th December, 1991. Sidings abound on both sides of the station although the nearby creamery on the up side no longer provides the considerable traffic it once did. Unlike Par or St Erth, this station has now lost all its fine GWR architecture which was tragically allowed to deteriorate over the years. Despite local protests, first the fine footbridge was demolished followed by the down platform buildings which had provided canopied roofing for both main line and the branch line bay platform. In 1981

Ex-GWR '14XX' class 0-4-2T No. 1419 at Lostwithiel with the Fowey branch auto-train on 12th September, 1958.   *Roger Joanes*

The only intermediate station was Golant Halt seen here in 1960 looking up towards Lostwithiel.
                                                                              Delma Prance

the up platform buildings were demolished. The waiting areas which act as replacements are almost an insult to what stood before and indeed an insult to the charming small town the station serves.

Branch line trains departed from the far side of the down island platform and ran independently parallel to the main line for a few hundred yards before curving away to the left to follow the banks of the Fowey river for the entire five miles, while the main line to Par and beyond climbs steeply up and away from the branch line. Since the closure of the branch to passenger traffic, freight trains coming out of the bay platform and its adjacent sidings now cross briefly onto the main line before turning onto the branch.

The solitary station of **Golant** along the line was a single concrete platform with a waiting shed gazing over the tidal river; behind was the picturesque village with its welcoming pub and church. With meandering mile upon mile of road access to Golant narrowly curvaceous, it is hardly surprising that local residents were so hurt by the line's closure to passengers although still open to commercial enterprise. No sign of Golant Halt now remains although it is fairly obvious where it once stood.

Continuing its riverside hug, the branch continued its journey to arrive after a few minutes amidst a plethora of sidings and signals at **Carne Point** before curving sharply into the single platform at **Fowey.** There was in fact a crossing loop here but with only one platform a passenger train could only cross with a freight train.

My first visit to Fowey was in 1957 when my parents were visiting our cousins Andrew and Lorna whose family lived nearby. I could not understand that this was called a terminus since there were no buffer stops which were the vital elements which epitomized to my 10-year-old mind what any proper terminus should be. It was cousin Andrew who tried to explain to me that a freight line also continued from Fowey in the other direction to Par. I think I remained confused but being a deputy headmaster I knew Andrew had to be right! Passenger trains had ceased on this route to Par as far back as 1929 although freight was to continue until this line closed in 1969, four years in fact after the passenger line to Lostwithiel. This freight

Ex-GWR '42XX' class 2-8-0T No. 4294 with a china clay train at Fowey on 12th September, 1958. An auto-train stands in the platform. *Roger Joanes*

line was then converted into a private road for china clay lorries, and remains as such today.

What an asset a passenger station would now be at Fowey where parking is far from easy and where tourists flock in the summer for sailing, painting, pasties and fishing, sight-seeing and holiday making. The old station building still struggles to maintain a dusty, ivy-clad identity just a few hundred yards from where the freight sidings now end amidst a fury of china clay activity. Heavy trains today move slowly into place as their precious cargo is loaded onto ships moored at what is the main deep water clay port in Cornwall.

Surely all would benefit with a simple reinstated passenger service which would not require huge financial outlay apart from the rebuilding of a small platform at Fowey and Golant.

Apart from at Lostwithiel and Golant, good vantage points along this line are hard to find, and even if access were easier at Carne Point it cannot be described as particularly attractive. However, the fine local artist Don Breckon not only caught on canvas what Lostwithiel station once looked like, but also captured immortal images of a single-coach push and pull passenger train making its way between Lostwithiel and Golant. In the distance of one such picture, on the opposite bank of the railway, stands, indeed almost paddles in the water, the ancient parish church of St Winnow … and what a place to stand and linger (*see front cover*).

I have several personal reasons for driving along the lanes to this wonderful oasis of divine peace overlooking the river. One might be that the local farm sells the most wonderful meat at very reasonable prices! Another would be to pay respects to former relatives who lie in peace in the churchyard; the one, Vice-Admiral Sir Charles Penrose, a great-grandfather who served with Lord Nelson, and the other my gentle and saintly cousin and Godfather Philip Bloy, fellow priest and like-minded railway enthusiast. Also because that same cousin Andrew who long ago tried to explain why Fowey was a buffer-less terminus now as a lay reader conducts Matins at this church. Finally because it is from here that the best view of the line can be captured. True it's not quite the same when today vast noisy clay-filled trains make their slow squealy progress along the water's edge as when those friendly little tank engines pulled and propelled their single coach along with abandoned ease.

But at least there is still a railway and perhaps, who knows in an age when there is renewed hope for our railways, one day there may be passenger trains again. Perhaps I should be praying more fervently to my Godfather and that other ancient Great Grandfather to persuade St Winnow to perform a miracle!

Chapter Ten

Still 'All Stations' to Barnstaple
... a withered finger lives on

Yeoford (junction) - 182m. 79ch. (from London Waterloo) - Coleford Junction (183m. 76ch.) - Copplestone (185m. 75ch.) - Morchard Road (187m. 47ch.) - Lapford (189m. 76ch.) - Eggesford 193m. 68ch.) - King's Nympton (197m. 64ch.) - Portsmouth Arms (200m. 55ch.) - Umberleigh - 204m. 67ch. - Chapleton (207m. 17ch.) - Barnstaple (211m. 43ch.) (all mileages from Waterloo)

Barnstaple

There can be few limbs which have suffered so much amputation and still held on to life as the so named 'Withered Arm', the title given, as already mentioned, by T.W.E. Roche, to the former Southern Railway's network, reaching its way up and into Devon and Cornwall. No longer do those finger-like tracks extend their way to Ilfracombe, Torrington, Halwill Junction, Bude or far distant Padstow.

Yet still hanging on by a veritable thread, is the stoical little line to 'Barnstaple'; alas, no longer do the name boards on the platform boast this to be 'Barnstaple Junction' as opposed to 'Barnstaple Town' or 'Barnstaple Victoria Road', once both on the northern side of the river. None the less Barnstaple still boasts its own, now single-tracked, terminus station. At the down end of what was once a busy up platform, one solitary buffer stop now emphatically insists there is no way forward to Fremington, Instow, Bideford, Torrington, and all stations to Halwill. Nor do trains any more curve away sharply to the right to cross Barnstaple bridge and away to steeply-gradiented Ilfracombe via a multitude of little level crossings. Nor again to the east do trains curve away in a northerly direction to find their way onto GWR tracks past the home of the first Jack Russell terriers at Swimbridge and on to South Molton, Dulverton and all stations to Taunton.

Today, Barnstaple is a shadow of its former self. A bare, trackless, tell-tale, island platform still gives a faint reminder of the former glories of this down platform where once both GWR and SR engines of various shapes and sizes rubbed shoulders before proceeding onwards in a variety of four different ways. Both signal boxes, one at each end of the platforms, have now gone while the once ample goods yard behind the still remaining up platform, is now a large car park. One sad, seldom used siding with its 3-lever ground frame, remains, stretching away for a couple of hundred yards in the up direction away from the station, bedecked at warmer times of year with a few rambling blue buddleias.

But if a shadow of the past it is, one has only to enter the still remaining, bright airy and clean booking office to discover that life still remains and that Barnstaple very much lives on! Well trained staff behind the ticket counter are happy to give advice and tap out information from their modern computer. The station still boasts periods of considerable activity when doors slam, buses and taxis pull up outside, and the high-ceilinged waiting room, filled to capacity, echoes to the voices of intending passengers who gradually spill out onto the wide, canopied platform, to await their train ... although only one train in and out, in only one direction, and from only one platform, so there is no confusion here as to which train to catch!

It has to be said that Barnstaple was never a very attractive station. The tall rock face on the south side, rather as at Okehampton, dominates the platform and casts it into an almost permanent shadow, a shadow which is underlined by the large

Barnstaple in 2010. How are the mighty fallen! Once an important through station now very much the end of the line as well as the final digit of the dear old 'Withered Arm'. *Author*

Yeoford in 1971 looking towards Coleford Junction just a mile away where lines diverge, one towards Plymouth and the other towards Ilfracombe. *Author's Collection*

canopy over the platform. Yet there remains a sense of quiet importance, as if to say 'I am Barnstaple, the alpha and omega of this line. I have a great past of which to be proud, and I still have an important part to play in the great scheme of things, so don't belittle me!'

Thus some 14 times or so each day a railcar or two-car dmu quietly and unostentatiously, slowly observes the speed restriction over the remaining points as it curves into the long platform, a platform, as at Newquay, which today is ridiculously long for such trains as these as it comes to stop opposite the station awning. Sometimes the driver is obviously in haste to make his way back to the front of his train for a quick return to Exeter. For if the train is running late with only a few minutes for the 'turn round', delay means missing connections back at main line Exeter as well as delaying the next train down the line with which it nearly always crosses at Eggesford, nearly half an hour away and now the only crossing point on the line before Crediton, 50 minutes away. At other times the driver can be more leisurely, disappearing into the station building to chat to the guard or colleagues, talk with passengers, or indeed replenish his trusty thermos, before ringing the Crediton signalman from the 'phone on the platform to say he is ready to depart. A miniscule hoot, a puff of exhaust, and once again the little train sets off, curving to the right and out of sight around the rock face, leaving the station to return to another period of peace until the next arrival, usually about an hour later.

Current arrival and departure times here are as follows:

Arrive: 06.59, 08.06, 09.39, 10.35, 11.35, 12.35, 13.37, 14.37, 15.35, 16.35, 18.07, 19.13, 20.08, 22.13, 23.59 (Fridays only)

Depart: 00.05 (Fridays only), 7.00, 8.43, 9.43, 10.43, 11.43, 12.43, 13.43, 14.43, 15.43, 17.08, 18.13, 19.16, 20.24, 22.16

The Line from Yeoford

I have probably taken more photos between Yeoford, once Yeoford Junction, and Barnstaple than on any other stretch of line in Britain, and now an individual small album is given over to photos of every station between the two. Over the past 50 years I have seen the line's decline from days when, between and including, every station from Yeoford to Barnstaple was caringly manned, the journey boasting 12 signal boxes plus one small level crossing box at Umberleigh. Today only Barnstaple is staffed; all signal boxes are gone. Station buildings with their cosy, musty, waiting rooms have all been sold off and modernized by their purchasers, leaving passengers to wait for their train in characterless glass shelters which afford little protection from rain and wind. Not a pleasant prospect when trains are delayed. The once spruce and cared-for station gardens are largely neglected with the possible exception of Chapleton. At rural Portsmouth Arms where once upon a time, in the now demolished waiting room, certificates adorned the wall proudly boasting awards for 'Best Kept Station', only wild flowers edge the still used down platform while ancient laurels bow their heads over the disused up platform, still discernible 30 years after the last train used the passing loop.

Yet the line lives on, still exuding tremendous charm for the would-be traveller, and despite the cutbacks one could not journey through more unspoilt countryside and verdant pastureland as the line crosses and recrosses the banks of the River Taw. Above all, here is a line where one can still linger, wait, and breathe in the atmosphere of a rural railway, despite the lingering ghosts of past busier days.

It is also good to note that not one station has closed between Yeoford and Barnstaple, amazing that is when one considers how tiny the communities are which surround such as Morchard Road, Portsmouth Arms or Chapleton, in comparison with other towns and villages which have long since lost their station. The Barnstaple line was not in fact scheduled for closure in the Beeching report, however, all intermediate stations beyond Crediton were so listed apart from Lapford and Eggesford.

In the early years of the last century when my father travelled twice each year from Plymouth to, now closed, Braunton, two steps down the line from Barnstaple, **Yeoford Junction** was the changing point for the North Devon line and a station of some importance. He often recalled three times asking a porter what time the next train was for the North Devon line and three times being told, quite simply, 'You've just missed it!' Well, no porter to ask now. This once busy rural junction with its extraordinary tall signal box peering over the top of the road bridge on the down side with an equally vast water tower, and lengthy sidings off the down platform is now but a shadow or less of its former glory. The old down island platform crumbles with disuse and the huge goods yard has long vanished under a variety of wild flowers and grasses, the gate of entry firmly padlocked. But at least there is an apology of a waiting room still standing on the up platform where trains from and to Barnstaple briefly pause. The station still gives an impression, if false, that it is still double track. In reality this is two single lines, the old up line serving trains to and from Barnstaple, the old down line being the already mentioned former main line to Okehampton, Tavistock and Plymouth. Along this line huge diesel-hauled stone trains make their way to and from Meldon Quarry while a small passenger service has been reinstated on summer weekends to Sampford Courtenay and Okehampton. The result of all this is that of course it is occasionally possible to see a freight train and a passenger train progressing together on parallel lines in the same direction! Both lines are under the control of Crediton where the one and only signal box on the whole line remains after leaving Exeter. No more semaphore signals even here, only coloured light ones in each direction, distant, home and starter, although there is still a real live human being who descends from the box to retrieve or deliver the token to the driver, Eggesford or Meldon-bound. And despite the modern panel inside the box, the actual structure remains as ever it was.

Curving away in the down direction and passing the tall signal box on the left, the train approached the down advanced starting signal with Coleford's split distant signals beneath, indicating the Plymouth line to the left and the Barnstaple line to the right, levers one and two from **Coleford Junction** signal box. Gradually straightening up for the clear run past this attractive box, closed in 1971 and already described in an earlier chapter, the train today charges straight ahead at this point while the line to Okehampton and Meldon curves off and away to the left. Until 1971 this was still double track for another few miles as the line curved past the stationless hamlet of Coleford and large rolling fields which still displayed the red-coloured soil of this part of Devon, attractive and distinctive to look at although not to be trodden into carpets at home where it can stubbornly stain! The down distant signal for **Copplestone** a little further on announced the approach to a long straight section through a deep cutting and under three road bridges, at the end of which was the attractive station, just two miles from Coleford. The station was typical of many along the line and in many ways almost identical to its neighbour Morchard Road. The main buildings were on the down side, north facing with the delightful signal box, with 10 levers just off the end of the up platform on the down end, and the small goods yard which included a goods shed and goods loop, off the down side of the down platform. Even the all important 'Atlantic Coast Express' from Waterloo had to slow here to pick up the first token of the journey and thus to gain entry to first of six single line sections, six that is until 1964 when it was reduced to five with the closure of Morchard Road box. There was a fine view of up trains as they made the approach up the hill towards Copplestone, which marked the summit of a fairly gentle climb all the way from Barnstaple, passing as it did the short up home signal which remained lower quadrant until the line was singled and the signal box closed in October 1971, the same day as Coleford Junction. The number of trains stopping here have varied considerably over the years since this was often one of the least patronized stations on the line, despite it being well positioned for the village. Even in the summer of 1995, of the 12 trains which passed through only one train on weekdays stopped in the down direction at 07.51 and one in the direction at 17.46. In recent years, however, there has been a good deal of development and the building of many new houses, not least around the station area. The result has been that by 2010 every train now calls here, even though by request, providing the station with an amazing increase of 14 trains each way per day with one extra down train late on a Friday.

6.16 Down	12.20 Up	17.50 Up
7.09 Down	12.49 Down	18.22 Down
7.43 Up	13.20 Up	18.55 Up
8.53 Down	13.49 Down	19.22 Down
9.22 Up	14.20 Up	19.53 Up
9.49 Down	14.49 Down	21.01 Up
10.20 Up	15.20 Up	21.26 Down
10.49 Down	15.49 Down	22.52 Up
11.20 Up	16.20 Up	23.16 Down (Fridays only)

Seldom could any rural station have had such an incredible increase of service and for anyone living at Copplestone today they are blessed with a better train service than they have ever had.

But back to pre-1971, the former up platform with its typical Southern Region waiting shelter faced more into the sun as did the signal box and thus when the up platform was taken out of use the location, for me at least, lost some of its character and today is a rather dark and sad little station.

Morchard Road, less than two miles from Copplestone was an almost identical design although with less goods facilities. Here too the main building was on the down side with signal box again just off the down side of the up platform with its half-dozen steps leading up to the box just as at Copplestone, although the frame here had an extra two levers. In 1995 the train service was almost as miniscule as at Copplestone; however, today all trains stop here apart from the first down train of the day. The station buildings are, as on all the intermediate stations, privately owned, renovated and look well cared for. Poor Morchard Road was the first station on the line to lose its signal box in 1964, which for a while remained standing sadly gutted at the end of the trackless up loop.

Because of the close proximity of the two neighbouring stations, Lapford and Copplestone, it was perhaps understandable that the signal box here was not entirely necessary although as John Nicholas points out in his fine book about the line, this was a busy place around 9 am in the morning when three trains passed here, the freight being shunted away into the small yard.

A down train for Barnstaple rushes through Lapford in 2003. At that time the loop was still *in situ* although generally out of use. *Author*

The author's parents (*left*) with Henry Williamson (*right*) and his family outside Georgeham church 1958. The 'Tarka' line was so named after Henry Williamson's famous book *Tarka the Otter* set along the Taw valley. *Author*

If Morchard Road and Copplestone were latterly rather dark stations facing away from the sun, **Lapford** had, and still has, an optimistic character, the main whitewashed station buildings on the up side here facing into the sun. Until 1970 the down platform was on the up side of the three-arched main road bridge, split away from the up platform on the down side, while the signal box was on the down side of the station with a distinctive signal alongside on which both the up home and the down advanced starter were mounted on the same post. The station was set on a fine one mile stretch of track, and still today this is a grand spot to watch trains pass by under the three bridges which embrace the location. Sadly, unlike Morchard Road and Copplestone, Lapford's services have been reduced, much to the upset of some locals. Again going back to 1995 eight of the 12 trains stopped here on weekdays, spread out through the day. Today only four trains stop on request at the beginning and end of the day. In the down direction to Barnstaple, after 07.17 nothing stops here until 17.27, although eight trains pass through. Two other down trains stop on request at 18.29 and 21.33. In the up direction the first two up trains of the day call at 07.35 and 09.16. Then again seven trains pass through with the next train due to call at 17.43 and 18.47. It seems strange that Lapford, so well situated for its village has suffered in this way, making life hard for would-be shoppers who might well be well served by a couple more trains in the middle of the day. As already mentioned this was one of only two intermediate stations on the line not recommended for closure by Beeching, and yet it is the one which today has lost its one time ample quota of stopping trains.

But it is a delightful spot at which to linger, and although remnants of the former sidings and down loop still remained until recently, albeit very overgrown, the sight of the ground frame still standing at the down end of platform with the levers and token instrument in place, give one a sense of hope that perhaps one day, the loop and/or the sidings might be reinstated for some purpose. Who knows!

The line now enters some of the prettiest scenery of the journey as it criss-crosses the river and heads towards Eggesford Forest. At this point too perhaps I should briefly reminisce about my favourite road, the A377. At the start of the book I wrote about our bi-annual holiday to Croyde in North Devon via Hatherleigh, Torrington and Bideford. One spring day post-Easter, late in the 1950s, there were serious road works between Torrington and Hatherleigh and my father decided we would return home to Tavistock another way. This was my first experience of the great A377 which not only followed the railway all 26 miles of the way from Barnstaple to Copplestone but was a quite stunningly beautiful valley road, especially in the spring. Primroses and daffodils lined the hedges and nodded their heads from the top of gardens walls, with woods and fields alive with budding energy as new growth burst into life. Later in the year old tables and wooden stands would be decked at the end of lanes and outside delightful cottages with all sorts of local produce for sale: eggs, honey, vegetables, colourful dahlias, fragrant sweet peas and a rich variety of fruit. Continually flirting with both road and railway the river Taw twists its way along the same valley, suddenly coming into view and then lost for a while behind the trees.

Over and above all this, it was along this road I was introduced for the first time to those eight little rural stations, Chapleton to Copplestone, set amidst the most wonderful lush scenery of the Taw valley. It was also around this time that I was privileged to meet the great Henry Williamson of *Tarka the Otter* fame who had been a patient of the my father's. I still have a treasured photo of him and his family which I took with my camera outside Georgeham church, as well as a wonderfully illustrated copy of his famous book, making this yet another reason for why this valley became so special. And of course here lies the reason why the railway today has been christened 'The Tarka Line'.

Returning to where we were on the journey, nowhere is the glory of the line more epitomized than over the eight miles between Lapford and King's Nympton. The Eggesford Forest merits a book of its own and only a few lines can be given over to it here. Created in 1919 from the Eggesford Estate, by 1956 the Forestry Commission had planted over a million acres of trees, an event marked by the Queen who unveiled a stone just off the main road on the Lapford side of Eggesford to mark this achievement and which can be glimpsed from the train, especially in less leafy winter, as it nears the down distant signal for Eggesford.

One of the most beautiful vantage points along the line can be found in the fields just below Eggesford church. I recall having a picnic here some years ago while I took photos and film of trains rushing down through the woods and slowly braking for the final curve into **Eggesford** station and I return here in the final section of the chapter.

Eggesford remains, as I suspect it always was, the aristocrat of the line. When the route was designed, the Earl of Portsmouth who then owned the estate, gave the land on condition that all trains should stop here. They still all do. Between Crediton and Eggesford it is now the only passing point on the line, indeed of the 14 trains which pass here in each direction in the current time table, 12 cross with another train. The main station buildings, curving back on themselves, are on the up platform. They are typical of the line's buildings although the house gave little privacy to the occupants with virtually no garden and the entrance opening out

Eggesford former signal box standing precariously over the river following the 1967 floods. The signalman had to escape through the window.   *Author*

immediately onto the main road. Indeed parking at this station at a busy time is not only difficult but somewhat dangerous. None the less the main buildings perch imperiously over the river, bridge and meadows in a beautiful position. In 1967 severe flooding destroyed part of the down platform and endangered the signal box structure to such an extent that it had to be closed. Had it not been for the level crossing, situated off a dangerous sharp bend on the main road, Eggesford's crossing loop might well have been gone forever and Lapford or King's Nympton might well have been the place where trains still cross today. For two years only the up platform was in use; but in September 1969 a new platform was opened, slightly staggered from the up platform in the down direction, and with it a new signal box close alongside the level crossing on the up side of the down platform. A new footpath ran behind the signal box, just above the river, giving access to this new platform. With this new signal box firmly established, within two years all the other boxes, apart from Barnstaple had been closed, although humble little Umberleigh Gates made it through until 1972, and Eggesford retained its box for another 18 years.

The extensive loop curved away from Eggesford over a long right-hand curve, with the up home out of sight of the box at a point where the line made its way through a sea of rhododendron bushes, to the right of which could be glimpsed the delightful Fox & Hounds hotel. In earlier days this impressive hostelry even boasted its own private siding stretching back from the down end of the up platform. On one occasion my parents stopped here for a drink and something to eat on the way home. On seeing me, the manager politely but firmly informed them that children were not allowed within the bar area but if I liked to go with him, the cook would be pleased to give me something to eat in the kitchen! I felt rather embarrassed I recall, although once in the kitchen I was made a huge fuss of and the manager refused to take any payment for the very good meal I was given, I think it was chicken!

Once beyond the Eggesford up distant, the countryside opens up and trains rattle their way past a fine collection of fields until nearing **King's Nympton**. My father still always referred to this station as South Molton Road, which was its name until St David's Day 1951. The 'Road' suffix of course signified that the station was a long way from South Molton itself, some eight miles away up a beautifully winding valley road to the north, a road which celebrates the glories of spring quite magnificently at that time of year.

If Lapford was 'optimistic' and Eggesford 'aristocratic', King's Nympton is in character essentially warm, cheerful and friendly. The turn off the main road can be difficult when the traffic is heavy, but once down the short drive there is plenty of parking space. In its heyday this was such a pretty station with well kept gardens which included pampas grass, a charming little 16-lever signal box on the down platform, and wisteria hanging over the front of the main station building on the up side. Although there were three sidings plus a small docking area, the layout was slightly cramped and the crossing loop relatively small. As at Morchard Road John Nicholas in his book gives good detail of those moments in the day when three trains converged here and the difficulties this caused when one train was rather long, 15 goods wagons being the limit. The station faced into the sun, over a field, across towards the river and although much has gone, even now it remains a happy place to sit on a sunny day. Like Lapford the train service today is not as good as it once was. Ten years ago almost every train stopped here. Today six down trains and five up call here by request, mainly at the start and end of the day, but unlike Lapford there are two trains in the middle of the day, one in each direction booked to stop at 13.02 up and 14.15 down, which do give shoppers an opportunity to make use of the station.

A final freight train ambles through Kings Nympton from Meeth in 1982.   *Author*

Miniscule Portsmouth Arms with an up train approaching in 2012; the former up platform still in evidence.   *Author*

Three miles further on, set on one of the few straight stretches of the line, was the utterly charming, cottage-like station of **Portsmouth Arms** which is named after a nearby pub. The main road, as at Eggesford, passes right alongside the station although the parking facilities here are slightly better. Entrance to the platforms from the small car park was once through the single-storey station building on the down platform, the walls of which were once adorned with certificates awarding this rural outpost the title of 'Best Kept Station' for several years. I recall this station with affection for two main reasons. The first is that this was one of the stations we stopped at on that first journey home from Croyde to Tavistock in the days when it was still fully signalled and I remember what an attractive place it was with beautifully kept flower beds, and everything appearing so neat and tidy, with its charming little signal box, also on the down platform, and a genial and welcoming signalman. The signal box had only 10 levers with the two home signals, levers Nos. 2 and 8, acting as point locks as well. The goods yard was the simplest on the line comprising of just one very long siding off the up side of the down platform with the last lever in the box, lever No. 10, controlling the ground signal for trains leaving the siding. The long siding was necessary when three trains met here since the loop only allowed for 20 wagons on freight trains.

To the north of the station are a couple of large fields leading down to the river, access to which is via a foot crossing on the up side of the station. To the north of the river the hills rise up steeply to the small village of Chittelhamholt and there is no better location from which to watch the train rattling along the one mile straight section than from here, high up on this hill.

On the edge of the village stands one of the best family-run hotels in the country, Highbullen, established by Hugh and Pam Neil in the 1960s and until recently run by their wonderful son and daughter, Martin and Colette. I have stayed here for over 30 years and it remains one of my favourite places anywhere I have been in the world set high up on a hill betwixt two magnificent Devon valleys, the one leading northwards way up to South Molton, the other stretching up towards Barnstaple and carrying the railway along with it. On still evenings one can still clearly hear the trains 'de-diddeley-dumming' up and down the valley for several minutes as they trundle through Portsmouth Arms.

I digress to this location simply because it was here that one of the most extraordinary experiences of my life took place in the early 1980s. Arriving one misty evening, I decided to have a quick swim before dinner. There was only one other person present, an elderly gentleman who was swimming methodically up and down the length of the small pool. We exchanged greetings and I plunged in and splashed around, with rather less discipline than the methodical gentleman, indeed I was out before him, and sat on the edge with a towel over my shoulders. Without warning he gave a shout and was obviously in some difficulty, suffering from cramp. The pool was not very deep and I was easily able to get back in and assist him to the side where I rubbed the afflicting, slightly varicosed leg, with a towel. He was very grateful and we sat on the edge exchanging pleasantries before we both set off to change for the evening meal. One needs to picture that here was an elderly gentleman, in a swimming costume, dripping wet and with wispy wet hair in disarray. But as I made my way to my room, a small bell was ringing at the back of my mind. 'I think I know this man!'

That evening at dinner the penny dropped, and it dropped when I *heard* his voice before actually seeing him, for it was the unmistakable voice of Laurence Olivier! After dinner he bought us champagne and talked long into the small hours; he was the most delightful and entertaining of company. The other extraordinary coincidence was that at one of the churches where I was rector at the time, Wimborne St Giles in Dorset, had a Communion chasuble which had belonged to his father who also had been a priest, and had given this to a former rector who had been a friend. Highbullen was a place Sir Laurence loved to visit and he had become a firm friend of the Neil family. The large room which he occupied on the ground floor with its magnificent view, gave him space, privacy and inspiration for writing his autobiography.

All this is almost irrelevant to the book were it not for the fact that next morning, as was often my wont, I drove down to Portsmouth Arms station before breakfast. There was Lord Laurence walking down the drive on an early morning constitutional. Winding the window down I explained I was going to look at one of favourite railway stations, would he care to come along? 'Why not?' was the reply after a slight hesitation, and down the long winding hill we went. It was a glorious morning and as we sat on the platform, alongside the milepost displaying the fact that we were 200 miles from Waterloo, and admiring the view, I explained that I was involved in the production of John Barton's 'Hollow Crown', a dramatic anthology of the Kings and Queens of England. Without a moment's hesitation he was on his feet and gave voice to the prologue of the work, from Shakespeare's *Richard II*, 'For God's sake let us sit upon the ground and tell sad stories of the death of Kings!'

What a sight it must have been for the sheep in the field opposite and the rooks overhead, for apart from me, that was the audience! And there he was, the greatest actor of his age giving me a solo performance on this tiny rural railway station. If only that original single-storey waiting room were still standing today, surely another 'first' certificate could have been added to those already there proclaiming that 'Laurence Olivier performed Shakespeare [if briefly] on this platform!'.

Sadly Portsmouth Arms was the third signal box to be abolished in 1966, making the block section now King's Nympton-Umberleigh. Sad too because since the station house was separate, off the end of the down platform, the station buildings were all demolished in the early 1980s, and today a modern glass waiting room is all that is offered to passengers and few trains stop here. In fact Portsmouth Arms and

Lord Olivier with Pam and Colette Neil at Highbullen Hotel high above Portsmouth Arms station and upon which platform he gave the author a solo performance from Richard II.   *The Neil Family*

Chapleton were always stations which had fewer trains stopping than most of the others. A current timetable for request stops here is:

Up	*Down*
07.16 (request stop)	One non-stop
Nine pass without stopping	07.43 (request stop)
18.28 (request stop)	Nine non-stop
Three non-stop	18.52 (request stop)
	One non-stop
	21.53 (request stop)
	One non-stop Fridays only

Despite all the deprivations over the years, Portsmouth Arms has, miraculously survived. Not only has it survived but there is still a wonderfully soporific atmosphere as one sits on the platform towards the end of a day, and whenever I am in North Devon there is still an irresistible urge to revisit this location. The long stretch in the up direction, at the end of which the down distant was once clearly visible, still reflects the sun on railcar windows as they pull towards the station. The phone box at the station entrance which featured in a many photographs is still *in situ*, as is the foot crossing towards the river. For many years the laurels on the old disused up platform grew taller and taller until a recent severe pruning, which has now restored the changeless view across the fields, as well as reawakening the possibility that there could still be a passing loop here. If ever there were a top 10 list of places at which to linger, Portsmouth Arms would have to be on it.

Continuing the journey towards Umberleigh the line crossed and re-crossed the river as well a succession of farm crossings. There were innumerable little crossings to fields along the line and a few which were tracks for vehicles had at one time actually had crossing keepers, such as Chenson crossing between Lapford and Eggesford and Higher Doomsford crossing between King's Nympton and Portsmouth Arms. Between Portsmouth Arms and Umberleigh there are no less than six farm crossings which were never manned but which today are connected by phone to Crediton signal box.

A quarter of a mile before **Umberleigh Station** was the one and only crossing box on the line after Crediton at **Umberleigh Gates,** guarding a small side road which runs parallel to the main road on the other side of the line. Within living memory this little box was simply a ground frame with all signals controlled from Umberleigh, while the ground frame had control of the siding off the up side of the station and a couple of ground signals. However, when Umberleigh box closed in 1971, Umberleigh Gates was given control of two home signals in each direction, a situation which lasted for another year and a half. The new down home was the former down outer home for Umberleigh while the up signal was a new lower quadrant signal erected just a few yards from the box. Signal buffs like myself rather hoped that this new investment meant that this little box might have had a longer life span. Alas no, and in November 1972 it was reduced to an automatic crossing, although the crossing keeper's cottage is still there.

Umberleigh station buildings are also still *in situ* although privately owned. Now just five miles from Barnstaple, the station retains something of its genteel atmosphere, the long down platform curving back on itself, with a large roomy car park. The river here is even closer than at Portsmouth Arms with the railway crossing over it just north of the station at a very good vantage point for watery-minded photographers. By now the Taw is growing wider and travelling faster, sensing an anticipation that journey's end is not far away where she will unite with her sister river the Torridge before crossing the bar at Westward Ho! and setting out to sea.

The seldom photographed Umberleigh crossing which gained its own independence for a short period after the closure of Umberleigh box and being the only crossing box on the line. Its two home signals were examples of GWR and SR variety. *Author*

Chapleton station looking towards Barnstaple, the former station house is on the former up platform. *Author*

The station is well positioned for the small village it serves, close to post office, tea shop and charming Rising Sun pub. All trains are booked to call here and there still remains a sense that this is an important point on the line, where until 1971 the single line sections came to an end, giving way to the final double track section to Chapleton and Barnstaple. Before the impressive 31-lever signal box was closed in the same year, placed in the middle of the former up platform, the station boasted four stop signals in the down direction and three in the up, together with working distant signals, and although visibility of trains from the platform was, and still is, limited in both directions, there was a fine view from the road bridge on the down side of trains approaching from Exeter from way beyond Umberleigh Gates.

Under a two-arched bridge with the once down starter standing tall on the wrong side of the down line to give better visibility as the train approached the station, the line crosses the river and is away across a wide valley of fields which is a mass of gold in the harvest season.

Two and a half miles on and the line curves sharply into **Chapleton**, the last station before Barnstaple and something of a loner along the line although there was it seems always a faithful handful of passengers. The station approach off the main road is on a sharp bend and it is easy to miss it; coming out from the bumpy station drive and back onto the main road was always a hazardous affair especially if turning right towards Barnstaple. On approaching the station through the trees the attractive and elegant station house faces one on the far side of the line at the end of the up platform. Of all the houses on the line this remains one of the most attractive and has been lovingly cared for with the original station name board well preserved. Although the main buildings were on the up platform, when the line was singled in 1971 it was the down platform which was kept in use, behind which stood the well-known Chappell and Walton sawmills which was to provide the station with considerable traffic. The attractive signal box was in the middle of the down platform and was provided with distant, home, starter and advanced starting signals in each direction. It closed in 1966, shortly before Portsmouth Arms, but long before was nearly always switched out with signals left 'off' unless freight trains were calling or on busy summer Saturdays. A foot crossing from the small car park takes walkers across the line into lush water meadows, often flooded in the rainy season. Today the same three down trains call here as call at Portsmouth Arms at 07.53, 19.03 and 22.03. In the up direction the first up train calls at 07.05 and a second at 17.14.

From the blind up direction trains still curve into view without warning while in the down direction the line runs for some four miles in an almost totally straight section, until the final curve into Barnstaple, having crossed the Taw for one last time as well as passing under the A377 at Newbridge at which point the road gradually pulls away from the line and enters Barnstaple about a mile away from the station.

Distant, outer home and gantried inner home signals, all in a neat straight line, welcomed down trains in towards Barnstaple, while to the right, until 1966, the former GWR curved in from Taunton, with the fine tall signal box, set slightly away from the line off the up platform, until 1987 when it too was closed.

Postscript from Eggesford – a farewell to signals

When on 1st November, 1987, the fine Barnstaple signal box closed, the only box left standing after Crediton was Eggesford. The signalling on the line had been gradually reduced since the closure of Morchard Road box in 1964. The order of box closures from then on was as follows:

The view from Eggesford's latter signal box with a train in the down platform. This platform was erected in 1967 following floods which had washed part of the original platform away.
Author

The interior of Eggesford signal box. Note the token instrument (*right*) and to its left the machine which was wound to provide power to the points at the Barnstaple end.   *Author*

Date	Signal box	Note
6th March, 1964	Morchard Road	
26th January, 1966	Chapleton	
3rd April, 1966	Portsmouth Arms	
18th August, 1968	Yeoford	
21st June, 1970	Lapford	a
26th July, 1970	King's Nympton	b
21st May, 1971	Barnstaple 'B'	c
21st May, 1971	Umberleigh	
17th October, 1971	Copplestone and Coleford Junction	
19th November, 1972	Umberleigh Crossing Gates	
1st November, 1987	Barnstaple 'A'	
1st December, 1987	Eggesford	d

Notes
a - When the signal box closed, two ground frames were installed at each end of the loop to allow access to what were then sidings to the Ambrosia factory, which ran off the old down loop. Although the loop has now been severed, the ground frames were until recently still *in situ*.
b - When the signal box closed, one siding remained on the up side for access to a fertiliser store with a two-lever ground frame and a boxed phone to Eggesford box alongside. This was removed in 1981.
c - This box controlled the west end of the station with lines to Halwill and Ilfracombe. The Ilfracombe line closed in October 1970 by which time the Halwill branch was reduced to freight only to Torrington and Meeth. In May 1971 therefore the signalling at the east end of Barnstaple was simplified, 'B' box closed and everything was controlled from the 'A' box at the east end.
d - In November 1967, as a result of flooding, part of the old down platform was washed away and the box had to be closed. The new box was opened on 28th September, 1969 and lasted for 18 years.

Eggesford therefore was the final box to close, one month after Barnstaple, and the last of the semaphore signals, two in each direction, were dismantled. The two on the up side had both remained upper quadrant from SR days while the two on the down side were Western style lower quadrant which replaced former signals after the flooding and the box being installed in 1969. Fixed distants had replaced the once working distants with the fine lower quadrant down distant signal being retained for this purpose. However, now the fixed distants were replaced by characterless boards with reflective distant signals affixed.

During the last week of November 1987, my mother and I had gone to have lunch at the Fox & Hounds just up the road, and around 3 pm we went back to park on the river side of the level crossing. This was a day or so before the box was finally closed and the area around the level crossing literally buzzed with orange clad railway engineers as they tinkered with points and wires, and putting the final touches to the token instruments which had been installed at the end of each platform in small metal cabins. For a late November afternoon it was a relatively mild day and there were still leaves on the trees, that autumn having been fairly mild. As the light began to fade I clicked away with my camera as up starter and down home signal received their final 'snip' never to be raised again. A down train was gingerly flagged across the crossing and tokens were given and received as usual. The down starter was still in operation and the train set off on its way off the long loop for the journey to Barnstaple which was now little more than one long siding. As the winter evening drew in the lights in the signal box were reflected off the orange jackets of the busying engineers. The signalman on duty was more than happy to allow me access to the box for the last time, indeed everyone was extraordinarily friendly and eager to explain how the new system would work.

That new system continues today as trains now approach from each direction following the course of the river. Down trains pause just before the crossing as the driver leans from his window to press a plunger which sets the descent of the barriers in motion. The train moves forward over the crossing, past the up platform and into the 'new' 1969 down platform where the driver alights and unlocks the metal cabin door giving access to the token instruments and to make contact with that distant god, the Crediton signalman. The Crediton token is replaced and if the up train has arrived he is able to withdraw the token for Barnstaple. Up trains curve into their platform where a similar process is put in motion, the metal cabin here being just a few feet from the level crossing. Once they are ready to depart, another plunger on the platform is pushed to again lower the barriers and the train is off curving to the left and then to the right, crossing the river and away towards Lapford. Standing a field away above the line, Eggesford church continues watch over each passing train, as it has done for some 160 years, bestowing on each a St Christopher's blessing.

As the sound of the trains' engines gently fade into the distance, the ceaseless voice of the river takes over until the countryside is once again disturbed and the process repeated about an hour later and only the first and last few trains of the day not crossing with another.

In 1964 a driver had 23 stop signals to guide him on his way from Coleford Junction to Barnstaple, nine working distants and one fixed distant for Barnstaple. In the up direction there were 22 stop signals and nine working distants. From 1st December, 1987, not one remained.

A final word

So the years have passed and times have changed as they always have and always will, for better or worse. Gone are the days when great 'West Country' class locomotives, named after so many stations they once served - *Braunton, Wrafton, Eggesford, Lapford* - with their familiar clanking axles and distinctive deep-throated whistles, coasted their way past thatched villages and humble, though homely, railway cottages; past primrose-clad cuttings, ancient oak woods and soaring pine forestries, over the Tarka-famed river and countless firmly-sleepered farm crossings.

Gone too are the sounds of coded bells, so clear in the summer when signal box windows are open wide, and rather less distinct in the winter when they are firmly shut! The two rings for 'Train entering section' and the 2-pause-1 to notify that the train has cleared the next station. Gone too the demanding pull of the black point lever with the accompanying thump of point rods to ensure a well-locked entrance into the loop, or the familiar bouncing 'clunk' of a signal arm to pronounce that all is safe ahead. No longer do the faithful Drummond 'T9' 4-4-0s simmer in small goods yards or single siding, while wagons are shuffled and clanked with their uncoupling and re-coupling, until all is in correct order, and then on to the next station where the process is repeated, as has happened for several generations 'as it was in the beginning but now never shall be ...'

Gone above all else is that often solitary, but oh so familiar, smartly waistcoated figure, the booking clerk, or porter, or signalman expectantly poised with staff or tablet in hand, to be swiftly exchanged with the engine crew, tangible assurance of safe passage to the next station. For at the heart of all the change, however necessary some change may have been, now remains a terrible facelessness, which makes it all so sad; that lack of the personal touch, that life blood which brought once loved little stations into life in the form of the resident railwayman who took time and trouble to ensure the station looked good year in and year out. Never in a million years can their worth be replaced by the crackling recorded voice of technology, (when it works that is!) which responds to the would be enquirer, invited to press a coloured plastic button: 'This station is (slight pause) King's Nympton. The next train in the direction of Barnstaple will be the (slight pause) 3.37 from Exmouth'. Oh dear!

... and yet!

When those of us who are of a certain age dig into our memories and call to mind those familiar horrid scars, softened by nature in the course of time perhaps, but then horrid indeed, when 20, 30, 40 years ago, long laid metal rails were ripped from even longer lying wooden sleepers, to leave behind bare ballast beds along so many hundred miles of ancient rural routes ... when we recall such wounded scenes, we *must* be grateful that here at least still beats a rural railway heart which does provide good service, as good as it has ever been, and where still the railway romantic can linger and enjoy. Still today there is the thrill to sit, late afternoon, on the empty platform at Portsmouth Arms, and gradually, at first almost sub-consciously, sense far away in the distance the echoes of a train from Barnstaple, making its way up the twisting valley to the north-west, still several minutes before coming into view; then a change of key as the sound strengthens while it passes over the river bridge just out of sight around the corner, before curving into view over the local farm crossing. The driver slows, uncertain as to whether I intend to board or not. My well-practised under-arm gesture indicating a non-intention is responded to by a brief toot of understanding, a wave, and a slight acceleration as the one or two coaches rattle gently through the platform with the few safe inches to spare, and then off and away down the long straight stretch as the rear cab catches the reflection of the evening sun before curving out of sight and on to more likely customers at such stations as King's Nympton and Eggesford.

Or indeed to sit in those idyllic sloping fields below Eggesford church with a proper pasty and a glass perched precariously amidst the tufts of grass, as a Barnstaple-bound train shoots out from the woods and across the river as the brakes are gently applied for final curve and over the station's level crossing beyond which another train is already standing waiting. Minutes later it too is on its way back past this contented observer and on to ever hopeful Lapford where until very recently it rattled over the rusting, disused points, past idle ground frames and away under bridge, under bridge and under bridge.

So despite the sadness of former days, everything that has changed and all that has gone, there must be some gratitude too that the little line to Barnstaple still lives and breathes, and still retains at heart the character of truly rural English branch line charm for all to savour and enjoy, enhanced of course with a proper pasty, a picnic basket, and a glass of chilled white wine with which to toast good health and long life to the passing trains.

Chapter Eleven

A Quick Scamper back into Dorset
... with a slight touch of Wiltshire

Exeter-Salisbury revisited ... plus a quick run down to Exmouth

Exeter St David's (172m. 35ch.) - Exeter Central (171m. 60ch.) - Exmouth Junction (170m. 52ch.) - Pinhoe (168m. 70ch.) - Whimple (163m. 26ch.) - Sidmouth Junction (159m. 46ch.) - Honiton (154m. 78ch.) - Seaton Junction (148m. 03ch.) - Axminster (144m. 64ch.) - Chard Junction (139m. 57ch.) - Crewkerne (131m. 53ch.) - Sutton Bingham (125m. 08ch.) - Yeovil Junction (122m. 69ch.) - Sherborne (118m. 22ch.) - Milborne Port (114m. 48ch.) - Templecombe (112m. 15ch.) - Gillingham (105m. 36ch.) - Semley (101m. 28ch.) - Tisbury (96m. 27ch.) - Dinton (92m. 02ch.) - Wilton South (86m. 21ch.) - Salisbury (84m. 02ch.)
(all mileages from Waterloo)

There was an impression given around 1967 that the ex-SR main line from Exeter to Salisbury was destined to be gradually run down while the Exeter to Paddington received the lion's share of input. And yet how short-sighted those cutbacks proved to be with the line today busier than ever and officialdom regretting the 1967 changes reducing the line to single track with crossing loops at Honiton, Chard and Gillingham, and retaining double track only between Yeovil and Templecombe through Sherborne. The folly of these decisions over the course of time have necessitated two more crossing places to be restored on the eastern side of Tisbury and through Axminster with the possibilities of more doubling to come.

One advantage, however, which the Salisbury route has always had over its ex-GWR rival is in its retention of some of the more rural locations. Places like Cullompton, Wellington or Somerton might well have retained their stations today had they been on the Waterloo line, whereas the likes of Whimple, Crewkerne or Tisbury might well have been swept away had they been on the Paddington route.

Despite the fact that the Salisbury route has now clawed its way back to again being a well-used main line rather than just an 'also ran', on account of its 11 generally small intermediate stations there remains a certain rural charm about this line.

Of course not all its stations were retained. As already noted Broad Clyst, Seaton Junction, Chard Junction, Sutton Bingham, Milborne Port, Semley and Dinton all fell under the axe as did Templecombe and Sidmouth Junction although these were later to be re-opened, Sidmouth Junction now re-named as Feniton. Of those others which closed, Broad Clyst may yet have a new lease of life if plans to build a new station to serve an expanding community comes about. With the closure of the Seaton branch there was little point in the retention of its remote main line junction. Chard Junction was possibly the odd man out for although the location was a mile or so away, the town was and is a substantial one and since the signal box and up platform were both retained it struck many as unfortunate that the station was not also kept in use. Sutton Bingham was possibly in the most beautiful setting of all the stations overlooking a reservoir, an absolute gem of a rural station on a main line, but its scattered community was tiny and the station little used. Semley was another small, scattered community. The station was also designed to serve Shaftesbury a mile or two up a long winding hill although it was argued it was as easy for Shaftesbury folk to make use of Gillingham with its fast growing community. Milborne Port was inconveniently situated and Dinton, although close to its village was considered too small to retain its station. Wilton South was another odd and unfortunate closure. This large suburb of Salisbury could be likened to the Pinhoe of Exeter and bearing in mind today's queues of traffic into Salisbury I cannot but wonder if one day this could one day be up and running again.

John Nicholas and George Reeve's trilogy of books about this line drip with minutiae of detail about all these stations and I do not intend, indeed I could not begin to try, to emulate them. I am merely lingering! So where might one still pause and enjoy the delights of rural railway charm on this line?

Before a quick romp down the main line there will be some who will want to point out an omission from all that has gone before. Despite the closure of all those little branch lines to Abbotsbury, Bridport, Lyme Regis, Seaton and Sidmouth, the little line to Exmouth lives on. Not only does it live on but over 30 trains a day make the ½ hour journey to and from the bustling seaside resort and it is a delightful run. Up the hill from Exeter St David's to the rather sombre Central station. Two minutes on to the diminutive **St James' Park Halt** before plunging into Blackboy tunnel and out at Exmouth Junction where the line turns off the main line. **Polsloe Bridge** sited high on an embankment lies on a straight section leading down the gradient from Exmouth Junction. Until 1973 the line was double track to Topsham but today only the old up platform is in use with the old down platform still *in situ* totally cloaked in a fine display of ivy! Another four minutes and the train comes to **Digby and Sowton** which was opened in 1995. Another station, Clyst St Mary and Digby Halt, once stood 400 yards north of this spot but closed in 1948. A metal bridge links the platform to the west side of the line where there is a large car park which serves as a 'park and ride' for the Devon and Exeter Hospital as well as for the station. Set in a cutting the station is built with concrete beams and the overall effect is somewhat austere, but it provides a service and that can't be bad.

Another four minutes and the line is away from the big city and the train enters the one crossing station on the line at the charming village of **Topsham**. With a regular half-hourly service through the day all trains cross here. The colour light signals are controlled from Exmouth Junction although the Grade Two listed signal box remains intact on the platform alongside the level crossing which it once controlled. To get a feel for the comings and goings of this busy little branch this is not a bad place to stop for a while. But for me the top marks for lingering must be at the next station just two minutes away at **Exton,** known as Woodbury Road until 1958. This is an absolute gem. So far as the station itself is concerned there is now little to see although until the end of World War I there had been a small signal box as well as a station master's house. In fact up to 1965 the station was staffed with porters. No sign of this now. The thing which makes this a lingering place is of course the setting which is quite stunning, set as it is on the very edge of the east bank of the Exe estuary. The changing colours of sea and sky, the continual changing mood of the water, and the view across to Starcross and Powderham on the west bank where main line trains skirt the water's edge between Exeter and Newton Abbot, all combine to make this a unique little station.

Lympstone Commando is explained by its name. The 224 ft-long platform was opened in 1976 for use of the Royal Marines stationed on the hill above the station. A bus shelter edifice adorns the platform but there is a guard hut at the entrance to the station where rather fierce looking men are at hand to make sure only soldiers get off the train. So definitely no resting here! Three minutes around the corner and there is **Lympstone Village**. This pretty little station somewhat went into decline once it became unstaffed in 1969. Until the early 1960s there was a goods loop opposite the station with a 12-lever signal frame in the booking office. The fine station buildings today have all gone and only a metal shelter remains.

The final five minute run into **Exmouth** is again along the water's edge with delightful views across the estuary. Once upon a time trains entered Exmouth from both Sidmouth Junction and Exeter; there were four platforms and a host of sidings. Today there is just one long single platform. The current picture is totally unrecognisable from the old. But there is a small booking office at the entrance to the station and at my last visit a most cheerful friendly lady was behind the window when I bought my return ticket to Exton.

The line is busy and flourishing. The views from the train are beautiful. I could linger for hours at Exton and possibly an hour at Topsham and yet it is sad to note how much this little line has lost by way of warmth and personality. So back to the main line passing Exmouth Junction and over the level crossing at **Pinhoe** whose signal box now is reinstated at Bere Ferrers and on to **Whimple**, the first rural station after leaving Exeter. The Beeching report wanted to close all stations between Exeter and Honiton but fortunately Whimple escaped the net. It is perfectly situated to serve its attractive village which lies just a mile off the main Honiton-Exeter road. Until 1967 the station was, as all others, double track but with the singling of the line between Pinhoe and Honiton, only the down platform was kept in use and the attractive wooden platform-based signal box was closed. However, there was a deceptive look to the station since the old up line was kept *in situ* to serve the sidings off the up side. This meant that passengers had to cross the line by the footbridge in order to catch their train. The sidings remained until as late as 1990. Two years later the track was re-aligned so that the up platform could be brought back into use. The down platform was demolished and the footbridge removed to Grateley, east of Salisbury.

Thus now, on a fine summer's day, this peaceful village station gazes happily southwards across Devon fields while the nearby church clock chimes out the hours over village shop, attractive houses and pubs. Gone are all the sidings in the up direction where once Whiteways Cider was one of the station's best customers. The line curves away to the left after a couple of hundred yards into a high cutting. In the down direction, however, there is a wonderful view of approaching up trains over an impressive two mile or more straight run.

For a number of years the number of trains stopping here was limited as was the case further up the line at Feniton or Tisbury. Today, however, of the 19 trains which pass in each direction 11 or 12 stop; this is roughly speaking one train stopping up and down every other hour although more do so at the beginning and end of the day. The rough rule of thumb in the current timetable is that trains which stop at Pinhoe do not stop at Whimple and Feniton and trains which stop at Whimple and Feniton do not stop at Pinhoe, although there are exceptions. Now privately-owned the station building is no longer part of the station itself but its white frontage gives a good backdrop to the scene, the only form of protection for passengers being a faceless, tasteless glass shelter with rather uncomfortable seats. Nonetheless Whimple remains a pleasant example of a quiet operational village station on a busy main line and for the station spotter it is worth a visit.

Of course for many railway enthusiasts **Feniton** will for ever be Sidmouth Junction. In fact it was Feniton upon its original opening in 1860 but only for one year until it became Ottery Road, later Ottery St Mary Sidmouth Road (that must have been a long station sign!) until finally Sidmouth Junction in 1874. In the old days until 1967 this was a large and impressive railway junction with its branch line curving away to the right off the up side of the down platform towards Ottery St

Mary, Tipton St Johns and Sidmouth. Thanks to the endeavours of the local Residents Association the station only closed for four years and in May 1971 Feniton was re-born and its initial five trains have now increased to 11 or 12. All this said it is not for me a station at which to linger. Possibly there are too many ghosts of the past and although efforts have been made to make the station work well (and it is well-patronized with just a 15 minute run to Exeter) the station has little personality, still less since centralized signalling which I shall mention at the end. So while I like to call here and see a passing train I do not loiter here.

Nor do I stay long at **Honiton,** not because I don't like it but rather having seen it I am happy to pass on knowing that I shall certainly come again and once more say 'hello' without staying too long. Honiton is a basic passing station situated high above the attractive town it serves. All sidings have now gone, occasional trains terminated here although such trains now usually go as far as Axminster.

The original station buildings have all vanished from Honiton and the single-storey booking office with its simple awning on the down side is comfortable, tidy and efficiently run.

Closed **Seaton Junction** was always a place at which to watch up trains from the concrete passenger footbridge as they roared down the 1 in 80 incline from Honiton curving through the hamlet of Umborne and towards the junction station. That view is still possible today and the concrete bridge remains *in situ*. But of course nothing stops here and Seaton Junction today is a spot at which to weep rather than to linger. I'm in two minds as to whether it is better to totally demolish an old station and put it out of its misery so that nothing remains or simply to let memories gradually fade through deterioration. Seaton Junction, after closure, lingered on for milk traffic for six years after which somebody seemed to just lock the door and went home. The station building today is in private hands but the whole area is sadly neglected. One comes here to mourn, to remember and then pass on.

Axminster with its renewed up platform and very long passing loop is a good place to watch trains passing but my favourite observing spot near here is three miles up the line. Between Axminster and Chard Junction until August 1967 were two manned level crossings protecting country lanes, **Axe Gates** and **Broom Gates** the latter being the closer to Chard Junction. The two were only half a mile apart so there was a mixture of home and distant signals surrounding each … very similar to Heddon Mill and Stoneybridge crossings on the Ilfracombe line. The original ground frame box at Axe Gates was replaced in 1949 by a small brick box which still, just, stands today and here amidst the rolling countryside on the Devon/Somerset border is a good place to stop the car, get out the sandwiches and pause awhile. There is nothing very dramatic about this spot but I find it attractive and peaceful. No signalman emerges from the locked box although a family of kittens did appear the last time I was there, took one look at me and vanished again under the building! But there is a moment of excitement as the nearby down distant for Axminster turns green, a disturbance of lowering barriers as a train appears in the far distance, charges across the crossing and is away to Axminster. Under the current timetable trains cross at Axminster just after the hour so it isn't long before the peace is again interrupted by an up train.

Just two miles up the line are the remains of **Chard Junction.** Until 2012 a resident signalman manned the modern signal box dating from 1982. As at Seaton Junction here was a reminder of a station that had seen grander days. Milk traffic here continued until 1980 but once that went the old up platform looked forlorn and forgotten. Only the signalman and signal box breathed any life into the place as the trains rushed by non-stop with the crossing loop seldom used and even less so since the introduction of the Axminster loop, most trains using the bi-directional up line. Today they have gone and Chard Junction is almost as lonely and sad a spot as Seaton Junction.

At just over 130 miles from London I always found **Crewkerne** a warm and welcoming station with a spacious booking office still in the original station building and wide and roomy platform and a very large station canopy to ward off inclement weather. Only the up platform remains in use, stretching under the main road bridge in the down direction against a grassy bank. One lonely coloured light home signal stands just beyond the down end of the platform. This, until recently, was controlled by Chard Junction and is to protect a small level crossing, Crewkerne Gates just a mile down the line which is approached on something of a blind curve on a rising gradient. The red light turns to green once the barriers have descended assuring the driver of a safe crossing. All trains call at Crewkerne with a train every hour in each direction. With such a good service on a line where timings are limited because of the single line sections, it would be hard to see how train services could be improved. However, the old down platform is still standing and this is an obvious place in the future where a further passing loop could be re-instated should the line continue to attract such good patronage.

For many years my son Ben and I would go and feed the ducks at **Sutton Bingham** reservoir after which we would walk up the road to the long-closed station. Vestiges of the old station were still visible even 20 years after closure although the building itself had long gone. The gates into the car park were left open wide, old rose bushes were still struggling for survival, the station cottages were still in use away from the station on the up side, and the platforms themselves were still just about visible with bits of old railway debris swallowed up in the undergrowth. The site of the old signal box with its gap under the platform was still discernible. This was a magic place. Today the station site is carefully wired off but in 1983 there was still unfettered if slightly dangerous access to the old platform. Another childhood memory came back to me whenever standing here. In 1961 my mother took me to London for a brief two day visit. The last train back to Tavistock, destination for the train Plymouth, left Waterloo at 7 pm. Having passed through Yeovil the train made an unadvertised stop at tiny Sutton Bingham. Our carriage had halted very close to the signal box situated on the down platform perched above the reservoir. and the guard who was talking to the signalman informed us that because of engineering works we would be stopping here for about 10 minutes. Sensing my interest the signalman invited me up into the box. It must have been during the summer holidays for though it was getting dark it was a beautiful evening and the water below was still just visible. The box, with that evocative paraffin smell, was warm and snug, very small with just 10 levers. I gathered that there was single line working through, I think, Crewkerne so we had to wait until that train had passed us at Sutton Bingham. I remember being allowed to pull levers for the up train, Nos. 2, 3 and 4 my later research tells me they must have been! I also recall not being able to pull lever No. 1 the distant signal and the signalman and guard being most amused. Small wonder since the up distant was 1,183 yards from the box and a tall order for a 14-year-old! All too soon for me the up train came through (up trains were usually given priority on the main line) and we were on our way again. It was the only time I visited Sutton Bingham station when operational. The station closed in 1962, one of the first on the line to do so, with the signal box closing in 1965. Trains still rush past this lovely spot but now only long strands of overgrowth are there to wave at the passing.

Yeovil Junction is not a pretty station but it commands respect as the largest station between Exeter and Salisbury with its long curving island platform and still a maze of sidings and outbuildings. Enthusiasts often gather here for steam days held on the far southern side of the station where a building is set aside for their use and for a souvenir and book shop. A connection remains between here and Yeovil Pen Mill and although there is no passenger service between the two stations, the line is often used for diversions when engineering work is being done on the former GWR Paddington route. Until 2012 the last remaining semaphore signals could be seen here guarding access to and from the spur down to Pen Mill. Again this is not a place I would choose to stay for long; it can also be quite a chilly spot if the waiting room is not open. However, on a fine day when the line is busy, a seat at the up end of the platform provides a good vantage point for passing trains.

Of all the stations along the line **Sherborne** is the one which has changed least over the years with its two curving platforms intact and with no singling of track although for a very brief period of time the line was single in the down direction through Yeovil to Chard Junction. However, within months double track was reinstated between Sherborne and Yeovil Junction.

The architecture of the down platform is nothing to write home about but the main building on the up platform is built of fine local ham stone and it is an impressive edifice. The station is well patronized not least by local schools for which the town is well-known. It is also one the best situated on the route with the historic and attractive town within easy walking distance and the fine Abbey church just a few hundred yards up the road, arguably one of the most beautiful churches of the west country. The station, built on a gentle curve, allows little view of approaching trains and again it is not a place I would chose to linger at for long although it is always worth a visit.

Many modern signal boxes were built along the line replacing old ones around the 1960s. These included Honiton, Gillingham, Semley, Tisbury and at Sherborne. Sadly many of these had very short life spans. Semley's new box only lasted five years - what a waste of money. Sherborne's lasted just 10, but remained standing until 2012 during which time it was used by various businesses. Similar boxes still remain *in situ* at Gillingham, Semley and Tisbury. Once Sherborne's box closed a tiny control panel for the crossing gates was erected at the end of the up platform and a distinctive bell would ring when a train was some five minutes away. The booking clerk on duty had to make it hot foot, come rain or shine, up the platform to the control panel, lower the gates and set the home and distant colour light signal. If he or she were the only person on duty this could be frustrating both for him or her as well as for passengers waiting to buy tickets. However, once set they could return speedily to the ticket office since signals and gates re-set themselves as soon as the train or trains had passed.

Many would say that the journey from here to the outskirts of Salisbury provide some of the best views of the journey. Climbing up away from Sherborne and passing Sherborne castles old and new the line touched briefly another 1 in 80 gradient before passing lonely **Milborne Port** closed in 1965, a charming rural station, somewhat out on a limb, but definitely a good lingering spot in the old days.

Templecombe, however, must be almost the best loitering point. To railway enthusiasts it is probably the most famous station on the line because of its associations with the Somerset & Dorset Joint Railway (S&D), long gone but never forgotten. After 1966 Templecombe became one of the most desolate sights anywhere. The station covered such a large area both on the SR line and also the S&D line that wherever one looked there was decay. Gradually, very gradually, all was cleared away until all that was left was a rather long, bleak platform, and a

The approach to Yeovil Junction from the front of a dmu in 1987. The fine signal box was closed and dismantled in 2012.   *Author*

The reopening of Templecombe station on 3rd October, 1983. The author is with a group of Sherborne students very early in the morning with distinguished ITV political commentator Tom Bradby second from the right in the back row, then in his last year at Sherborne.   *Author*

rather forlorn looking signal box. But again thanks to the persistence of local residents and others with a love for Templecombe, in 1983 the station re-opened amidst much rejoicing. There was much to be done in rebuilding a new waiting room and maintaining an attractive garden but done it was.

I recall driving an ancient minibus with a crowd of teenagers from Sherborne school to see the first train stop on 3rd October. A kindly signalman allowed us all into the box and a photo was duly taken. Amongst those assembled was the now distinguished ITV political editor Tom Bradby. The interior of Templecombe box was almost unique. One climbed the stairs to find oneself in the first half of the box which was a booking office; the other half contained the 18-lever signal frame with a home and distant signal in each direction and the points on the down end for trains to leave or enter the double line section to Yeovil. There was also access to a short siding. Down trains could be signalled to use the up line, which was bi-directional, if there was no up train between Templecombe and Yeovil. But with the increased number of trains on the line this latterly seemed to happen rather less than had been the case.

The newly-constructed station building, as modern stations go, is very pleasant to behold and it blends in well with the extensive garden area which adorns the platform. As ever, in the up direction the line stretches away for as far as the eye can see and from the footbridge there is the most wonderful vantage point from which to view passing trains. Looking westwards there is another good view of the whole campus, station, signal box and points leading off into double track, with the line stretching away towards Milborne Port before curving away to the right. Although a purist in many ways for the old days, I have to admit that here is a station which has been tastefully restored and it is a fine place to abide awhile.

Gillingham, like Honiton, is a neat and tidy crossing station with a fine view of trains coming up from the down direction. Like Sherborne it is perfectly situated to the town it serves with the exterior of the main building still as it ever was on the up platform. The booking office is well kept and warm in wintry days. But having seen and enjoyed it for many years, again like Honiton, it is not a place at which to stay although it will always be a place to which I shall return from time to time.

My final lingering point, now just in Wiltshire, is **Tisbury.** Here is another example of a charming small town station which only just avoided closure. For a while only five trains a day called here with the impression being made that it was doomed. However, with the 22 mile gap between Salisbury and Gillingham people continued to support their station and today some 23 trains stop here in each direction with the exception of the final up train of the day which zooms through half an hour after midnight. The station commands a lovely view over its town being situated on the southern edge. It is a pity that when the line was singled it was the up platform that was used since the view from the platform is over an unattractive concrete factory complex, the land of which had been sold off by the railway. Had the down platform been retained the view would have been superb.

The selling off of this site meant that when it was realised a new loop had to be built there was not enough room at the station. Thus in 1986 a new crossing loop was built east of Tisbury station just out of sight around the corner with the up home signal at the end of Tisbury's platform. Most trains cross here just after the hour with the result that an up train arrives at Tisbury more or less on the hour, disappears around the corner and after a couple of minutes the down train appears, creating around the o'clock much activity on the platform and in the booking office.

From here the line makes its way for the 20 minute run to Salisbury through closed Dinton and Wilton. But before I end this section there is one more very special observing spot. A mile west of Tisbury was the charming setting for **Tisbury Gates.** This was one of the last crossings on the line to retain its signalling. Situated in the Nadder valley not far from the river amidst a lush setting of rolling fields this remains a most charming place. Like most crossings on the line there was a distant and home signal in each direction. Tisbury's down advanced starting signal had been combined with the Tisbury Gates down distant and vice versa the Tisbury up distant was combined with Tisbury Gates up home. The box with its six-lever frame had been provided with a wheel to control the gates and even after the gates were replaced by half-barriers signalling remained in place for a number of years, although signals were usually left 'off' for trains and the gates opened for occasional passing road traffic. Today this remains a delightful spot at which to linger. The crossing keeper's house is where it ever was and the actual crossing box still stands where it ever did.

So here is a main line which still retains its rural attraction, a line which is doing well and which I suspect will continue to develop with the reintroduction of another crossing loop or two at, possibly, Crewkerne or Seaton Junction, if not the relaying of double track over longer stretches.

In 2012 all signal boxes were closed between Exmouth Junction and Salisbury, that is to say at Honiton, Chard Junction, Yeovil Junction, Templecombe and Gillingham to be controlled centrally from Salisbury and latterly Basingstoke. As a signalling enthusiast I find this desperately sad. One reason is pure nostalgia of course. Another is I am not convinced that centralizing signalling is the safest way of running a railway. Thirdly it is sad when hard working railwaymen after many years of faithful service are either made redundant or are moved away from locations to which they feel they have some loyalty. But above all it is the continuing facelessness which encroaches over the system. During the early months of 2014 the story will be repeating itself as loyal signalmen and women will be made redundant, or at best have to find far distant jobs, from Poole, Hamworthy, Wareham, Wool and Dorchester, on the Waterloo to Weymouth line.

Tisbury Gates box in 1980 looking in the down direction. The box is still still *in situ* today although non-operational. *Author*

In some places the signalmen was the last figure of human contact left at a station and it is the personal contact between the railway employees and the public which makes things work. I use the word 'encroachment' because hand in hand with the withdrawal of signalman is the talk of withdrawal of guards on trains. I hope this may not be true. But what I do note is that more and more of the smaller stations' booking offices are now open for fewer and fewer hours. From personal experience of the line about which I have been writing, the men and women who worked as booking clerks at Sherborne, Gillingham, Templecombe and Tisbury gave wonderful service to the public. They were helpful, informative, friendly, and wonderful ambassadors for the railway. The hours at all these stations seem to have been cut to be replaced by faceless machines which for many are not easy to use, not least at night or in bad weather. I am sure somebody is going to tell me about the importance of 'good progress'. All I can say is if progress does not go hand in hand with positive face to face human relationships in the workplace, then it can never be called 'good' and if 'progress' then I would question to what end is such progress for.

Castle Cary to Dorchester – a remaining cross-country link

Castle Cary (129m. 46ch.) - Sparkford (134m. 29ch.) - Marston Magna (136m. 29ch.) - Yeovil Pen Mill (141m. 27ch.) - Thornford Bridge Halt (144m. 36ch.) - Yetminster (145m. 45ch.) - Chetnole Halt (147m. 52ch.) - Evershot (149m. 76ch.) - Cattistock Halt (153m. 18ch.) - Maiden Newton (154m. 8ch.) - Grimpstone & Frampton ((157m. 56ch.) - Bradford Peverell & Stratton Halt (158m. 72ch.) - Dorchester West (161m. 63ch.)

I have never been quite clear in my mind when a full-bodied main line becomes a cross-country line or even when a cross-country line becomes a branch line. Possibly there was a clearer distinction in bygone days. I was always led to think that the Somerset & Dorset line was a cross-country line rather than a main line. I am sure wiser folk than I will correct me, but if that is so then I imagine the same must apply to the line which still runs from Westbury to Weymouth. Certainly it goes cross-country but then so do main lines. But perhaps what gives it its definition is that it goes across and links main lines. In the case of the Westbury to Weymouth line it crosses and connects to three main lines: Penzance to Paddington, Exeter to Waterloo and Weymouth to Waterloo. For the purpose of this section, however, I concentrate just on the area from Castle Cary to Dorchester.

Having already said that the ex-SR to Salisbury was better at preserving some small stations than the GWR main line, I now have to retract slightly. There are two stations on the Paddington line which still have undoubted rural charm. One is Pewsey in Wiltshire which is certainly an epitome of small town railway elegance while the other is **Castle Cary**. This latter station remains a 50 per cent gem.

The GWR architecture on the up platform is perfect and while the new building on the down platform does not really do justice to the building it should complement nonetheless Castle Cary remains a charming rural junction with fields sloping up to its small town on the hill above. Yes, we could well to linger here. Not all trains on the main line stop; many charge through at great speed appearing from the down direction under a road bridge on what always strikes me as a rather sharp bend for so fast a train. In the up direction towards Bruton the line curves away to the right of the platform before a long straight run alongside refuge loops. Gone

Right: The author's son Ben aged four watches from Yeovil Pen Mill signal box as Ken Christmas exchanges tokens with the driver of a Weymouth bound train in 1984. An up train waits in the up platform.

Author

Below: The view from the down end of Yeovil Pen Mill in 2007 where lines to Weymouth and to Yeovil Junction twist away together left and right. These lower quadrant signals have since been changed to upper quadrant.

Author

since February 1985 are the beautiful semaphore signals which once adorned the station which greedy Westbury panel swallowed up but I won't go on about that.

One seldom has long to wait here before something comes along the main line and every so often a slightly smaller train makes its way quietly into the down island platform and waits for the signal to indicate the direction off the main line and onto the line for Yeovil Pen Mill. Already it will have stopped at Frome and Bruton, stations on the main line but which are usually only served by the Weymouth branch train.

The typical wide, open countryside from Castle Cary to Yeovil is exemplified in the miles that follow. Two fine old stations along the line are now as if they had never been, **Sparkford** and **Marston Magna**. Both stations closed in 1966, two years before the line was singled, freight having been withdrawn a few years earlier. Cars zooming along the A303 at Sparkford are hardly aware of crossing a railway let alone of the fact that there was once an attractive rural station here. The passing driver might just be aware of the former United Dairies building to the north of the road bridge which once provided considerable traffic for the station, now the home of a publishing company; apart from this nothing remains of the old station itself. Nor is there any sign of Marston Magna's attractive stone-built station tucked away half a mile from the village it served on the little lane to Rimpton. Both stations had once been busy freight centres with milk, coal, cattle feed, livestock, tree trunks for the saw mill at Sparkford and huge casks of cider at Marston Magna. The sidings here were greatly extended in 1940 for the War Department but all sidings were removed in 1962, the same year as Sparkford's sidings were taken out of use. Sadly Marston Magna became one of those stations which died slowly and by the end with no freight, no staff, no signal box, the state of the station was a sorry sight with grass creeping along the platform and ivy up the walls. The only reminder today of its existence is the former station master's house.

The long straight sections on the Castle Cary to Yeovil section provide good views from the over-bridges along the route with the yellow light of the Yeovil down distant signal visible from far away for the driver before the long s-bend into **Yeovil Pen Mill**. This station remains an oasis of an almost bygone age in a county which has lost so much of its railway history. Here is a station which has so much which many others have lost. There are still proper semaphore signals together with a proper signal box and even, not so long ago, and a proper signal box cat. There are original station buildings, no second rate bus shelter waiting rooms, with a booking office and even at certain hours of the day a refreshment room.

Many sidings have been removed although some are still *in situ*, generally unused. It is an odd station since it not only has an up platform alongside the main station building, there is also a down island platform which makes the up platform bi-directional under an all embracing roof. In no way could Yeovil Pen Mill be described as pretty, but it is unique, slightly cosy and a 'one-off'. Once upon a time this was the northern end of a strange triangle which embraced the three stations of Yeovil, Junction, Town and Pen Mill. The 'Town' station was probably the one which would today have been of most use to the general public but which is (dare I say 'of course') the one which closed.

At the end of the station in the down direction a bridge crosses the line with the Yeovil to Sherborne road. Just beyond, the old line to nearby Yeovil Town once curved away to the right and if one takes the footpath across the field alongside and follows the old track bed it is still possible to find signs of the old line which escaped the engineer's blowtorch.

As the Weymouth line curves under the bridge, the line to Yeovil Junction branches off to the right to then run parallel for three-quarters of a mile before climbing up to the junction station. There is a long left-hand curve away from Pen Mill with the two up home signals for both lines some 900 yards out. Here the line from the old town station would have come in from the right to pass lonely Yeovil South Junction signal box. This brick-built box (and junction) was erected in 1943 to help the war effort and enabling trains from Pen Mill to have access to the Exeter-Salisbury line. Latterly it was seldom used and the legendary George Pryer tells the story of discovering millions of flies in the box after a long period of its being switched out and having to walk back to Yeovil to buy cans of fly killer before anyone could be persuaded to enter the box.

A regular shuttle service once ran between the three Yeovil stations, This has long gone although some simple service between Pen Mill and the Junction would certainly make life easier for those who now have carry luggage from station to bus in order to get from one station to the other. However, the rail link is in regular use when engineering work is taking place on the Paddington line or when there are excursion trains.

A little way further on from South Junction the Weymouth line goes under the Waterloo main line soon passing from Somerset into Dorset. Four of the eight stations between Yeovil survived the Beeching cuts. The first along the route was **Thornford Bridge Halt.** Chetnole, two stops further along the line, and Thornford once both had staggered wooden platforms with a road bridge in-between. When Cattistock Halt closed in 1966, Cattistock's two platforms were taken to Thornford and Chetnole to replace the ageing wooden up platforms. Two years later in 1968 when the line was singled the remaining wooden down platforms at each station were discarded. Thornford was opened as late as 1936 and is situated about a mile from its village with access down a steep flight of steps.

When living in Sherborne in the mid-1980s, my young son Ben would often be awake by six o'clock and on certain days we would drive down to Yeovil Pen Mill and catch an early morning down train to one or other of the stations. This down train crossed with an up train at Maiden Newton and we would get off at either Thornford, Yetminster or Chetnole. Occasionally we would go to Maiden Newton jump off the train and run over the bridge to catch the waiting up train. Ben gave each station a name. Thornford Bridge was always 'Slippery Steps Station' since he once fell near the bottom of the steep flight. Yeovil Pen Mill was 'Ken's Station' after a signalman with the delightful name of Ken Christmas and who was very fond of Ben. Yetminster was 'William's Station' after a black and white cat of that name who used to often be in the station car park.

Thornford was probably lucky to retain its station since **Yetminster** with its larger community was only one mile away. Opened in 1857 this was a much more substantial station, very much along the same lines as Marston Magna and Sparkford with a 27-lever signal box, considerable freight, and facilities for banking engines to help trains from here up to Holywell tunnel. The station was well situated for its village and was well used by passengers. Over the years the facilities became fewer and with the singling of the line in 1968 the signal box was taken out of use. The station became unmanned the following year. A modern glass bus shelter is all that now remains on the former up platform and this once attractive and well-cared for station is soul-less and sad. Of course we must be grateful there is still a station here but its edifice is hardly becoming for such an attractive Hardyesque Dorset village.

Two miles on is **Chetnole Halt** and this is a wonderful spot. The station is some half mile up the road from its village. Here is the epitome of a truly rural halt which has survived. It is similar to Thornford but the setting is more attractive. Approaching the station from the village there is the impression that the station is sitting in the middle of a field. There is a fine view from the road bridge in both directions, set as it is on a long straight section climbing up towards the summit at Evershot. Like Thornford too there are steep steps from the bridge giving access to the platform and in the summer there is a profusion of wild flowers in the hedgerows around the station. Ben's name for Chetnole was 'Misty Station', a title derived from one early spring morning when

Tilly (Till Eulenspiegel) sits happily at the top of the steps leading down to ultra rural and attractively positioned Chetnole Halt in 1988.   *Author*

the whole station and fields around were submerged in a sea of mist and dampness which was slowly evaporating into a cloudless blue sky above. It is interesting to reflect on the fact that many stations which suffered least from modernization and rationalization are the small halts which have survived such as Chetnole since they have always been small and therefore have lost least. Chetnole was another late arrival being opened in 1933. As at Yetminster and Thornford, almost all trains are booked to stop here but only by request.

After a climb of about two miles through lush Dorset countryside the line enters a deep cutting announcing the approach to Holywell tunnel, 308 yds long and at 500 ft above sea level, the summit of the line between Yeovil and Maiden Newton. situated a quarter of a mile on the up side of the site of **Evershot station.** This wooden-built station was an absolute joy, beautifully cared for with a fine display of roses and colourful flower beds. Opened at the same time as Yetminster in 1857 Evershot was situated in the tiny hamlet of Holywell. The village it was named after was some distance from the station, and its remoteness and low number of passengers, the parish of Evershot only registering 149 in population, was the reason it was closed in 1966. Just as Evershot village continues to be one of the chocolate box gems of Dorset, used as the backdrop for a number of films, so the station was considered a showpiece. Today nothing of it remains and down trains rattle on down the hill, alive with country colour and flavour, for another three miles before curving past the village of **Cattistock** with its magnificent church tower. Of the little halt here too nothing remains. When it opened in 1933 the platforms were wooden. These were replaced in 1959 but were only to survive seven years before the station closed and the platforms resurrected at Chetnole and Thornford. The station was poorly patronized and with **Maiden Newton** less than a mile away there was little wonder that there was no chance of survival.

Maiden Newton has already been described in the earlier chapter relating to the Bridport branch which closed in 1975. For another 13 years the signal box remained open with two stop signals in each direction. Ben's name for Maiden Newton was 'Bill's Station' named after Bill Love a relief signalman who would always allow us into the box and whom Ben and I liked very much. The box, however, finally closed on 15th May, 1988 and I was able to capture the last time the up home signal was pulled. Apart from the signalman, the station was unmanned by this time and with the closure of the box there was not even a signalman to breath a little life into the place. Small metal cabins were erected at the end of each platform in order to allow the driver to obtain tokens for trains to continue on to Dorchester or Yeovil.

A flurry of activity occurred along the line during the 2012 Sailing Olympics down in Weymouth with a number of extra trains and a fluttering of Union Jacks along the route, but on normal weekdays the timetable remains relatively quiet with eight trains each way spread out over a long day. The timetable in 2012 at Maiden Newton ran as follows:

05.57 Up	11.43 Up	16.47 Down
07.05 Up	*Trains crossing*	17.54 Up
07.58 Down	13.44 Down	18.45 Down
09.18 Up	13.46 Up	19.44 Down
10.37 Down	*Trains crossing*	20.45 Up
11.41 Down	15.33 Up	22.44 Down

I retain so many happy memories of this station in busier days that it must always remain a special and a favourite place to loiter, and loiter one must if you want to see a train since there are some long gaps in the day. Despite the empty signal box which still remains, as do the station buildings (although looking a trifle weary and unloved), this is still a good place to be; the station still has a nice feel about it. The walk up Station Road from the village is much as it ever was and as the final slope towards the main building comes into view there is still a leap of excitement in the heart, well mine at any rate. Here is still a good old-fashioned village crossing station and thank you dear God!

The one signal that remains is the colour light ex-down starter some yards away from the end of the down platform now controlled from Dorchester. Two further closed stations lie on the seven miles between Maiden Newton and Dorset's capital. Overlooking the Frome valley with a vista of fields rivers and woods, the quiet station of **Grimstone and Frampton** was another station opened in 1857 and closed in 1966. It was set on a sharp s-bend curve with one siding, the red-brick signal box being on the down end of the up platform. I only visited the station once just before closure. The signal box had closed although armless signal posts were still standing and the booking office on the down side was firmly locked, the station being unstaffed for the final six months of its life. But what a peaceful spot, not dissimilar to Evershot's atmosphere and it was one of those stations where 'the memory kind'a lingers'. Here was a real touch of railway solitude where one might have been inspired to write a poem. There was an attractive brick built waiting shelter on the up platform. While I was there an up train ambled in, stopped, and moved on. Nobody got on, nobody got off. Just a nod to me from the guard who looked surprised to see anyone, knowing that within a few weeks no train would ever be stopping here again.

Three miles before Dorchester stood **Bradford Peverell and Stratton Halt,** a tiny station with a large name board! In fact 'stands' would be better than 'stood', for although the station closed in that dreadful month of widespread railway annihilation of October 1966, the station remains *in situ* today. As motorists drive away from Dorchester towards Yeovil, as they pass under the railway near Stratton and glance up to the right there are the two staggered concrete platforms still standing. Until 1959, as at Cattistock, the station was timber built before being changed for concrete, to last just seven years of passenger usage. The joint population of these two villages is well over 800, larger than Thornford or Chetnole and one cannot help but wonder if a case could be made for the re-opening of the halt which would surely be a great benefit for Dorchester-bound shoppers.

From Grimstone and Frampton to Bradford Peverell and Stratton the main road hugs the railway line before passing under it. From this point road and rail gradually move away from each other, the line hugging the side of the hill before plunging into a tunnel on the north side of Dorchester and arriving at **Dorchester West.** This station, dating from 1857, in its heyday was a fine structure built to last and I recall being hugely impressed by a succession of three starting signals in the down direction each having a distant signal beneath, these latter controlled from Dorchester Junction box which could just be spotted beyond the road bridge carrying the road to Weymouth. The fine red-brick 29-lever signal box was at the up end of the down platform, unusually positioned away from the main sidings which were on the down side. Down trains often paused here for a short time waiting for the line towards Weymouth to clear. This still occasionally happens today although the unmanned station now has a melancholy air about it as happier and busier days are remembered when a plethora of staff served the station. A coloured light signal controlled from the signal box at Dorchester South half a mile away, now guards departure from the down platform and another at the end of the up where the double track turns into single for the journey north to Maiden Newton.

At that momentous time of change for this line in 1968 I had an odd reply to a comment I had made from a signalman at Maiden Newton with a beautiful gentle Dorset accent whose name I cannot recall. Amidst the sadness of closed stations, miles of double track displaced to make it single, empty signal boxes, unmanned stations and armless signals, I, the sad romantic, observed the tragedy of it all. His reply was simply, 'Well yes. But did you know young man, you can still survive with one kidney?' It was an answer I didn't quite grasp at the time but it has always stuck in my mind. So much had been taken away, and yet there is still life here. Of course he went on to explain that was exactly what had happened to him and he was glad to be alive.

So this attractive cross-country line lives on and at least Castle Cary and Yeovil Pen Mill some of the time still have human beings around to remove some slight facelessness. Much has gone, as will be obvious, but there are still wonderful views and still the occasional magic moment. Yeovil Pen Mill remains an unsung hero to the lost world of the GWR and perhaps one should not whisper its name too loudly in case some bureaucrat in a far off railway dictatorship-land suddenly wakes up one morning and discovers there is still a crossing station in Somerset which needs to be 'modernized'! Too late has that moment come for staff-less Maiden Newton, although here too there is still enough personality for this village passing place to hold its head high and remind folk that 'I am still a station to be reckoned with'. But if you want to linger, then Chetnole Halt is the place to be, preferably on a warm summer's day and for choice as an up train appears in the far distance on its way towards the summit, alas without a banking engine. And rest in peace Sparkford, Marston Magna, Evershot, Cattistock, Grimstone and Frampton, Bradford Peverell and Stratton Halt. 'At the going down of the 'last train' and in the evening, we will remember you'.

The delightful and gentlemanly Bill Love lived near the crossing at Chard Junction. He was a relief signalman seen here at Maiden Newton in 1988, the same year the box closed.
Author

Epilogue

A Dozen Red Railway Roses
My top 12 West Country loitering places

The original title of this book was to have been *Loitering with Intent* and I still like it, not least because my son encouraged it. However, the publishing powers that be felt this was not an appropriate title and I humbly bow to their good judgement. So, if you have noticed the 'loitering' word appearing on various occasions, that is the reason. To loiter (there it is again) on a pretty rural station waiting for the train which may still be many minutes or more away, is one of the great pleasures of life. It slows me down and gives me time to catch up with life and myself. So I offer 12 places where I could happily loiter and not be bored. Nobody has to agree with the list but it may encourage some interesting discussion for those love this sort of thing and immense boredom for those who don't!

This is an impossible task and I know that the day after this book has gone to print, and for ever after, I shall be worrying if I should have made other choices. But at the end of the day a decision has to be made, or in this case 12! My choice is of course very subjective. So, dear reader, here goes, in alphabetical order. Please bear in mind I am looking for peaceful, rural railway settings, and therefore stations or level crossings which are in no way fussy, ostentatious or over-busy. They are places where I enjoy waiting quietly for the trains, even if I have to wait a little while! It is very much a list of 'small is beautiful'!

1 – Bere Ferrers (Plymouth to Gunnislake)

It was either here or Bere Alston; but there had to be a station on the list from my formative teenage days. With nine trains each way a day, this half way point of the line is the best example I know of a small rural station, once part of the big main line to Waterloo, which has graciously grown into a small branch line halt while retaining its character, largely thanks to the station's owner who has put his own mark upon this enchanting station. *Only alternative, Bere Alston.*

2 – Causland Halt (Liskeard to Looe)

The epitome of a timeless ex-GWR halt, a single platform in a beautiful valley with hardly a house in sight. Perfection. I never ever get tired of this place. *No other choice although Coombe Junction Halt would be a close second.*

3 – Chetnole Halt (Weymouth to Castle Cary and Westbury)

An extraordinary survivor on a line which has been hugely downgraded over the years. A single concrete platform (once wooden) which looks as if it is growing out of a field. Fine views from the road bridge in a beautiful Dorset setting. *Maiden Newton would have once won the prize until it lost its signal box.*

4 – Eggesford (Exeter to Barnstaple)

Although I already have Portsmouth Arms on the list on the same line, I have to include Eggesford as well. Although the original down platform has been replaced by a modern one following floods , the setting over the river and with a view over the bridge, across to fields beyond and up to the parish church is fabulous. At almost every hour of the day trains up and down cross here and for a few minutes there is a flurry of activity. Then there is only the sound of the river for another hour, when there is a repeat performance.

5 – Exton (Exeter to Exmouth)

The station itself is nothing to look at but what a view over the Exe estuary with a constant stream of activity of both changing tides , movement of boats and an endless supply of wildlife make this a memorable stop. Four trains pass through each hour and if that were not enough one has only to gaze across the estuary to Starcross to watch the Exeter-Plymouth trains whistle by.

6 – Goonbarrow Junction (Par to Newquay)

For an award winning A* overgrown footpath, the track leading to the south side of Goonbarrow with its hidden stile over the track, must be top of the list. Having got there however, this is wonderful spot at which to watch trains use the only remaining crossing loop on the Newquay branch. *Other choice might have been Luxulyan at the very heart of its little village.*

7 – Lelant Saltings (St Erth to St Ives)

Others might well choose a spot further down the line towards Carbis Bay but there is something about this long, curving modern platform that captivates me. There is still a semaphore signal at the up end, the outer home for St Erth and towards the end of the day there is a wonderful tranquillity here and, as at Exton, a cacophony of bird calls.

8 – Liskeard (Paddington to Plymouth and Penzance)

I felt I had to include something on a main line which was both rural and which still held its character. This is a busy station at the edge of its town, but there remains a rural flavour, some nice architecture, semaphore signals, an adjacent branch line, and some very friendly staff. *I might also have chosen Lostwithiel, Par, or St Erth ... well done Cornwall!*

9 – Portsmouth Arms (Exeter to Barnstaple)

A favourite since childhood when it was awarded the prize for the 'Best Kept Station' on the Southern Region for several years. Now a diminutive request halt bereft of all former architecture. And yet it remains such a special place. *King's Nympton and Lapford are also contenders along the line ... see also (4) Eggesford.*

10 – Saint Winnow Church (Lostwithiel to Carne Point (Fowey))

Not a station but a viewing point and you may well have to wait a while looking from the church across the river since this is now freight only. If you read the section about this line you will realise why it is included for personal reasons. But even without those reasons this is a fabulous spot to see the clay trains go by and to recall the days when the tiny passenger trains sauntered by via Golant. (*See front cover.*)

11 – Templecombe (Waterloo to Salisbury and Exeter)

This poor old SR route is such an old friend and it has been so messed about with, but I must include some place on it. Templecombe is a historic place which, like Bere Ferrers has had to change identity over the years. It is not as it once was and yet there is still a charm about the place, not least because of the love and care which locals have poured into it. And to stand on the bridge in the evening light and see a down train appear from the very far distance over a vast straight section, through the platform and pass from single to double track still gives me great pleasure.

12 – Yeovil Pen Mill (Westbury to Castle Cary and Weymouth)

This is not a pretty station but it has great atmosphere. I have also experienced most friendly staff. This is a final bastion of Somerset semaphore signalling. There is an island platform as well as a beautifully quirky bridge from up platform to the island platform. There is a fine signal box at the up end. There can be long periods of quiet but it gets exciting when trains are diverted from the Salisbury line and take the former branch which ran from here to the junction.

Tail Lamp

Tucked away in the pages of the Old Testament in the Song of Solomon runs the charming verse, 'Many waters cannot quench love, neither can the floods drown it'. And if that is so then my little dog Gigi, who, like her springer spaniel predecessor Tilly, has loitered with me on so many an occasion, would also want to say that many waters cannot quench the fascinating scent of a closed branch line as can be seen from the photograph below where she delights in those waters which flood the entrance to Torpantau tunnel, close to the long closed station of the same name, surely one of the remotest stations of Wales.

So what to say by way of conclusion? When talking about railways there is the danger is of being over pessimistic or unduly sentimental about days past. Over the years I have developed an odd antennae which lodges somewhere deep in my brain and which suddenly leaps into action as I drive along a road or lane I have never travelled before as a little voice in my head tells me 'a railway once ran alongside here'. And I may stop the car, get out and there, possibly amidst a row of unkempt trees or in the middle of a field, is indeed the track-bed of a long forgotten railway line, or even the vague remains of a workman's hut. And a little further on at the next village there is that little giveaway as off to the right appears a turning into the eternally optimistic 'Station Road' where once villagers made their way in sun and rain to that their own little station which could take them to a bigger world and back again.

And it is sad. But in reality we know that it was ridiculous to suppose that the Trouble House Halts, the Torpantaus, the Meeths or Goonbarrow Halts of this world could ever really be justified today. We cannot be too hard on poor old Lord Beeching who was given

a job to do and, to be fair, did it all too well. The blame lies of course much more with the Ernest Marples of that era who, being far more interested in the roads than the rails, swallowed most of the report hook, line and sinker without much real thought for the future. And we are the poorer for it. It could have been implemented so much better.

But life moves on and the good news is that railways are on the up. I have to say I am personally not bothered about, nor impressed by, trains which go faster. I have always been puzzled by this obsession of 'going faster'. Why is it after all that despite the fact we have more and more facilities at our fingertips to make life easier than even just 50 years ago, people appear to have less and less time. Why is it that more working days are lost by people suffering from stress than for any other reason? We don't need to go faster. All that going faster seems to achieve is to make us go even faster. We need to slow the pace so that human beings can catch breath and catch up, and train travel does that in a beautifully civilized manner. 'Let the train take the strain' was that fabulous catchphrase but it does not do that by having to go faster.

So I do not lose heart. Despite the criticisms that are often made of our railway system it generally remains a wonderful way by which to travel and for those of us more interested in the smaller rural lines, as already indicated, there are still many wonderful little stations and stretches of line, not only in the West Country but further afield around Britain. I do say again that the facelessness of the rural lines continues to depress me; the lack of personal contact and the loss of those wonderful men and women whose livelihood not only depended on the railway but whose life was the railway and who gave their all in its service. They are still around of course, but often one has to travel far to find them.

Overall however railways are on the up, and that is good. New stations are opening up, old ones are being revived, and there are many hopes in many pipelines, even though some of those hopes may just be dreams. But dreams can come true.

I have generally avoided too much reference to preserved lines since this is a different world and worthy of another book. But here of course the old traditions do live on. Beautiful little stations such as Corfe Castle on the Swanage Railway, Staverton on the South Devon Railway or Crowcombe on the West Somerset Railway, retain that timeless rural charm, lines where hundreds of courteous volunteers, guards, porters, signalmen, drivers and suchlike, in their smart uniforms, are reminders that being of service to passengers is the hallmark of a good railway and nothing is too much trouble.

I end with one final memory slightly further away from the confines of this book, although still on an ex-GWR route. A week before writing this tailpiece I visited the Brecon Mountain Railway once again. Although as yet without signals (which for me personally is the perfect tailor's finish to any railway as you may have gathered!) it is an utterly beautiful line. Currently trains travel down from Pant through Pontsticill to then terminate and run round at Dol-y-Gaer; but the track is now laid a further two miles up into the Brecon mountains as far as Torpantau and it was to this spot for the first time, along tiny twisting roads and through high rolling forested hillsides that my course was set on 18th August, 2013. And I want to end here because there is something magically symbolic about this spot.

The setting is utterly remote but so very beautiful. The trackbed terminates against a large grassy hillock with two buffer stops and a run-round loop, the remains of the original station being a couple of hundred yards further on. The new miniscule low-level platform and loop line are both cradled by grassy banks full of wild flowers and fluttering butterflies, with an endless supply of interesting smells for Gigi! If ever there was a beautiful place at which to pause for a magical view and savour an anticipatory atmosphere like some rare vintage wine, it is surely here. No trains as yet, the tracks are rusty and silent. But yet here, at this remotest of spots, is a wonderful symbol of railway promise for the future and a joyous anticipation of things to come. So whatever the losses may be, and there are many, there is also great hope. Thus I trust that, God willing, for many years to come I shall continue that intense of pleasure of allowing time to stand still, as 'I loiter with intent' and await for the train, no matter for how long!

Glossary

Atlantic Coast Express (ACE) – This wonderful express train journeyed from Waterloo to Padstow with coaches being shed on the way for Bude, Ilfracombe, Plymouth and Torrington. It stopped in 1964 having originally been introduced by the Southern Railway in 1926. Latterly its title has been used on Paddington to Newquay services which many purists feel is not quite correct, Newquay being very much an ex-GWR line and not ex-SR!

Bay platform – This is a platform often used for branch line trains at their main line station or for trains which terminate at a station. They are usually found at a through station but on the other side of a full length platform with buffer stops at the end.

Block system – Railways are divided into definite intervals of space, each space being known as a 'block section'. A signal box is at each end of the section and only one train at a time is allowed into any one section on the same line, apart from an emergency situation. A train enters the section at the final signal which it passes on leaving the station. For many stations there is simply one such signal, known as the starting signal. But there can be as many as three or even more, these known as starter, advanced starter, outer advanced starter. Whichever is last marks the start of the block section to the next station or signal box.

Chain – A measurement of distance often used on the railway. There are 80 chains in a mile.

Coloured-light signal – As opposed to a manually operated semaphore signal, this is an electrically-operated signal whose light (red, yellow or green) makes visibility easier both during the day and even more so at night or in poor weather.

Diesel multiple unit (dmu) – There is no locomotive as such on the front, the driver controlling the train from the very front of the train from a driving cab.

Distant signal – This is a yellow warning signal which can be situated anything from a quarter of a mile to over a mile or more before the next station or signal box. If the distant signal is 'off' (at 'proceed') it indicates that the next (stop) signal is also off. If at caution it warns the driver he may have to stop at the next signal. On the smaller lines, often branch lines where there is a speed restriction, the distant signal is often fixed permanently at caution or 'on'. Both examples can be seen on the Swanage Railway. Semaphore distant signals are yellow with a v-shaped notch at the outer end.

Down line and up line – Trains are either travelling in the down or up direction. Trains moving towards London are always up trains and trains away from London are down trains. Thus even if a train is travelling up towards Scotland it is still a down train. This description started long before railways having indicated the direction of stage coaches. (In South Wales, however, a down train runs down the valley and an up train up the valley.)

Gate box or crossing box – A signal box whose only function is to guard a level crossing.

Great Western Railway (GWR) – This started as the London to Bristol Railway in the 1830s. As the years went by it not only grew hugely but also incorporated many smaller companies. At its height in the 1920s it covered 3,025 route miles. It became part of British Railways in 1948.

Ground frame – A small set of mechanical levers away from a signal box, covered or out in the open. The levers control points in and out of sidings with possibly ground signals as well. These points are unlocked by a lever in the nearest signal box or by a special key which can be slotted into the side of the point levers in order to allow the points to be pulled.

Ground signal or ground disc – A small disc-shaped signal with a red or yellow stripe across its face. These are used to control movements in or out of sidings or where a train is being crossed over from one line to another. Ground signals are usually at ground level but can also be attached to a main running signal. Occasionally ground signals can be seen in the shape of a miniature semaphore signal.

Home signal – A red stop signal which controls the exit from the block section, thus it is positioned at the approach to a signal box or station. Where there is a junction or several sidings at the approach there may be an outer and inner home signal, or even more.

Island platform – A platform with lines on both sides of it as at Yeovil Pen Mill.

Light railway – A railway which has been built rather more simply than is normally required. Speed on such a line may be limited and signalling of a minimum such as no distant signals, open frames (no signal box) and more ungated level crossings. Curves may be sharper than usual and gradients steeper. The Torrington-Halwill line was a good example of this.

Mixed Train – A train which carries both passengers and freight. These were especially to be found on branch lines.

On and off – A signal is said to be 'on' when it indicates 'stop' or in case of distant signals 'caution' and 'off' when it indicates 'proceed'.

One engine in steam – A delightfully old-fashioned expression but one still sometimes used. It indicates a line along which only one train may travel at a time. The St Ives branch is a good example of this and the latter days of the Bridport branch. The driver carries a (usually) wooden staff to show he alone has authority to travel the line. This he returns to the signalman once he vacates the line.

Passing loop/crossing loop – A place on a single line (usually at a station but not always) where two trains are able to pass each other.

Pull off – To pull a signal lever, and hence the signal arm, over to the 'off' (proceed) position.

Quadrant, upper and lower – To indicate signals either move up 45 degrees from the horizontal position or down 45 degrees. Why up or down depended on the region of the line and when it was introduced. The Great Western Railway in particular used lower quadrant signals. Upper quadrant signals were introduced from America and some consider them safer since in extreme conditions ice or snow can force a lower quadrant signal downwards, giving a false impression to a driver.

Signal levers – Every signal box is different. There may be scores of levers or half a dozen. Red levers indicate red stop signals. Yellow levers indicate yellow distant signals and are usually at the extreme ends of a box. Black levers indicate points and blue levers indicate a facing point lock (FPL). FPL levers secure more firmly a point which a train is to run over, slightly similar to dropping the latch on a yale lock to ensure greater security. Levers which electrically operate a point or a signal are slightly shorter than the manually operated ones. White levers indicate they are no longer in use; there are sadly all too many of these today in many boxes.

South Devon Railway – The original line ran from Totnes to Ashburton. When it began its life as a preserved line it was initially called the Dart Valley Railway. Sadly the Buckfastleigh to Ashburton section was given the chop because of road improvements although there are rumours it could be re-instated one day. It runs along the banks of the Dart from Totnes to Buckfastleigh via Staverton.

Southern Railway (SR) – Formed in 1923, this incorporated the London & South Western Railway (LSWR) as one of is constituents, and was the great rival of the Great Western Railway. Although both the LSWR and GWR became part of British Railways in 1948 the rivalry lingered for a while, and indeed friendly banter still continues today as can be heard when the GWR tank is running on the Swanage Railway.

Split-armed distant signals (splitting distants) – At the approach to a junction usually only one distant is provided. It is only pulled for the main line and is left at caution for the branch line or the line over which there is a very definite speed restriction. If, however, the speed round the junction were allowed to be 40 mph or more a second 'splitting' distant would be provided on a bracket, the arms being positioned to show the more important route.

Starting signal – See under 'Block System'.

Stop signal – Any form of signal which when 'on' tells the driver he must not pass this point unless given specific instructions otherwise from the signalman on duty.

Tail lamp – A red lamp or light placed on the last coach or vehicle of any train day or night to show the train is complete. Every signalman controlling semaphore signalling watches for this at every passing train. On one occasion on one particular railway no lamp could be found and somebody produced a pair of red pyjamas! My lips are sealed as to who and where.

Tarka Line – The name given to the Exeter-Barnstaple line travelling, as it does, the haunts of Henry Williamson's *Tarka the Otter*.

Train token, tablet or staff – 'What have you just handed the driver?' is one of the most asked questions to any signalman, not least on the Swanage Railway. Although being gradually superseded by more modern methods this is still used on the railway system and not least on preserved lines. It is a tried and tested system which ensures the safe passage of a train over a single line section. It is only used on lines where there is single track. What passengers see is a large hoop which the signalman exchanges with the driver. This is merely a kind of handbag and is of no real value other than convenience. The tablet or token which it contains is what matters. A tablet is tablet-shaped, circular and made of metal. The token is a large metal key. Both perform the same function, and that is to give the driver of a train the visible permission to continue to the next block post (station or signal box) where he will surrender that key or token and be given another. The token or tablet is replaced in machines in the signal box once received and another can only be taken out when the single section of line is clear to the next signal box. Thus only one tablet or token can ever be removed at any one time. The staff did exactly the same job but was a long metal object which fitted into a differently shaped machine. With a one train only line, the staff may be wooden with a small metal key attached.

'Withered Arm' – An expression which has become part of railway jargon. In 1967 as the Southern Region's network west of Exeter was gradually being destroyed, the late T.W.E. Roche produced a fabulous book to which he gave this title thus verbally describing the shape of the five tentacles which had reached from Exeter westwards.

Wrong Side (reference to signals) – The normal position for a signal is on the left-hand side of the line. However, there are many places where this does not happen. A signal is said to be on the 'wrong side' when it is on the right-hand side of the track. This is normally so positioned in order to give the driver a better view of the signal. A fine example of this is with the magnificent down home signal at Corfe Castle where the signal is at the end of a deep cutting. To have placed it on the left would have made it virtually impossible to have been seen by the driver until a few feet away. Placed where it is he can view the signal for a long distance before the cutting is reached.

Acknowledgements

As well as those to whom thanks have been given and to whom this book is dedicated, the author would like to thank those who have generously contributed photographs. Also:

Mr & Mrs Greg Brown of Hole station; Dr the Revd Martin Connop Price, priest and Oakwood author, for his ongoing friendship and encouragement; Jane & Ian Kennedy for their support to a new author; Simon Lang for his enthusiastic support over the years; Sir William McAlpine for his kind help; Valerie Quant, daughter of the late Frank Quant of Tavistock; John Snell of Bere Alston; Christine Stewart for her clarification on some of the finer points; Professor Christopher Caseldine of Exeter University for his geographical guidance, all those kind and courteous signalmen who have welcomed me into their signal boxes; members of the Swanage Railway, whose professionalism has continued to keep me on my railway toes, these include Mike Whitwam, Steven Jenkins, Alan Greatbatch, Mick Gould and Roger Pleasant, also photographer Andrew P.M. Wright, and to the ever cheerful Barry Light, the Swanage Railway's permanent way genius, whose good humour and fount of knowledge makes early mornings in a signal box an even greater pleasure!

Bibliography

The Branch by Bernard Mills, Plym Valley Railway Co.
Branch Line Memories (two volumes), Eric R. Shepherd, ARK Publications
The Branch Lines of Devon by Colin G. Maggs, Amberley Publishing
The Bridport Railway, Brian Jackson and Mike Tattershall, Oakwood Press
Devon Railway Stations by Mike Oakley, Dovecote Press
Great Scenic Railways of Devon and Cornwall, Michael Pearson, Wayzgoose Press
Great Western Branch Termini by Paul Karau, Oxford Publishing Co.
  (originally in two volumes but subsequently available as one)
Great Western Railway Halts, Kevin Robertson
  (Vol. 1 published by Irwell Press. Vol. 2 by KRB Publications)
Great Western Railway Stations 1947, R.J. Smith, Amadeus Press
Growing up on the Railway in the South West, Grace Horseman, ARK Publications
An Historical Survey of Great Western Stations, R.H. Clark, Oxford Publishing Co.
An Historical Survey of Selected Southern Stations, G.A. Pryer & G.L. Bowring, Oxford Publishing Co.
An Illustrated History of the North Cornwall Railway, George Reeve
  (based on the book by David Wroe), Irwell Press
In the Tracks of the ACE, Jeffrey Grayer, Noodle Books
The Kingsbridge Branch, Dermot Reynolds & Ken Williams, Oakwood Press
The Launceston Branch by G.H. Anthony, revised and extended by S.C. Jenkins, Oakwood Press
Lines to Torrington, John Nicholas, Oxford Publishing Co.
The Liskeard and Looe Branch, Gerry Beale, Wild Swan Publications
Main Lines to the West (Vols. 2 & 3), John Nicholas & George Reeve, Irwell Press
The Newquay Branch and its Branches, John Vaughan, Oxford Publishing Co.
The North Devon Line, John Nicholas, Oxford Publishing Co.
The North Devon Line, John Nicholas & George Reeve, Irwell Press
The Okehampton Line, John Nicholas & George Reeve, Irwell Press
Passengers Once More … Southern England, Terry Gough, Silver Link Publishing
The Plymouth & Launceston Railway by Anthony R. Kingdom, ARK Publications
Plymouth and Launceston, T.W.E. Roche, Branch Line Handbooks
Rails to Newquay, Railways - Tramways - Town - Transport, John Vaughan, Oakwood Press
The Railways, Quarries and Cottages of Foggintor, Kath Brewer, Hedgerow Print
The Salisbury to Exeter Line, Derek Phillips & George Pryer, Oxford Publishing Co.
Signal Boxes of the London & South Western Railway, George Pryer, Oakwood Press
Track Layout Diagrams (various), R.A. Cooke, published by the author
The Westbury to Weymouth Line, Derek Phillips, Oxford Publishing Co.
The Withered Arm, T.W.E. Roche, Forge Books
The Yelverton to Princetown Railway, Anthony R. Kingdom, Forest Publishing in association with ARK Publications